Data Mining and Exploration

Student Edition

Kimberly Seefeld, EdD

Table of contents

Data Mining and Exploration

Student Edition

By Kimberly Seefeld, EdD

Published under **DataJoyAI** imprint

Companion resources for this book are available at:

DataJoyAI

https://datajoyai.com

Edition: First Edition
ISBN: 978-1-969233-38-8

Chapter 1

Data Mining in the Age of AI

1.1 Learning Outcomes

1-1. Explain the concept of data mining and its evolution from manual analysis to AI-enhanced techniques.

1-2. Identify and differentiate types of data (numeric, binary, text, image, audio, video, categorical, time series, and spatial) and describe how AI improves analysis for each.

1-3. Describe the AI-enhanced data mining process, including data exploration, preprocessing, mining, postprocessing, and application of knowledge.

1-4. Recognize modern tools and platforms for AI-powered data mining, including traditional software, programming languages, AutoML, and no-code/low-code solutions.

1-5. Discuss ethical considerations and limitations in AI-enhanced data mining, including bias, privacy, transparency, and responsible AI practices.

1.2 Introduction

In this chapter we'll delve into the essence of data mining and cover some fundamental aspects that have been transformed by artificial intelligence. Our primary goal is to articulate what data mining entails in today's AI-enhanced landscape and set the stage for further study.

Data mining can be defined in a few ways depending on the perspective, but in 2025, it has become deeply intertwined with artificial intelligence and machine learning. Firstly, data mining can be viewed as a process. From this angle, data mining is akin to a search for patterns within a dataset, but now we have AI algorithms helping us find patterns we never could have discovered manually. Whether consumer data revealing purchasing behaviors through recommendation systems or medical data unveiling disease-symptom correlations via machine learning, the essence remains the same: identifying patterns within data. This perspective emphasizes the core aspect of data mining—uncovering meaningful patterns. In essence, data mining still mirrors the process of mining for gold, where the objective is to extract valuable insights from a vast expanse of data, but now we have much more sophisticated tools to help us dig.

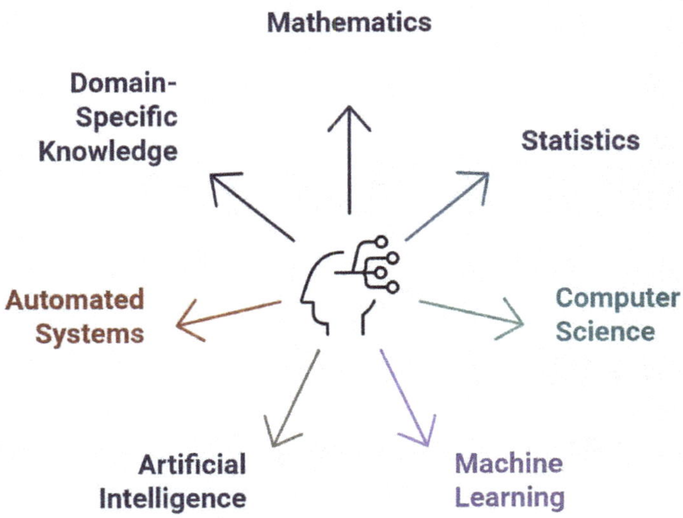

Academically, data mining is an interdisciplinary field that employs techniques from mathematics, statistics, computer science (including database management and programming), machine learning, artificial intelligence, and automated systems, along with domain-specific knowledge from fields like business and healthcare. Contrary to popular belief, data mining isn't solely a realm of mathematics or computer science, and it certainly isn't just about AI either. To set the stage for this book, it's crucial to understand that much like data analytics itself, data mining uses techniques from many academic disciplines, with AI serving as a powerful enhancement rather than a replacement for fundamental analytical thinking.

1.3 History of Data Mining

To understand the history of data mining, it's essential to recognize that it's not entirely a novel field and has evolved over decades, with the most recent evolution being the integration of artificial intelligence. Data mining has roots that stretch back quite a while, though not in the AI-enhanced context we typically associate with it today. Let's review some key highlights to provide perspective on its evolution.

1.3.1 Early Computing (1960s–1980s)

The origins of data mining can be traced back to the 1960s. Early computing machines, though primitive by today's standards, hinted at the potential for automating analytical tasks. Before this period, data management primarily relied on manual processes, with information stored in physical documents within office settings.

However, the landscape began to shift in the 1970s, marking the initial steps towards what we now recognize as data mining. As we moved into the 1970s, there was a gradual shift towards computerized data management. While still in its infancy, the concept of automating analytical processes became increasingly feasible with the emergence of rudimentary computing technology.

By the 1980s, data mining began to take shape as a defined practice. Desktop computers became increasingly prevalent. Shapiro, in the late '80s, introduced the concept of "knowledge discovery in databases" (KDD), which essentially encompasses what we now know as data mining. Despite the term "data mining" being coined earlier by Fedman, KDD became synonymous with the process of uncovering patterns and relations within data.

1.3.2 The Internet Boom and Big Data (1990s–2000s)

The 1990s witnessed a proliferation of computer usage, with desktop computers becoming commonplace. While internet usage was still in its nascent stages, the widespread adoption of desktop computers laid the groundwork for the digital age to come. Alongside this technological boom, businesses began to recognize the value of leveraging data for profit. In a capitalist society like America, where value and profit are paramount, the importance of data surged.

As businesses embraced data-driven decision-making, the late '90s and early 2000s witnessed a surge in interest and investment in data analytics. With the proliferation of internet usage, businesses recognized the potential of data to uncover valuable insights, particularly in areas such as sales and customer behavior analysis.

In essence, the 1990s marked a turning point where the convergence of technology, business needs, and academic research propelled data mining into the forefront of innovation and profitability.

Moving into the 2000s, coinciding with the internet boom, there was a notable emergence of open-source data mining tools, exemplified by the advent of R, a freely available platform. The accessibility of such tools democratized data analysis, driving increased adoption due to their cost-effectiveness. The early 2000s saw the publication of seminal works in data mining, such as a prominent textbook released in 2003. These resources played a pivotal role in the proliferation of data mining courses and the subsequent expansion of the field.

Moreover, the concept of "Big Data" gained traction during this period, reflecting the exponential growth in data volume facilitated by the internet explosion. While the term lacks a precise definition, it underscores the unprecedented scale of data collection and the challenges and opportunities it presents for analysis and utilization. Technological advancements also played a crucial role, with platforms like Apache Hadoop simplifying the storage and processing of large datasets. This development marked a significant milestone in handling the burgeoning volumes of data generated in the digital age.

1.3.3 Cloud Computing and Machine Learning Integration (2010s)

As we entered the 2010s, cloud computing emerged as a transformative force. This shift from local server-based infrastructure to cloud-based data storage revolutionized data management practices. The advent of cloud computing facilitated the creation of vast data warehouses, housed in secure facilities known as the "cloud." This shift paved the way for unprecedented scalability and accessibility of data resources.

The early 2010s witnessed a remarkable surge in machine learning and artificial intelligence (AI) technologies. The rise of social media platforms like Facebook further fueled the demand for data analysis tools. However, this period also saw controversies surrounding data privacy and collection practices, exemplified by incidents involving Facebook.

In 2011, IBM showcased the capabilities of AI through its computer Watson, which famously competed on Jeopardy. This demonstration highlighted the power of machine learning and natural language processing in solving complex tasks. Additionally, Google's release of TensorFlow in 2015 marked a significant milestone in open-source machine learning libraries. TensorFlow quickly emerged as one of the most widely used tools in the field, reflecting its versatility and effectiveness in various applications.

The midpoint of the decade saw the emergence of deep learning as a dominant paradigm in AI research. This sophisticated approach to machine learning, characterized by hierarchical layers of neural networks, revolutionized various domains, including computer vision and natural language processing.

1.3.4 The AI Revolution (2019–Present)

A significant breakthrough occurred in 2019 with the release of language models for natural language processing. Unlike computer languages with fixed meanings, natural language presents challenges due to its semantic complexities. This development enabled computers to comprehend contextual nuances, paving the way for innovations like chatbots and AI applications.

The release of ChatGPT in late 2022 marked a watershed moment. For the first time, sophisticated AI capabilities became accessible to the general public, not just data scientists and researchers. This democratization of AI has fundamentally changed how we think about data mining. Now, anyone can use AI tools to help analyze data, generate insights, and even write code for data analysis.

Today, in 2025, we're seeing the integration of AI throughout the data mining process. Automated machine learning platforms can now handle much of the technical work that previously required extensive expertise. AI can automatically clean data, select appropriate algorithms, and even interpret results. However, this doesn't mean human expertise is obsolete—rather, it means we can focus more on asking the right questions and understanding the business context of our findings [[1]].

Cloud computing has streamlined data access and analysis for businesses by decentralizing data storage and enabling remote access via the internet. Consequently, the 2010s and 2020s have witnessed the evolution and expansion of data mining, with continuous advancements in techniques and tools. While data mining lays the groundwork for artificial intelligence, the latter encompasses broader domains like natural language processing and other computational aspects.

However, with progress comes responsibility. The 2020s have brought heightened awareness of privacy concerns and ethical considerations surrounding data usage, especially when AI systems are making decisions that affect people's lives. As data analytics professionals, it's crucial to navigate these issues ethically and responsibly.

1.4 Types of Data in the AI Era

Data has many different types, and the AI revolution has expanded our ability to work with all of them more effectively.

First, there's **numeric data**, which aligns with what's typically encountered in introductory statistics classes. Numeric data lends itself well to analysis using basic statistical methods, and now AI algorithms can find complex patterns in numerical data that would be impossible for humans to detect manually. However, it's important to note that data analytics, including data mining, encompasses more than just numerical data.

Binary data, for instance, traces back to the fundamental language of computers, comprised of zeros and ones. This form of data underpins the digital world, functioning at the most elemental level of computing processes. AI systems work extensively with binary data, not just for computation but also for representing yes/no decisions and categorical features.

Text data represents another significant category, often referred to as unstructured data. This includes a vast array of information found in textual formats, such as social media posts, emails, and documents. Analyzing text data used to present unique challenges due to its unstructured nature, but advances in AI, particularly large language models like ChatGPT, have revolutionized our ability to extract insights from text. Modern AI can understand context, sentiment, and meaning in ways that were impossible just a few years ago.

Image data is also considered unstructured data, but AI has transformed how we work with images. Computer vision algorithms can now automatically identify objects, faces, and scenes in images. This has applications ranging from medical diagnosis to quality control in manufacturing.

Audio data is another type of unstructured data, representing sound and speech. AI-powered speech recognition and audio analysis have made it possible to automatically transcribe conversations, analyze customer service calls, and even detect emotions in voice patterns.

Video and movie data combine both image and audio data and are similarly categorized as unstructured data. AI systems can now analyze video content for everything from security monitoring to content recommendation systems.

Categorical data, on the other hand, encompasses discrete, qualitative information, like colors, genders, or species. While not as lengthy as textual data, categorical data provides valuable insights into various attributes and characteristics. AI systems have sophisticated ways of handling categorical data, converting it into numerical representations that machine learning algorithms can process effectively.

Time series data is another essential type, capturing observations collected over sequential intervals. This data is crucial in analyzing trends and patterns over time, particularly in domains such as sales forecasting and economic analysis. AI has greatly enhanced our ability to work with time series data, with machine learning algorithms that can detect complex temporal patterns and make accurate predictions about future values.

Spatial data is another significant type of data, which is commonly used in mapping the Earth. Organizations like the UN have been heavily involved in this field. Although most of the Earth's surface has likely been mapped using GPS coordinates, spatial data still plays a crucial role in geographic and environmental studies. AI has enhanced our ability to analyze location-based patterns and optimize routes and logistics.

Each type of data presents its own set of challenges and opportunities for analysis. Understanding these distinctions is essential for effectively leveraging data analytics techniques to derive actionable insights. The key difference in the AI era is that techniques of data mining can now be applied to all kinds of data more effectively, with AI serving as a powerful tool to uncover patterns that would be impossible to find manually.

1.5 AI-Enhanced Data Mining Process

The data mining process we're following is inspired by the CRISP-DM (Cross-Industry Standard Process for Data Mining) methodology, but it has evolved significantly with the integration of artificial intelligence and automation. While CRISP-DM provides a specific algorithm for data mining, our approach is adapted and modified to incorporate modern AI capabilities. The general pattern remains the same, though the specifics have been enhanced by intelligent automation.

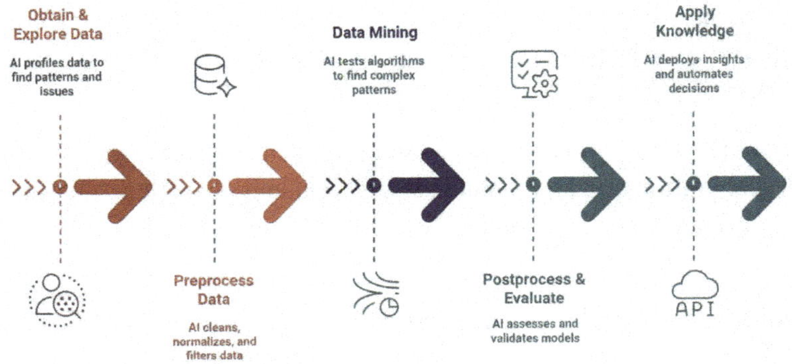

1.5.1 Step 1: Obtain and Explore Data with AI Assistance

The initial phase involves gathering and examining the data, but now we have AI tools to help us do this more efficiently and thoroughly. Typically, data still comes from a database or data warehouse system maintained by IT professionals. An analyst will either receive the data from IT or retrieve it directly using SQL or related technology. Once the data is obtained, the analyst uploads it into the software tool they will use for analysis. This tool may be the same for all steps of the data mining process or different software may be used for different tasks.

What's changed is that AI can now help with the exploration process. Modern data mining tools can automatically generate comprehensive data profiles, identify potential quality issues, and even suggest which variables might be most important for analysis. AI algorithms can quickly scan through large datasets to identify patterns, outliers, and relationships that might take humans much longer to discover.

During this phase, the data should be thoroughly explored to understand its structure and contents. This includes generating summaries such as frequency distributions, creating visualizations, and analyzing variables to gain a comprehensive understanding of the dataset. AI-powered tools can now automate much of this exploratory work, creating interactive dashboards and highlighting key insights automatically.

1.5.2 Step 2: Data Preprocessing with Intelligent Automation

This step involves cleaning and transforming the data to prepare it for analysis, but AI has revolutionized how we approach preprocessing. Essential pre-processing tasks include modifying data, handling missing values, and other necessary preparations, but now many of these tasks can be automated or semi-automated using AI.

Pre-processing is crucial for ensuring that the data is suitable for data mining and may involve several activities:

Cleaning/Reformatting/Transforming Data: AI can now automatically detect and correct many types of data quality issues. Machine learning algorithms can identify inconsistent formats, detect likely errors, and even suggest corrections. This doesn't replace human judgment, but it makes the process much more efficient.

Reducing Dimensionality: AI has advanced techniques for automatically identifying which variables are most important and reducing the complexity of datasets while retaining essential information. Modern algorithms can handle much larger datasets than traditional methods.

Filtering/Subsetting Data: AI can help identify which subsets of data are most relevant to the analysis and automatically filter out noise or irrelevant information.

Normalizing Data: AI systems can automatically determine the best methods for adjusting data values to a common scale, ensuring consistency and improving the performance of data mining algorithms.

Automated machine learning platforms can now create entire preprocessing pipelines that adapt to different types of data automatically. However, human expertise is still crucial for understanding the business context and ensuring that the preprocessing makes sense for the specific problem being solved.

1.5.3 Step 3: AI-Powered Data Mining

The core focus of this book lies here, but the landscape has changed dramatically with AI integration. This step now involves not just applying clustering, association, and classification techniques, but also leveraging advanced machine learning algorithms, deep learning, and automated model selection to find patterns in the data.

Modern AI systems can automatically try multiple algorithms, compare their performance, and select the best approach for a given dataset. This doesn't mean that understanding the underlying techniques is less important—quite the opposite. Understanding how these algorithms work is crucial for interpreting results and knowing when to trust AI recommendations versus when human judgment is needed.

AI has also expanded the types of patterns we can discover. Deep learning algorithms can find complex, non-linear relationships in data that traditional methods might miss.

Natural language processing can extract insights from text data, and computer vision can analyze images and videos as part of the data mining process.

1.5.4 Step 4: Postprocessing with AI-Enhanced Evaluation

In this phase, we evaluate the effectiveness of the models created during data mining, but AI has enhanced our ability to do comprehensive evaluation. Post-processing now involves several key steps enhanced by artificial intelligence:

Assess Model Performance: AI can automatically evaluate models using multiple metrics and provide comprehensive performance reports. However, understanding what these metrics mean and how to interpret them in the business context remains a crucial human skill.

Validate the Model: AI can help ensure that models are both sensible and effective by automatically checking for common problems like overfitting, bias, and data leakage. Explainable AI techniques can help us understand why models make certain decisions.

Make Adjustments: Based on automated evaluation, AI systems can suggest adjustments to improve model performance. Some platforms can even automatically retune models or try different approaches.

The goal of post-processing remains ensuring that the models are reliable and can provide meaningful insights, but AI has made this process more thorough and efficient.

1.5.5 Step 5: Application of Knowledge with Intelligent Systems

This step involves using the insights gained from data mining to make informed decisions or solve specific problems, but AI has transformed how we deploy and use these insights. The knowledge derived, often in the form of a new model, is applied for practical and productive purposes, but now this can happen automatically and at scale.

Modern applications might include:

Implementing Automated Solutions: AI systems can automatically apply models to new data as it arrives, making real-time decisions or recommendations without human intervention.

Informed Decision-Making: AI can help translate model outputs into business recommendations, though human judgment remains crucial for strategic decisions.

Continuous Improvement: AI systems can automatically monitor model performance and retrain models as new data becomes available, ensuring that insights remain accurate over time.

The key difference in the AI era is that this process can now operate continuously and automatically, with models updating themselves as new data arrives and business conditions change. However, human oversight remains essential to ensure that automated systems are working correctly and making decisions that align with business objectives and ethical considerations.

1.6 Modern Tools for AI-Enhanced Data Mining

There are many software tools used in data mining, and the landscape has been transformed by artificial intelligence, but the underlying theory of data mining remains constant. This is why this book isn't tied to any specific software—the theoretical foundations you will learn will stay relevant, even as you encounter new AI-powered tools and technologies.

Data mining tools can be broadly categorized into several types, each serving different aspects of the data mining process, but now many of these tools incorporate AI capabilities.

1.6.1 Traditional Tools Enhanced with AI

Firstly, there's general-purpose software like Microsoft Excel and Google Sheets. While these aren't dedicated data mining tools, they now offer AI-enhanced capabilities. Excel has integrated AI features for data analysis and pattern recognition, and Google Sheets includes machine learning-powered suggestions and automated insights. For basic data manipulation and cleaning tasks, which are essential components of data wrangling, these tools remain useful and are now more powerful with AI integration.

Next, we have statistical software, including tools like SPSS (IBM), SAS, and Minitab. While these have been available longer than dedicated data mining tools, they now integrate advanced AI and machine learning functionality. However, they are primarily proprietary and may have costly licenses. SAS is recognized for its high cost but now includes comprehensive AI capabilities, while SPSS is frequently utilized in academic disciplines such as psychology and social sciences and has added machine learning features. Mastering these tools effectively can be challenging due to their complexity, but they now offer more automated features to help users.

Another noteworthy category is data visualization and business intelligence (BI) tools. Examples include Tableau and Power BI, which excel at swiftly and effectively presenting data for insights and now include AI-powered analytics. Modern versions of these tools can automatically suggest visualizations, detect patterns, and even generate natural language explanations of data trends. While Tableau is esteemed for its visualization capabilities and now includes AI features, Power BI has expanded beyond its initial constraints and includes sophisticated machine learning integration.

1.6.2 Programming Languages with AI Integration

In addition to these tools, programming languages such as Python and R play a crucial role in modern data mining and have extensive AI libraries. Python has become the dominant language for AI and machine learning, with libraries like scikit-learn for traditional machine learning, TensorFlow and PyTorch for deep learning, and automated machine learning libraries that can handle much of the technical work automatically.

R offers robust capabilities for data manipulation, analysis, and modeling, making it a favored choice among data scientists and analysts, and now includes extensive machine learning and AI packages. Proficiency in programming languages like R and Python unlocks opportunities for more customized and advanced analytics tasks, including cutting-edge AI techniques.

However, the level of programming expertise needed varies depending on the specific role and industry. For example, advanced data science roles may require more extensive programming knowledge compared to applied analytics roles, where programming skills may be less critical. The good news is that AI is making programming more accessible, with tools that can automatically generate code and help users implement complex analyses without extensive programming knowledge.

SQL also plays a significant role in data mining for data wrangling and retrieving data from databases, and many modern database systems now include built-in machine learning capabilities.

1.6.3 AI-Native and Automated Platforms

A new category of tools has emerged specifically for AI-enhanced data mining. Automated machine learning (AutoML) platforms like H2O.ai, DataRobot, and Google AutoML can automatically handle much of the data mining process, from preprocessing to model selection and deployment [[2]]

Another excellent choice for data mining is specialized software like Orange, an open-source tool that operates on Python but provides a user-friendly visual programming interface. Although it functions on Python in the background, you aren't required to directly code in Python to utilize it. Orange has a longstanding history of over two decades and enjoys widespread adoption in research, biology, and medical sectors. Recent versions include AI and machine learning capabilities, allowing you to focus on the analytical work rather than the technical implementation.

Cloud-based platforms like Amazon SageMaker, Google Cloud AI Platform, and Microsoft Azure Machine Learning provide comprehensive AI-powered data mining capabilities without requiring extensive infrastructure setup. These platforms can automatically scale to handle large datasets and provide access to cutting-edge AI algorithms.

1.6.4 No-Code and Low-Code AI Tools

Perhaps the most significant development is the emergence of no-code and low-code AI platforms that make sophisticated data mining accessible to users without extensive technical backgrounds. Tools like DataIku, Alteryx, and Knime provide drag-and-drop interfaces for building complex data mining workflows that incorporate AI and machine learning.

These tools democratize access to AI-powered data mining, allowing business analysts and domain experts to leverage sophisticated techniques without needing to become programming experts. However, understanding the underlying concepts remains important for interpreting results and making good decisions about which techniques to use.

The key insight is that while AI has dramatically enhanced the capabilities of data mining tools, the fundamental principles of data analysis remain important. The most effective approach often combines the power of AI automation with human expertise and domain knowledge.

1.7 Ethics and Limitations in the Age of AI

The Rise of AI in Data Mining

Artificial intelligence has transformed data mining, allowing analysts to uncover patterns in massive datasets that were previously impossible to process. Unlike traditional statistics, which rely on carefully designed studies, random sampling, and controlled experiments, AI often works with unstructured and non-random data collected for convenience rather than scientific rigor. This can introduce biases that AI systems may amplify, making ethical awareness more critical than ever.

Exploration vs. Hypothesis Testing

Data mining is fundamentally exploratory. Instead of testing a hypothesis, it looks for patterns, trends, and relationships in data. This approach can reveal valuable insights, but it also carries a high risk of false patterns—apparent correlations that are actually the result of chance or biased data. AI accelerates this risk by processing vast amounts of information quickly, increasing the likelihood of mistaking noise for meaningful signals.

Bias and the Amplification Effect

AI algorithms are powerful because they can find patterns without direct human guidance, but this flexibility can amplify existing biases. Data from sources like social media or online activity often overrepresent certain groups, such as younger, wealthier, or more educated individuals. If AI systems are trained on these datasets, they can produce conclusions that misrepresent broader populations and lead to unfair or discriminatory outcomes. Bias in data, algorithms, or human interpretation can all influence results, and AI can magnify these effects at scale.

Legal and Regulatory Considerations

The ethical challenges of AI are compounded by evolving laws and regulations. Privacy, consent, data ownership, and algorithmic transparency are ongoing concerns. The European Union's General Data Protection Regulation (GDPR) and the California Consumer Privacy Act (CCPA) set legal standards for handling personal data. The EU AI Act, implemented in 2024, goes further by classifying AI systems by risk and imposing strict requirements for high-risk applications, including credit scoring, hiring, and medical decision-making.

Real-World Implications

AI-powered predictive systems influence many areas of daily life, from mortgage approvals and hiring decisions to medical diagnoses and policing practices. When these systems are trained on historical data that reflect societal inequities, they can perpetuate discrimination, even without malicious intent. The "black box" nature of many AI models makes it difficult to understand how decisions are made, which can hide biased or flawed reasoning from human oversight.

Practical Limitations of AI

AI systems are not perfect. They can overfit to training data, struggle when patterns change over time (concept drift), or be manipulated through adversarial attacks. They are also highly dependent on data quality; incomplete, biased, or inaccurate datasets can produce misleading results. The sophistication of AI can mask these problems, making them harder to detect and correct.

Responsible Practices in AI Data Mining

Ethical vigilance must guide every step of AI-enhanced data mining. Analysts should question where the data comes from, who is represented or excluded, and whether observed patterns are meaningful or artifacts of bias. Transparency, fairness, and human oversight are essential. Organizations should implement governance frameworks with bias audits, clear documentation, and continuous monitoring to ensure that AI systems perform fairly across different populations.

The Human Role in Responsible AI

While AI can process vast datasets and detect patterns humans cannot, it cannot replace human judgment, domain expertise, or ethical reasoning. Responsible data mining requires more than technical skill; it demands a commitment to fairness, accountability, and awareness of broader societal impacts. Ethics is not an optional add-on—it is central to ensuring that AI-driven insights are reliable, fair, and beneficial to society.

1.8 Key Terms

Data Mining: The process of discovering meaningful patterns, correlations, or trends in large datasets, often using statistical, computational, and AI methods.

Artificial Intelligence (AI): The simulation of human intelligence in machines, enabling tasks like learning, reasoning, and pattern recognition.

Machine Learning (ML): A subset of AI where systems learn patterns from data and improve performance without explicit programming.

Big Data: Extremely large datasets that cannot be easily managed, processed, or analyzed using traditional methods.

CRISP-DM: Cross-Industry Standard Process for Data Mining; a methodology for data mining workflows, including business understanding, data preparation, modeling, evaluation, and deployment.

Preprocessing: The stage of cleaning, transforming, and preparing raw data for analysis.

AutoML: Automated machine learning platforms that handle data preprocessing, model selection, training, and evaluation with minimal human intervention.

Explainable AI (XAI): Techniques that provide human-understandable explanations for AI decisions, enhancing transparency and trust.

Convenience Sampling: A non-random method of data collection based on accessibility, often leading to biased datasets.

Bias Amplification: The phenomenon where AI systems magnify biases present in training data, potentially resulting in unfair or discriminatory outcomes.

No-Code/Low-Code Platforms: Tools that allow users to build data mining and AI workflows using graphical interfaces rather than extensive programming.

1.9 Review Questions

1. How has data mining evolved from its early days to the AI-enhanced era of 2025? Provide at least two key milestones.
2. Explain the difference between structured and unstructured data. Give examples of each and describe how AI assists in their analysis.
3. List and briefly describe the five steps of the AI-enhanced data mining process. How does AI improve each step?
4. Identify at least three modern tools or platforms for AI-enhanced data mining. Describe one key feature of each that demonstrates AI integration.
5. Discuss at least two ethical challenges in AI-powered data mining. How can practitioners mitigate these risks in practice?
6. What is bias amplification in AI systems, and why is it particularly important to monitor in high-stakes domains like finance or healthcare?
7. Why does human expertise remain essential even when using AutoML or fully AI-driven data mining platforms?

1.10 Lab 1 Setup for Python

1.10.1 Introduction

This lab will guide you through setting up Python, which you will need to complete all lab exercises in this course. Don't worry if you're new to programming—modern AI tools like ChatGPT and Claude can help you focus on concepts while assisting with coding when needed.

This book provides code in Python for labs but **does not require any specific Python implementation**. Instructors and students may use whatever Python environment works best for them, provided it supports the required packages and allows students to complete exercises accessibly.

Python can run in **local IDEs**, **cloud notebooks**, or **hybrid environments**, and accessibility considerations (screen readers, keyboard navigation, alternative outputs) should be observed to support all learners.

1.10.2 Choosing a Python Environment

Here are common Python options you may encounter:

Environment	Description	Pros	Considerations
Local IDEs (VS Code, PyCharm, Thonny, RStudio)	Installed on your computer; supports scripts and projects	Powerful, flexible, offline	Must be installed; setup may require more guidance; check accessibility support
Cloud Notebooks (Google Colab, JupyterHub, Binder)	Run Python in a web browser	No installation required, easy collaboration, access from multiple devices	Accessibility may vary; interactive outputs (plots, widgets) may need descriptive alternatives
RStudio with Python support	Primarily for R but can run Python alongside R	Useful for mixed-language labs or statistics-heavy exercises	Not required; adds complexity if Python-only work is sufficient
Other platforms	Examples: Repl.it, Anaconda Navigator	Easy access, beginner-friendly	Check which packages are supported and how to save/share work

> **Instructor Note:** This course is implementation-agnostic. Students can choose any environment that meets the requirements, and instructors should provide guidance for installation, accessibility, and usage based on local policies.

1.10.3 General Python Setup

Regardless of the environment, students will need:

1. **Python 3.9 or newer** (3.11 recommended)

2. **Core packages** for data manipulation, visualization, and machine learning

3. **Text processing packages** for NLP tasks

1.10.3.1 Core Python Packages

- `pandas` – Data manipulation
- `numpy` – Numerical computing
- `matplotlib` – Basic plotting
- `seaborn` – Statistical visualization

1.10.3.2 Machine Learning & Statistics

- `scikit-learn` – ML algorithms
- `scipy` – Scientific computing

1.10.3.3 Text Processing & NLP

- `nltk` – Text processing
- `textblob` – Natural language processing
- `wordcloud` – Word cloud generation

1.10.3.4 Specialized / Optional

- `mlxtend` – Association rule mining
- `plotly` – Interactive visualization
- `opencv-python` – Image processing
- `pillow` – Image handling

  Instructor Note: Package installation commands differ by environment. For local IDEs, use `pip install <package>`. In cloud notebooks, `!pip install <package>` or environment-specific commands may be used.

1.10.4 Getting Help

1.10.4.1 When You're Stuck:

1. **Read the error message** - It usually tells you what's wrong
2. **Check your imports** - Make sure all packages are installed

3. **Use AI assistants:**
    - "ChatGPT, I'm getting this error: [paste error]. How do I fix it?"
    - "Claude, explain this Python code: [paste code]"
4. **Ask classmates** - Share your Colab notebook or screenshots
5. **Check package documentation** - Most packages have great examples online

1.10.4.2 Useful Prompts for AI Assistants:

- "Explain this Python error and how to fix it: [error message]"
- "What does this code do? [paste code]"
- "How do I install [package name] in [RStudio/Colab]?"
- "Convert this code to work with my dataset: [paste code]"

1.11 Conclusion

Data mining has evolved dramatically from its early manual and statistical roots to the AI-enhanced techniques of today. What was once a labor-intensive search for patterns has become an automated, intelligent process capable of handling vast, complex, and diverse datasets. AI now empowers analysts to uncover patterns in numeric, categorical, text, image, audio, video, time series, and spatial data—patterns that would have been impossible to detect manually. This evolution has not replaced human expertise but rather amplified it, allowing professionals to focus on interpretation, context, and decision-making.

The AI-enhanced data mining process—from data exploration and preprocessing to mining, postprocessing, and application—illustrates how automation and machine learning tools can improve efficiency and insight generation. Modern platforms, ranging from AutoML and programming libraries to no-code AI tools, make sophisticated data analysis accessible to a broader audience, yet understanding the underlying principles remains essential. Ethical considerations, including bias, privacy, and transparency, must guide every stage, ensuring that AI-driven insights are accurate, fair, and socially responsible.

Ultimately, the AI era of data mining represents a balance between technological power and human judgment. While AI can process unprecedented amounts of data and reveal hidden patterns, human oversight, domain knowledge, and ethical awareness remain critical. By integrating AI responsibly, analysts can unlock the full potential of data mining, transforming raw information into actionable knowledge that drives informed decisions and innovation across industries.

1.12 References

[1] MIT Sloan Review. (2025). *Five Trends in AI and Data Science for 2025.* https://sloanreview.mit.edu/article/five-trends-in-ai-and-data-science-for-2025/

[2] DataCamp. (2025). *25 Top MLOps Tools You Need to Know in 2025*. https://www.datacamp.com/blog/top-mlops-tools

[3] GTG Legal. (2025). *Data Mining and Ethical AI - Navigating the EU Regulations*. https://gtg.com.mt/technology-lawyers-regulations-ethical-ai-data-mining/

Chapter 2

Descriptive Statistics

2.1 Learning Outcomes

2-1. Compute and compare measures of center and dispersion.

2-2. Interpret variability in data distributions and explain how dispersion affects business and analytical conclusions.

2-3. Identify skewness, kurtosis, and deviations from normality using graphical and numerical methods.

2-4. Use AI-supported analysis to detect unusual variability patterns and inform data-driven decisions.

2.2 Introduction

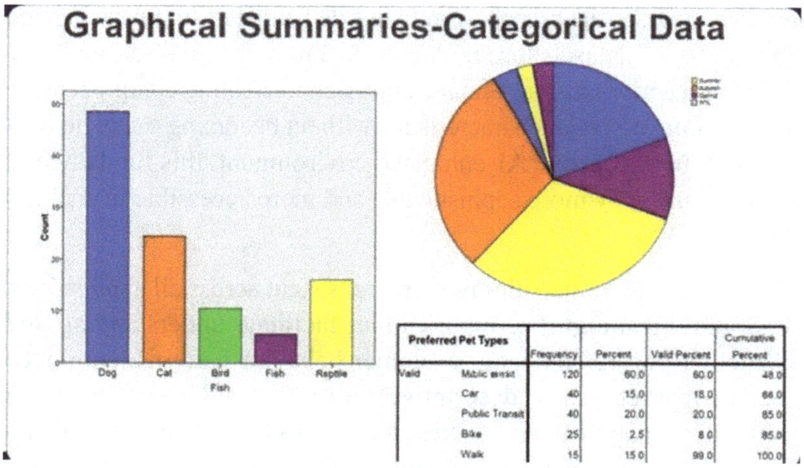

Descriptive statistics serves as the foundation for understanding and summarizing data effectively, providing essential insights that guide all subsequent analytical work. In today's AI-enhanced analytical landscape, these fundamental statistical concepts have evolved from manual calculations and basic visualizations to sophisticated, automated systems capable of instantly profiling datasets, detecting complex patterns, and generating actionable insights. However, while the tools have advanced dramatically, the core principles remain unchanged: we seek to understand what our data reveals, identify the stories it tells, and uncover the patterns that may be hidden within its structure.

This chapter introduces you to descriptive statistics as your first systematic conversation with any dataset—the critical initial step where you become acquainted with your data's characteristics before proceeding to more complex analytical techniques. Modern AI-powered tools have transformed this process, making it both more powerful and more accessible, while simultaneously increasing the importance of understanding these fundamental concepts. As AI systems generate increasingly sophisticated analyses, your ability to interpret and contextualize descriptive statistical measures becomes more crucial than ever.

The integration of artificial intelligence into descriptive statistics represents a paradigm shift in how we approach data exploration. Where traditional methods required extensive manual effort to calculate basic measures and create simple visualizations, contemporary AI-enhanced platforms can generate comprehensive data profiles in seconds, automatically identifying key patterns, potential data quality issues, and interesting characteristics that warrant further investigation. This technological advancement doesn't diminish the importance of understanding descriptive statistics—rather, it amplifies the need for statistical literacy as AI tools can generate vast amounts of information that requires skilled interpretation.

2.3 Introduction to Descriptive Statistics

Descriptive statistics encompasses the branch of statistics dedicated to summarizing and describing the main features of datasets through numerical measures and visual representations. This discipline functions as a systematic approach to creating comprehensive profiles of your data, revealing essential characteristics without becoming overwhelmed by individual data points. In the current AI-enhanced environment, this fundamental process has become simultaneously more sophisticated and more accessible to analysts across all skill levels.

The primary objective of descriptive statistics remains consistent across all applications: to transform raw data into meaningful summaries that facilitate understanding and decision-making. Whether you're analyzing customer behavior patterns, employee performance metrics, or market trends, descriptive statistics provides the essential foundation for all subsequent analytical work. These techniques help identify data distributions, detect unusual patterns, understand variability, and establish baseline measures that inform more advanced statistical modeling and machine learning applications.

2.3.1 Role in Data Mining and AI

Descriptive statistics plays an increasingly critical role in modern data mining and artificial intelligence applications, serving multiple essential functions that support the entire analytical pipeline. First and foremost, it provides the foundational understanding necessary before implementing sophisticated machine learning models or advanced AI techniques. Without this fundamental comprehension of data characteristics, even the most advanced algorithms may produce misleading or inappropriate results.

In traditional analytical workflows, data scientists and analysts would spend considerable time manually calculating means, constructing frequency tables, and generating basic visualizations to understand their datasets. Contemporary AI-powered tools have revolutionized this process, enabling the generation of comprehensive data profiles within seconds while automatically identifying key patterns, potential quality issues, and interesting characteristics that merit further investigation [1]. This technological advancement doesn't eliminate the need for understanding descriptive statistics—quite the contrary. As AI tools become capable of generating increasingly complex information, the ability to interpret and contextualize these results becomes more important than ever.

Modern AI systems utilize descriptive statistics as fundamental inputs for more sophisticated analyses. Machine learning algorithms require comprehensive understanding of data distributions, outlier identification, and pattern recognition—all of which depend heavily on descriptive statistical measures. When training AI models, these systems automatically calculate extensive descriptive statistics to optimize performance and make informed decisions about data processing approaches. The quality and appropriateness of these automated decisions depend directly on the accuracy and relevance of the underlying descriptive statistical analysis.

Furthermore, AI-enhanced descriptive statistics can handle substantially larger datasets and identify patterns that would be impossible to detect through manual analysis. These systems can automatically segment data, identify subgroups with distinct characteristics, and suggest which descriptive measures are most relevant for specific datasets and analytical objectives. This capability extends the reach and impact of descriptive statistics far beyond traditional limitations.

2.3.2 Difference Between Descriptive and Inferential Statistics

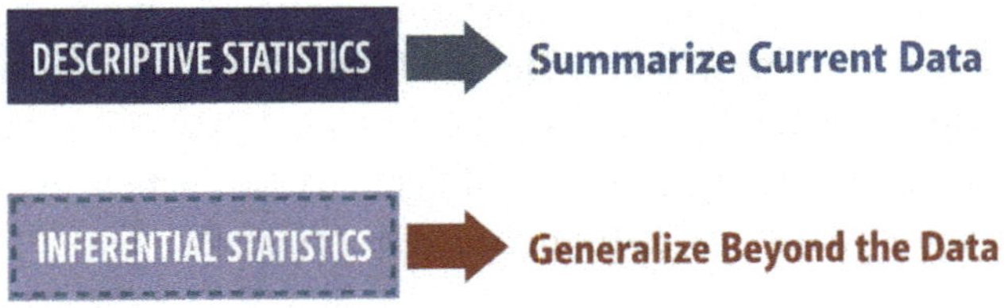

Understanding the fundamental distinction between descriptive and inferential statistics remains crucial for proper interpretation of analytical results, particularly as AI systems have begun to blur some traditional boundaries between these approaches. This distinction affects how we interpret results, make decisions, and communicate findings to stakeholders.

Descriptive statistics focuses exclusively on summarizing and describing data that you currently possess. It addresses questions such as "What characteristics does my dataset exhibit?" and "What are the primary features of my current data?" For example, when analyzing sales data from your organization, descriptive statistics would reveal the average sale amount, identify the most common purchase categories, and quantify how sales performance varies across different time periods or geographic regions. These analyses make no claims about populations beyond the data at hand.

Inferential statistics, conversely, utilizes sample data to draw conclusions about larger populations from which the sample was drawn. It addresses questions such as "Based on my sample data, what conclusions can I draw about the broader population?" and "How confident can I be in these broader conclusions?" Using the same sales example, inferential statistics might help predict future sales trends, determine whether a marketing campaign significantly increased sales performance, or assess whether observed differences between regions are statistically meaningful rather than due to random variation.

In the contemporary AI era, this traditional distinction has become more fluid and complex. Modern AI systems frequently combine descriptive and inferential approaches automatically, generating outputs that include both descriptive summaries and inferential insights within the same analysis. For instance, when an AI tool generates a comprehensive data profile, it might include traditional descriptive summaries such as means and distributions alongside inferential insights such as trend predictions, anomaly detection, and pattern recognition that extend beyond the immediate dataset.

Despite this technological convergence, understanding the fundamental difference between descriptive and inferential approaches remains essential because it helps you interpret AI-generated results correctly and understand when you can trust various types of conclusions. Descriptive results can be accepted with confidence when the data quality is good, while inferential conclusions require additional considerations about sampling methods, population characteristics, and statistical assumptions.

The sophistication of modern AI-enhanced descriptive statistics lies in its ability to handle substantially larger datasets while identifying patterns that would be impossible to detect manually. These systems can automatically segment data, identify subgroups with different characteristics, and suggest which descriptive measures are most relevant for specific analytical contexts and business objectives.

2.4 Frequency Tables and Distributions

Frequency tables and distributions represent fundamental tools in descriptive statistics that have been significantly enhanced by AI-powered analytical capabilities. These techniques help organize and quantify data patterns to reveal insights that might remain hidden in raw numerical datasets. Understanding how to create, interpret, and leverage these tools forms the foundation for more advanced statistical analysis and data-driven decision making.

The primary purpose of frequency analysis is to systematically organize data to reveal how often different values or categories appear within your dataset. This organizational approach transforms potentially overwhelming collections of individual data points into manageable summaries that highlight important patterns, trends, and anomalies. Modern AI-enhanced tools have expanded these capabilities dramatically, enabling automatic pattern detection, optimal grouping strategies, and intelligent highlighting of unusual characteristics that warrant further investigation.

2.4.1 Tabular Summaries

Frequency tables organize data systematically to display how often each value or category appears within your dataset—essentially creating a comprehensive inventory of your data's composition. For categorical variables such as employee departments, a frequency table reveals the distribution of employees across different organizational units, providing immediate insights into organizational structure and resource allocation.

Consider the following employee dataset that demonstrates typical organizational data structure:

Table 2.1: Sample Employee Data (first 6 rows)

Employee ID	Department	Quarterly Sales	Satisfaction	Years Experience
EMP001	Sales	42.8	9.4	14
EMP002	Support	105.9	8.0	14
EMP003	Engineering	88.8	7.6	4
EMP004	Support	56.5	7.0	9

Employee ID	Department	Quarterly Sales	Satisfaction	Years Experience
EMP005	HR	116.3	6.4	8
EMP006	Sales	95.7	7.6	6

The corresponding frequency table for department distribution reveals organizational composition:

Table 2.2: Department Frequency

Department	Frequency
Engineering	12
HR	6
Marketing	9
Sales	15
Support	8

Traditional frequency table creation could be extremely time-consuming, particularly when working with large datasets containing thousands or millions of observations. Contemporary AI-powered tools have revolutionized this process, generating comprehensive frequency tables instantaneously for all variables while automatically detecting optimal groupings and highlighting unusual patterns that merit further investigation.

Modern AI systems extend far beyond simple counting procedures. For continuous variables, these systems can automatically determine ideal bins or breakpoints that reveal meaningful patterns in the data. For example, when analyzing customer ages, an AI tool might automatically create age brackets such as 20–29, 30–39, 40–49, and so forth, while simultaneously highlighting clusters, gaps, or unusual concentrations in the data that might indicate distinct customer segments or data quality issues.

The power of AI-enhanced frequency analysis becomes particularly evident when dealing with complex categorical data. Consider customer purchase frequency analysis: a traditional frequency table might simply display how many customers made 1, 2, or 3 purchases within a specific time period. An AI-enhanced system could automatically identify that customers making 3 or more purchases exhibit fundamentally different behavioral patterns compared to occasional buyers, suggest appropriate customer segmentation strategies, and flag unusual patterns that might indicate data entry errors, fraudulent activity, or other anomalies requiring attention.

AI systems also provide significant advantages when working with categorical data that may contain inconsistencies or variations. For instance, if employee department names are recorded inconsistently (such as "HR" and "Human Resources"), AI can automatically combine these categories and flag rare or unusual categories that may require special attention or data cleaning procedures.

2.4.2 Histograms and Bar Charts

Visual representations of frequency data have undergone dramatic transformation through AI-enhanced analytical capabilities. Histograms effectively display the distribution of continuous variables such as customer age or monthly spending patterns, while bar charts present counts of categorical variables such as employee departments or customer satisfaction ratings. These visualizations transform numerical summaries into intuitive visual patterns that facilitate rapid pattern recognition and insight generation.

Traditional histogram creation required careful manual decisions regarding bin width, scaling, and formatting—choices that could significantly affect interpretation and potentially lead to misleading conclusions. AI-powered visualization tools now make these critical decisions automatically, optimizing visual presentations to emphasize the most important patterns while maintaining statistical accuracy. These systems can generate multiple complementary views of the same data to help analysts explore different aspects of distributions and identify patterns that might not be apparent in any single visualization.

For example, when analyzing customer monthly spending patterns, an AI system might automatically create histograms showing spending ranges, highlight clusters of high-spending customers that represent valuable market segments, and detect gaps or unusual spikes that suggest outliers requiring further investigation. Similarly, for employee performance data, AI-generated histograms of quarterly sales could reveal that most employees fall within a moderate sales range while identifying high performers who create a long tail in the distribution, suggesting opportunities for best practice sharing or performance improvement programs.

AI-enhanced bar charts extend significantly beyond simple counting and display capabilities. These systems can automatically sort categories by frequency to highlight the most important groups, identify significantly different categories that warrant special attention, and suggest combining or splitting categories based on underlying patterns in the data. For example, a bar chart of customer satisfaction scores could automatically highlight that most customers provide scores of 4 or 5, while very few provide scores of 1 or 2, and AI could suggest grouping low scores for focused analysis of problem areas and improvement opportunities.

Consider the following customer dataset that illustrates typical business data characteristics:

Table 2.3: Sample Customer Data (first 6 rows)

Customer ID	Age	Satisfaction Score	Monthly Spend
1	43	5	152.98
2	30	2	167.13
3	41	2	150.99
4	59	3	83.30
5	47	5	179.46
6	42	5	165.44

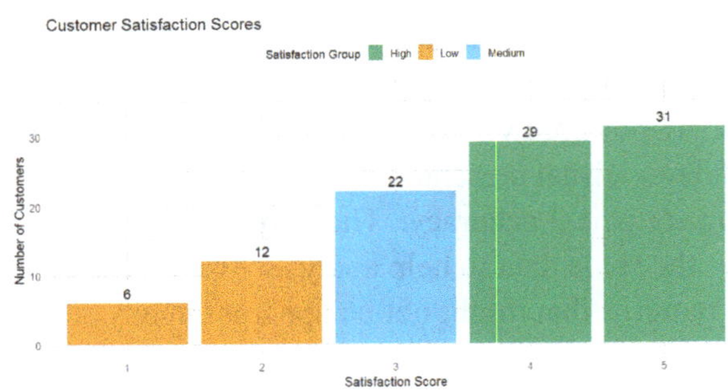

The true power of AI emerges when handling multiple variables simultaneously. AI systems can automatically generate cross-tabulations that reveal relationships between different categorical variables, identify interaction effects that might not be apparent when examining variables individually, and create sophisticated visualizations showing how frequencies change across different subgroups. For instance, these systems could automatically create charts showing satisfaction scores by customer age group or quarterly sales performance by department, instantly highlighting patterns that require attention and suggesting follow-up analyses that could provide additional insights.

2.5 Measures of Central Tendency

Measures of central tendency provide essential information about the "typical" or "average" values within datasets, representing some of the most commonly used and widely understood descriptive statistics. AI has significantly enhanced both the calculation of these measures and the interpretation of their meaning within broader analytical contexts. Understanding these measures and their appropriate applications forms a crucial foundation for all subsequent statistical analysis and data-driven decision making.

The fundamental purpose of central tendency measures is to identify representative values that summarize the overall level or location of data distributions. These measures help answer questions about what constitutes a typical observation, where the center of the distribution lies, and how to best characterize the overall level of the variable being analyzed. However, different measures of central tendency can provide different perspectives on the same data, and understanding when to use each measure is crucial for accurate interpretation and effective communication of results.

2.5.1 Mean, Median, Mode

The following table presents key descriptive statistics for quarterly sales performance across employees:

Table 2.4: Quarterly Sales Descriptive Statistics for Employees

Statistic	Value
Mean Quarterly Sales	86.40000
Median Quarterly Sales	85.30000
Standard Deviation	23.43631
Maximum Quarterly Sales	139.20000
Minimum Quarterly Sales	27.30000

The mean (arithmetic average) represents the most familiar and widely used measure of central tendency. Calculation involves summing all values and dividing by the number of observations—a conceptually simple process that becomes complex in its interpretation and application. While this calculation appears straightforward, AI has significantly enhanced our understanding of when the mean provides appropriate representation and when it might be misleading or inappropriate for specific analytical contexts.

For example, in the employee dataset, the mean quarterly sales across all employees is calculated by summing all individual sales figures and dividing by the total number of employees (50). AI systems can automatically detect when a few extremely high sales values are skewing the mean upward and suggest the median as a more representative measure of typical employee performance. This automatic detection capability helps prevent misinterpretation of results and ensures that analytical conclusions accurately reflect underlying data patterns.

The median represents the middle value when data is arranged in ascending or descending order, providing a measure that is often more representative than the mean when dealing with outliers or skewed distributions. For instance, if most employees achieve quarterly sales around 80–100 units but one or two exceptional performers achieve extremely high sales exceeding 200 units, the median provides a better sense of typical employee performance while the mean would be artificially inflated by the exceptional performers.

The mode identifies the most frequently occurring value within your dataset, representing the most common observation. For categorical data, this often provides the most meaningful measure of central tendency. In customer satisfaction analysis, the mode of satisfaction scores reveals the most common satisfaction level among respondents, providing direct insight into typical customer experiences. AI systems can automatically detect multiple modes (bimodal or multimodal distributions) that indicate distinct subgroups within the data, such as highly satisfied versus dissatisfied customers, suggesting the need for segmented analysis approaches.

Modern AI systems can automatically determine which measure—mean, median, or mode—best represents your specific data characteristics and provide clear explanations for their recommendations. For example, in customer satisfaction analysis, most customers might provide scores of 4 or 5, with fewer providing scores of 1 or 2, resulting in a bimodal distribution. In such cases, AI could calculate separate means for each group and flag that a single overall mean might not accurately represent the diversity of customer sentiment, suggesting alternative analytical approaches that better capture the underlying patterns.

2.5.2 Weighted Averages

Weighted averages become essential when not all observations carry equal importance or when different observations should contribute differently to the overall summary measure. For instance, in employee performance analysis, you might want to weight average quarterly sales by years of experience, giving greater influence to seasoned employees' performance patterns when calculating overall performance benchmarks.

AI systems can automatically suggest when weighted averages are appropriate based on data characteristics and analytical context, calculate multiple weighting schemes to explore different perspectives, and demonstrate how these different choices affect results and interpretations. In customer satisfaction analysis, satisfaction scores could be weighted by monthly spending levels, providing a clearer picture of high-value customers' experiences and ensuring that business decisions appropriately prioritize the most economically important customer segments.

Time-weighted averages represent another powerful application where more recent observations receive greater weight than older ones. This approach proves particularly valuable in business analytics where trends change over time and recent performance may be more predictive of future outcomes than historical patterns. AI systems can automatically implement various time-weighting schemes and help analysts understand how different approaches affect their conclusions.

The true power of AI lies not merely in performing these calculations efficiently, but in contextualizing the results within broader business and analytical frameworks. AI systems can automatically compare your dataset's central tendency measures to industry benchmarks, historical trends, or similar datasets, helping you determine whether your employees' sales performance or customer satisfaction scores represent typical patterns or unusual situations that warrant further investigation and potential action.

2.6 Measures of Dispersion

While measures of central tendency reveal information about typical values within datasets, measures of dispersion provide crucial insights into the variability or spread of data around those central values. Understanding dispersion is essential because two datasets can exhibit identical means while displaying dramatically different levels of variability, leading to completely different interpretations and business implications. The combination of central tendency and dispersion measures provides a comprehensive picture of data characteristics that supports informed decision-making and appropriate analytical choices.

Dispersion measures help answer critical questions about data consistency, reliability, and risk. High dispersion might indicate inconsistent performance, diverse customer preferences, or high uncertainty, while low dispersion suggests consistency, predictability, and homogeneity. These insights directly impact business decisions, risk assessments, and strategic planning processes across all organizational functions.

2.6.1 Range, Variance, Standard Deviation

The range represents the simplest measure of dispersion, calculated as the difference between the largest and smallest values in the dataset. For example, in our employee dataset, quarterly sales might range from 27 to 139 units, demonstrating the full spectrum of employee performance variation. However, range can be misleading because it depends entirely on extreme values and provides no information about the distribution of values between the extremes.

Table 2.5: Employee Quarterly Sales

Statistic	Value
Minimum	27.30000
Maximum	139.20000
Range	111.90000
Standard Deviation	23.43631
Interquartile Range	31.07500
MAD	23.12856

Variance measures how much each observation deviates from the mean on average, providing a comprehensive measure of overall spread that considers all data points rather than just extremes. For instance, if most employees achieve quarterly sales close to 85 units but a few demonstrate extreme values, the variance captures that overall variability pattern. However, variance is expressed in squared units, making it less intuitive for direct interpretation and communication to non-technical audiences.

Standard deviation represents the square root of variance, returning the measure to the same units as the original data and making it much more interpretable. For example, if the standard deviation of customer monthly spending is $41, we understand that most customers spend roughly $41 above or below the mean spending level. Standard deviation is far more intuitive than variance for interpretation and communication, and AI-powered tools can automatically flag unusually high variability that might indicate inconsistent performance, diverse customer behavior, or potential data quality issues.

Table 2.6: Customer Monthly Spend

Statistic	Value
Minimum	51.36000
Maximum	252.86000
Range	201.50000
Standard Deviation	41.61633
Interquartile Range	55.71500
MAD	41.00872

Modern analytical systems can also calculate robust measures of dispersion such as the median absolute deviation (MAD), which is less sensitive to extreme values than standard deviation. This proves particularly useful when some employees demonstrate extremely high sales performance or when a few customers exhibit unusually high monthly spending that might skew traditional measures of variability.

2.6.2 Interquartile Range (IQR)

The interquartile range (IQR) measures the spread of the middle 50% of observations, providing a robust measure of dispersion that is not affected by extreme values. For example, in customer spending analysis, the IQR of monthly spending might span $120–$180, showing where most typical customer spending falls while ignoring outliers that might represent unusual circumstances or data errors.

Values that fall more than $1.5 \times$ IQR above the third quartile or below the first quartile can be automatically flagged as potential outliers. AI-enhanced analysis can automatically identify these outliers and suggest whether they represent data errors, unusual but valid behavior patterns, or important business patterns that warrant special attention and analysis.

2.6.3 Boxplots, Density Plots, Violin Plots

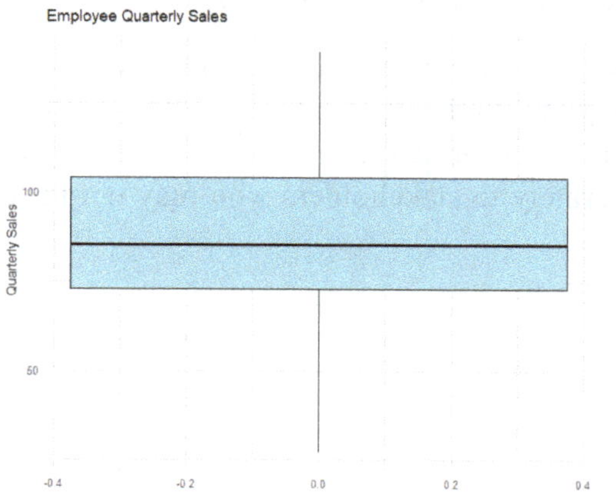

Boxplots provide highly effective visualizations for displaying data distribution characteristics, clearly highlighting medians, quartiles, and potential outliers in a compact, easily interpretable format. In our employee quarterly sales example, boxplots would show that most employees cluster around the median performance level, with a few high performers exceeding 120 units and creating an extended upper tail in the distribution.

These visualizations provide compact, easily readable summaries of data variability and help identify unusual values that may represent either data errors or interesting patterns worthy of further investigation. The visual format makes it easy to compare distributions across different groups, time periods, or other categorical divisions.

Density plots provide smoothed views of data distributions, making it easy to compare overall shapes across different groups and identify multiple peaks, skewness, or other distributional characteristics that might not be apparent in summary statistics alone. Violin plots combine boxplot summaries with density information, showing both summary statistics and the full distribution shape in a single visualization.

In practice, AI tools can automatically determine when these alternative visualizations provide more informative perspectives than standard boxplots, but for our sample data, the boxplots alone clearly highlight the key dispersion patterns and outlier characteristics. The real advantage lies in AI-assisted interpretation: subtle patterns, differences between groups, or unusual concentrations in the data can be automatically detected and highlighted, drawing attention to insights that might otherwise be missed in manual analysis.

2.7 Shape of Distributions

Understanding the shape of data distributions is crucial for choosing appropriate analytical techniques and interpreting results correctly. Distribution shape reveals important characteristics about data symmetry, concentration, and tail behavior, all of which have significant implications for analysis selection, interpretation validity, and decision-making processes. The shape provides insights into underlying data-generating processes and helps identify when standard analytical assumptions may be violated.

Distribution shape affects virtually every aspect of statistical analysis, from the choice of summary measures to the selection of appropriate modeling techniques. Understanding these characteristics enables analysts to make informed decisions about analytical approaches and communicate results accurately to stakeholders who may not have technical statistical backgrounds.

2.7.1 Skewness and Kurtosis

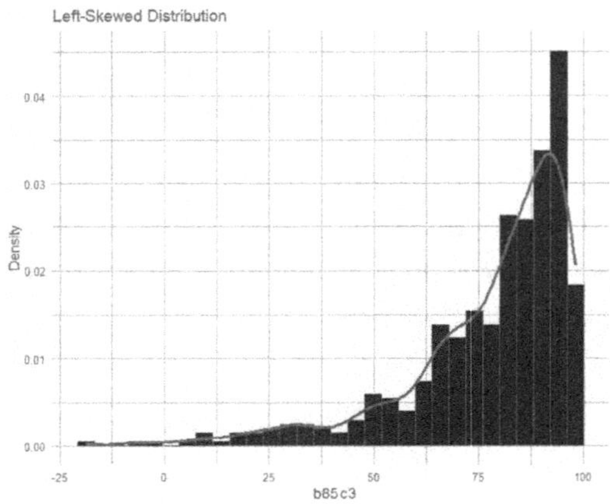

Skewness measures asymmetry in data distributions, providing quantitative assessment of whether data tends to cluster toward one end of the range. Right-skewed (positively skewed) data exhibits a long tail extending toward higher values, while left-skewed (negatively skewed) data shows a tail extending toward lower values. Perfectly symmetric distributions exhibit zero skewness, though real-world data rarely achieves perfect symmetry.

Kurtosis measures the "tailedness" of distributions, indicating whether a distribution has heavy tails (high kurtosis) or light tails (low kurtosis) compared to a normal distribution. High kurtosis suggests that extreme values occur more frequently than would be expected in a normal distribution, while low kurtosis indicates that extreme values are less common than normal expectations.

Understanding these measures helps analysts choose appropriate summary statistics (such as median versus mean for skewed data) and detect extreme values that could significantly affect business decisions. AI systems can automatically calculate skewness and kurtosis, highlight unusual patterns that warrant attention, and suggest data transformations or robust analytical methods that are less sensitive to distributional assumptions.

2.7.2 Normal vs Non-Normal Distributions

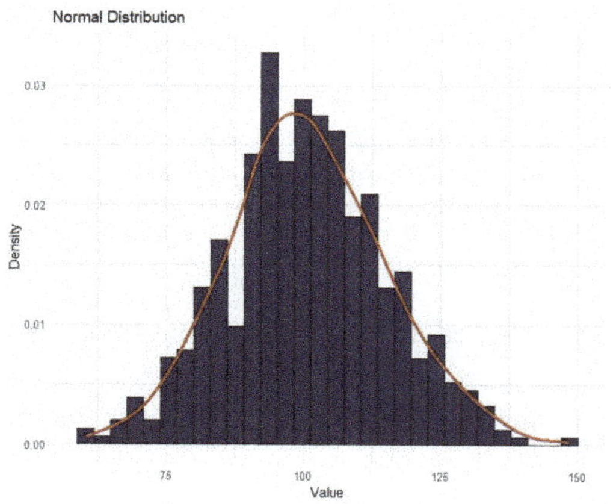

The normal distribution—commonly called the "bell curve"—represents a symmetric distribution where most values cluster around the mean, and the probability of extreme values decreases smoothly and predictably toward the tails. Many traditional statistical methods, including t-tests, ANOVA, and linear regression, assume that data follows approximately normal distributions because these methods rely on specific mathematical properties of the normal curve, such as predictable probabilities within 1, 2, or 3 standard deviations of the mean.

Understanding normality is important because it affects how well traditional statistical methods perform and how accurately they estimate probabilities and confidence intervals. When data is approximately normally distributed, the mean and median are very close to each other, and the standard deviation provides a meaningful and interpretable measure of variability that can be used to make probability statements about future observations.

In practice, real-world business data rarely follows perfect normal distributions. Sales figures, customer wait times, monthly spending, and employee performance often exhibit skewness, multiple peaks, or heavy tails that deviate from normal expectations. Detecting departures from normality allows analysts to choose robust analytical methods, apply appropriate data transformations, or use AI-enhanced analytics that can adapt interpretations to actual data characteristics rather than relying on potentially inappropriate distributional assumptions.

Modern AI systems can automatically assess normality using multiple statistical tests and visual assessments, suggest appropriate analytical approaches based on actual data characteristics, and provide interpretations that account for distributional properties. This capability ensures that analytical conclusions are based on appropriate methods and that business decisions are supported by valid statistical inference.

2.8 Summary Statistics with Tools

Having established the theoretical foundations of descriptive statistics, we now explore how these concepts are implemented in practice using modern analytical tools, particularly those enhanced by artificial intelligence. The landscape of statistical computing has transformed dramatically from the era of manual calculations and basic spreadsheet functions to sophisticated, AI-powered platforms that can generate comprehensive analytical insights with minimal user intervention.

The evolution of statistical software has democratized access to advanced analytical capabilities while simultaneously increasing the importance of understanding fundamental statistical concepts. As tools become more powerful and automated, the ability to interpret results correctly and understand the assumptions underlying different analytical approaches becomes increasingly critical for effective decision-making.

2.8.1 Using R/Python for Quick Descriptive Summaries

Python has emerged as the dominant programming language for data analysis, with its extensive libraries providing powerful tools for data manipulation, analysis, and visualization. The pandas library, in particular, offers comprehensive functionality for generating descriptive statistics with minimal coding effort. With just a few lines of code, analysts can generate comprehensive descriptive summaries of entire datasets, including all the measures discussed in this chapter.

The describe() function in pandas automatically generates count, mean, standard deviation, minimum, quartiles, and maximum for all numeric variables in datasets. However, modern Python libraries extend far beyond basic summaries. Libraries such as pandas-profiling can automatically generate comprehensive data reports that include distribution plots, correlation matrices, missing value analysis, and potential data quality issues—essentially providing complete data profiling capabilities that would require hours of manual work.

R remains a powerful platform for statistical analysis, with extensive libraries specifically designed for descriptive statistics and data exploration. The summary() function provides quick overviews of data characteristics, while specialized packages like psych offer detailed descriptive statistics with additional measures and visualizations. R's particular strength lies in its statistical heritage and the depth of its analytical capabilities, making it especially valuable for complex statistical analysis and research applications.

The real revolution has emerged from AI-enhanced versions of these traditional tools. Modern platforms can automatically generate appropriate code in R or Python based on natural language descriptions of analytical objectives. Analysts might simply request "show me the distribution of customer ages by geographic region" and the AI system will automatically generate the appropriate code, execute the analysis, and interpret the results in business-relevant terms.

What makes modern AI-enhanced programming environments particularly powerful is their ability to automatically suggest relevant analyses based on data characteristics and analytical context. When working with time series data, these systems might automatically suggest trend analysis and seasonality detection. When analyzing categorical variables with many levels, they might recommend grouping strategies or dimensionality reduction techniques that simplify interpretation while preserving important information.

2.8.2 AI-Assisted Descriptive Analytics

The emergence of automated data profiling tools has revolutionized approaches to descriptive statistics, enabling comprehensive analysis of datasets that would be impractical to analyze manually. These AI-powered systems can automatically scan entire datasets and generate comprehensive profiles that would require hours or days to create using traditional methods.

Modern AI profiling tools automatically detect data types and suggest appropriate analytical approaches, identify potential data quality issues such as missing values or inconsistent formatting, calculate appropriate summary statistics for each variable based on its characteristics, generate relevant visualizations that highlight important patterns, detect relationships between variables that might not be apparent in univariate analysis, and flag unusual patterns or outliers that warrant further investigation.

For example, when uploading a customer dataset to an AI profiling tool, the system might automatically detect that customer age exhibits a bimodal distribution suggesting two distinct customer segments, that purchase amounts are highly correlated with customer tenure indicating loyalty effects, that there are unusual patterns in geographic distribution that might indicate data collection issues or market opportunities, and that certain product categories show much higher variability in customer satisfaction scores than others.

These tools don't replace the need to understand descriptive statistics—they amplify the ability to apply these concepts at scale and identify patterns that might be missed in manual analysis. Understanding what the AI is communicating and knowing how to interpret and act on its findings remains crucial for effective analysis and decision-making.

AI-assisted analytics also excel at comparative analysis, automatically comparing datasets to historical data, industry benchmarks, or similar datasets to provide context that helps analysts understand whether their descriptive statistics indicate normal patterns or unusual situations requiring attention. This contextual information is often as valuable as the statistics themselves for making informed business decisions.

Modern AI systems can also automatically generate natural language summaries of descriptive statistics, transforming tables of numbers into readable reports. Instead of presenting only numerical summaries, these systems can generate reports stating insights such as "Customer satisfaction scores are normally distributed with a mean of 7.2 out of 10, which is slightly below the industry average of 7.5. However, there's significant variation across product categories, with electronics customers showing much higher satisfaction than clothing customers."

2.8.3 AI-Driven Visualization Tools

The landscape of data visualization has been revolutionized by AI-powered platforms that can automatically generate appropriate visualizations based on data characteristics and analytical objectives [3]. These tools extend far beyond traditional charting software by incorporating intelligence about what visualizations work best for different types of data and analytical questions.

Modern AI visualization platforms can automatically detect the type of data being analyzed (categorical, continuous, time series, etc.), suggest the most appropriate visualization types for specific analytical objectives, automatically optimize visual design elements such as colors, scales, and layouts for maximum clarity and impact, generate multiple complementary views of the same data to highlight different aspects and patterns, and create interactive visualizations that allow for deeper exploration and analysis.

For example, when uploading customer transaction data, an AI visualization tool might automatically create a comprehensive dashboard that includes time series plots showing transaction trends over time, geographic maps displaying transaction patterns by location, distribution plots showing the range and concentration of transaction amounts, and correlation matrices showing relationships between different variables that might indicate business opportunities or operational issues.

These AI systems can also automatically detect and highlight anomalies or interesting patterns in visualizations, drawing attention to insights that might otherwise be overlooked. They might automatically circle outliers in scatter plots, highlight unusual trends in time series data, or use color coding to draw attention to categories that behave differently from others.

One of the most powerful features of AI-driven visualization is the ability to automatically generate insights from visual patterns. Modern systems can automatically detect trends, seasonality, correlations, and anomalies in visualizations and generate natural language descriptions of their findings. This capability bridges the gap between visual pattern recognition and actionable business insights, making advanced analytical capabilities accessible to users without extensive statistical training.

AI visualization tools also excel at creating personalized dashboards that adapt to specific user needs and interests. These systems can learn from user interactions with visualizations to understand what types of insights are most valuable and automatically prioritize similar patterns in future analyses. This personalization capability ensures that analytical outputs remain relevant and actionable for different stakeholders with varying information needs.

The integration of natural language processing with visualization has created tools that allow users to ask questions in plain English and automatically receive appropriate visualizations as answers. Users might ask "How do sales vary by season and region?" and receive an automatically generated set of visualizations that comprehensively answer the question while suggesting follow-up analyses that could provide additional insights.

Interactive AI-powered visualizations can also automatically suggest follow-up questions or analyses based on current viewing patterns. If a user is examining a time series plot that shows an unusual spike in activity, the system might automatically suggest drilling down to identify what caused the spike or comparing it to similar periods in historical data to understand whether the pattern represents a recurring phenomenon or a unique event.

2.9 Key Terms

Descriptive Statistics – Methods for summarizing and describing data characteristics, including measures of central tendency (mean, median, mode) and dispersion (range, variance, standard deviation, interquartile range). Focuses on **existing data**.

Inferential Statistics – Methods that use sample data to make **predictions or conclusions** about a larger population, accounting for uncertainty.

Central Tendency – Measures that indicate the "typical" value of a dataset. Includes mean, median, and mode.

Dispersion – Measures of variability that describe how spread out data is around central values. Includes range, variance, standard deviation, IQR, and MAD.

Skewness – Quantifies asymmetry of a data distribution; indicates if data is concentrated toward one side.

Kurtosis – Measures the "tailedness" of a distribution; indicates the likelihood of extreme values.

Frequency Table – A tabular summary showing the count of observations for each value or category.

Histogram / Bar Chart / Boxplot / Violin Plot / Density Plot – Visual tools to display distributions and variability; AI-enhanced tools automate optimal binning, highlighting, and insights.

AI-Enhanced Analytics – Modern systems that automate descriptive statistics, identify patterns, detect outliers, and provide actionable summaries.

2.10 Review Questions

1. What are the main differences between descriptive and inferential statistics, and why is this distinction important?
2. How do measures of central tendency and dispersion complement each other in summarizing a dataset?
3. Why is it important to detect skewness or kurtosis before interpreting central tendency measures?
4. How do AI-enhanced tools improve frequency tables, visualizations, and outlier detection?
5. In what situations would the median be a more appropriate measure of central tendency than the mean?
6. Explain how interquartile range (IQR) and median absolute deviation (MAD) provide robust measures of variability.
7. How can AI-generated descriptive statistics influence business decisions differently than traditional manual summaries?

2.11 Lab 2: Descriptive Statistics

Descriptive statistics are essential for making sense of data by summarizing its main features in a clear and meaningful way. Even in today's world of advanced data mining and AI tools, understanding these basic concepts is critical for correctly interpreting results. Before applying complex models, analysts must first explore and understand their data. In this lab, you will use descriptive statistics as a starting point to examine patterns, trends, and key characteristics within a dataset.

2.11.1 Demonstration

We'll start by importing the essential Python libraries for our analysis:

```
import pandas as pd
import numpy as np
import matplotlib.pyplot as plt

# Set up display options for cleaner output
pd.set_option('display.max_columns', None)
pd.set_option('display.width', None)
```

We'll work with an employee dataset containing quarterly sales, satisfaction scores, and experience levels. This mirrors the type of business data commonly analyzed in modern AI systems.

```
# Create employee dataset matching textbook examples
np.random.seed(42)  # For consistent results

# Generate realistic employee data
employees = {
    'employee_id': [f'EMP{str(i).zfill(3)}' for i in range(1, 51)],
    'department': np.random.choice(['Sales', 'Support', 'Engineering',
    'HR', 'Marketing'],50, p=[0.30, 0.16, 0.24, 0.12, 0.18]),
    'quarterly_sales': np.random.normal(86.4, 23.44, 50).round(1),
    'satisfaction': np.random.uniform(1, 10, 50).round(1),
    'years_experience': np.random.randint(1, 20, 50)
}

df_employees = pd.DataFrame(employees)

# Display first 6 rows as shown in textbook
print("Employee Dataset (first 6 rows):")

print(df_employees.head(6))
```

Output:

```
Employee Dataset (first 6 rows):
employee_id   department  quarterly_sales  satisfaction  years_experience
    EMP001       Support            103.7           9.0                 3
    EMP002     Marketing             90.4           5.9                 4
    EMP003            HR             83.7           8.3                19
    EMP004   Engineering             79.3           9.1                 3
    EMP005         Sales             51.7           3.9                19
    EMP006         Sales             69.5           2.0                 7
```

This table shows the first six rows of an employee dataset, including employee ID, department, quarterly sales, satisfaction score, and years of experience.

2.11.1.1 Step 1: Frequency Tables and Distributions

Frequency tables organize data systematically to display how often each value or category appears within your dataset. They create a comprehensive inventory of your data's composition.

```
# Create frequency table for departments
dept_freq = df_employees['department'].value_counts().sort_index()
print("Department Frequency Table:")
print("=" * 30)
for dept, count in dept_freq.items():
```

```
    print(f"{dept:<12} | {count:>2}")
print(f"\nTotal Employees: {len(df_employees)}")
```

Output:

```
Department Frequency Table:
==============================
Engineering  | 12
HR           |  4
Marketing    |  7
Sales        | 19
Support      |  8

Total Employees: 50
```

This frequency table reveals the distribution of employees across different organizational units, providing immediate insights into organizational structure and resource allocation.

We can also express these frequencies as percentages to better understand proportions:

```
# Convert to percentages
dept_percent = df_employees['department'].value_counts(normalize=True)
 ↪ * 100
print("\nDepartment Distribution (%):")
print("=" * 30)
for dept, pct in dept_percent.sort_index().items():
  print(f"{dept:<12} | {pct:>5.1f}%")
```

Output:

```
Department Distribution (%):
==============================
Engineering  |  24.0%
HR           |   8.0%
Marketing    |  14.0%
Sales        |  38.0%
Support      |  16.0%
```

Bar charts and histograms transform numerical summaries into intuitive visual patterns:

```
# Bar chart for department distribution
plt.figure(figsize=(10, 6))
dept_freq.plot(kind='bar', color='skyblue', edgecolor='black')
plt.title('Employee Distribution by Department')
plt.xlabel('Department')
plt.ylabel('Number of Employees')
```

```
plt.xticks(rotation=45)
plt.tight_layout()
plt.show()

# Histogram for quarterly sales
plt.figure(figsize=(10, 6))
plt.hist(df_employees['quarterly_sales'], bins=10, color='lightgreen',
         edgecolor='black', alpha=0.7)
plt.title('Distribution of Quarterly Sales')
plt.xlabel('Quarterly Sales')
plt.ylabel('Frequency')
plt.grid(True, alpha=0.3)
plt.show()
```

2.11.1.2 Step 2: Measures of Central Tendency

Measures of central tendency are statistics that describe the center or typical value of a dataset. Rather than examining every individual data point, they provide a single number that represents where the values tend to cluster. The most common measure is the mean, or average, which is calculated by adding all the values and dividing by the total number of observations, although it can be influenced by extreme values. The median identifies the middle value when the data is arranged in order and is less affected by outliers, making it useful for skewed distributions. The mode represents the most frequently occurring value and is especially helpful for identifying common or repeated outcomes. Together, these measures offer different ways to understand what is typical within a dataset.

Let's explore how to use these metrics with our sample dataset.

```
# Calculate measures of central tendency for quarterly sales
sales_data = df_employees['quarterly_sales']
mean_sales = sales_data.mean()
median_sales = sales_data.median()
mode_sales = sales_data.mode()

print("Quarterly Sales Analysis:")
print("=" * 40)
print(f"Mean Quarterly Sales    | {mean_sales:.5f}")
print(f"Median Quarterly Sales  | {median_sales:.5f}")
print(f"Standard Deviation      | {sales_data.std():.5f}")
print(f"Maximum Quarterly Sales | {sales_data.max():.5f}")
print(f"Minimum Quarterly Sales | {sales_data.min():.5f}")
```

Output:

```
Quarterly Sales Analysis:
========================================
Mean Quarterly Sales    | 86.33600
Median Quarterly Sales  | 87.00000
Standard Deviation      | 21.53751
Maximum Quarterly Sales | 123.10000
Minimum Quarterly Sales | 25.00000
```

```
# Understanding what these numbers mean
difference = abs(mean_sales - median_sales)
print(f"\nDifference between mean and median: {difference:.2f}")
if difference < 2:
    print("The mean and median are close, suggesting fairly symmetric
     ↪ data")
    print("Both measures represent typical performance well")
else:
    print("The mean and median differ significantly")
    print("This suggests the data may be skewed by extreme values")
    print("Consider which measure better represents 'typical'
     ↪ performance")
```

Output:

```
Difference between mean and median: 0.66
The mean and median are close, suggesting fairly symmetric data
Both measures represent typical performance well
```

2.11.1.3 Step 3: Measures of Dispersion

Measures of dispersion describe how much the data varies or spreads out around the center. While measures like the mean or median tell you what is typical, dispersion tells you how consistent or inconsistent the values are. Two datasets can have the same average but feel completely different if one is tightly clustered and the other is widely spread out.

The range is the simplest measure of spread and is calculated as the difference between the maximum and minimum values. It gives a quick sense of the total spread, but it is very sensitive to extreme values. The variance measures how far each value is from the mean on average, using squared differences, which makes larger deviations more impactful. Because variance is in squared units, it can be harder to interpret directly. The standard deviation solves this by taking the square root of the variance, bringing the measure back to the original units of the data. It is the most commonly used measure of dispersion because it provides an intuitive sense of how far values typically deviate from the mean.

```
# Calculate dispersion measures
minimum = sales_data.min()
maximum = sales_data.max()
data_range = maximum - minimum
std_dev = sales_data.std()
variance = sales_data.var()

print("Dispersion Measures for Quarterly Sales:")
print("=" * 40)
print(f"Minimum                    | {minimum:.5f}")
print(f"Maximum                    | {maximum:.5f}")
print(f"Range                      | {data_range:.5f}")
print(f"Standard Deviation         | {std_dev:.5f}")
print(f"Variance                   | {variance:.5f}")
```

Output:

```
Dispersion Measures for Quarterly Sales:
========================================
Minimum                  | 25.00000
Maximum                  | 123.10000
Range                    | 98.10000
Standard Deviation       | 21.53751
Variance                 | 463.86439
```

The interquartile range (IQR) is a powerful measure of variability that focuses on the "middle" of a dataset rather than its extremes. Instead of being influenced by unusually high or low values, the IQR captures the spread of the central 50% of observations by measuring the distance between the first quartile (Q1) and the third quartile (Q3). This makes it especially useful in real-world data, where outliers can distort other measures like the range or standard deviation. By examining the IQR, we gain a clearer picture of where most observations fall and how tightly they are grouped. It also serves as the foundation for a common method of detection of outliers, helping us identify values that fall far outside the typical range of data.

```
# Calculate quartiles and IQR
Q1 = sales_data.quantile(0.25)
Q3 = sales_data.quantile(0.75)
IQR = Q3 - Q1

print(f"\nInterquartile Range Analysis:")
print(f"First Quartile (Q1)        | {Q1:.5f}")
print(f"Third Quartile (Q3)        | {Q3:.5f}")
print(f"Interquartile Range        | {IQR:.5f}")
print(f"\nIQR Interpretation:")
```

```
print(f"25% of employees sell less than {Q1:.1f} units")
print(f"25% of employees sell more than {Q3:.1f} units")
print(f"The middle 50% of employees sell within a {IQR:.1f} unit
↪  range")
```

Output:

```
Interquartile Range Analysis:
First Quartile (Q1)       | 74.37500
Third Quartile (Q3)       | 102.95000
Interquartile Range       | 28.57500

IQR Interpretation:
25% of employees sell less than 74.4 units
25% of employees sell more than 103.0 units
The middle 50% of employees sell within a 28.6 unit range
```

Outlier detection using the 1.5 × IQR rule:

```
# Identify potential outliers
lower_bound = Q1 - 1.5 * IQR
upper_bound = Q3 + 1.5 * IQR
outliers = sales_data[(sales_data < lower_bound) | (sales_data >
↪  upper_bound)]

print(f"\nOutlier Detection:")
print(f"Lower boundary: {lower_bound:.2f}")
print(f"Upper boundary: {upper_bound:.2f}")
print(f"Number of potential outliers: {len(outliers)}")
if len(outliers) > 0:
    print(f"Outlier values: {list(outliers.round(2))}")
```

Output:

```
Outlier Detection:
Lower boundary: 31.51
Upper boundary: 145.81
Number of potential outliers: 1
Outlier values: [25.0]
```

2.11.1.4 Step 4: Visualizing Distributions

Boxplots are one of the fastest ways to understand how data is distributed, especially when comparing groups like departments. Instead of listing numbers, a boxplot turns key statistics into a visual summary. Each part of the boxplot tells a specific story about the data. The line inside the box represents the median, which is the typical value for that group. The box itself spans from the first quartile (Q1) to the third quartile (Q3), showing where the middle 50% of values fall. This is the same range captured by the IQR, so a taller box means more variability among typical observations.

The "whiskers" extend outward from the box to show the range of values that are still considered typical. They do not always go all the way to the minimum and maximum—instead, they stop at values within $1.5 \times$ IQR from the quartiles. Any points beyond the whiskers are plotted individually and flagged as potential outliers, meaning they are unusually high or low compared to the rest of the data.

When you compare multiple boxplots side by side, like sales across departments, you can quickly see which groups have higher typical performance (median), which are more consistent (smaller boxes), and which have unusual values (outliers). This makes boxplots especially useful for spotting differences that would be hard to see in raw numbers alone.

```
# Create boxplot by department
plt.figure(figsize=(12, 6))
df_employees.boxplot(column='quarterly_sales', by='department',
↪  figsize=(12, 6))
plt.title('Quarterly Sales Distribution by Department')
plt.suptitle('')  # Remove automatic title
plt.ylabel('Quarterly Sales')
plt.xticks(rotation=45)
plt.tight_layout()
plt.show()
```

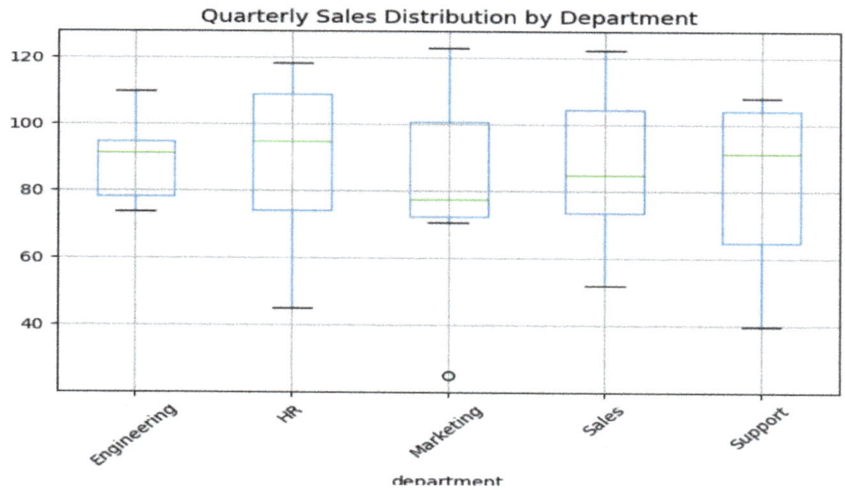

The boxplot shows that Engineering has the most consistent sales with a narrow middle 50% range, while HR and Support exhibit wider variability among employees. Marketing has the lowest median sales and includes a clear low-performing outlier, indicating an unusually low quarterly result.

2.11.2 Practice

For these exercises create a dataset that represents 50 customers with age, monthly spending, and satisfaction data.

```
# Customer dataset for analysis
np.random.seed(123)
customers = {
    'customer_id': range(1, 51),
    'age': np.random.randint(18, 75, 50),
    'monthly_spend': np.random.normal(150, 41.62, 50).round(2),
    'satisfaction_score': np.random.choice([1, 2, 3, 4, 5], 50,
        p=[0.05, 0.10, 0.15, 0.35, 0.35])
}

df_customers = pd.DataFrame(customers)
print("Customer Dataset (first 6 rows):")
print(df_customers.head(6))
```

2.11.2.1 Lab 2 Questions

1. Show the print of the first 6 lines of the data you created.
2. Create a frequency table of the satisfaction scores and describe what it tells you about customer sentiment.
3. Calculate the mean, median, and mode for monthly spending. Indicate which measure best represents typical customer spending and explain why.
4. Create a histogram of customer ages. Describe any patterns you observe in the age distribution.
5. Calculate the standard deviation and interquartile range (IQR) for monthly spending. Explain what these numbers indicate about variability in spending.
6. Divide customers into three age groups: Young (18–35), Middle (36–55), and Senior (56+). Calculate the mean, median, and standard deviation of monthly spending for each group. Compare the groups and describe any patterns.
7. Create side-by-side histograms showing the distribution of monthly spending for each age group. Discuss any differences you observe.
8. Identify outliers in monthly spending for each age group using the $1.5 \times$ IQR rule. Describe any patterns of unusual spending across age groups.

2.12 Conclusion

Descriptive statistics form the **foundation of all data analysis**, enabling analysts to understand the characteristics of datasets before making inferences or predictions. Measures of central tendency and dispersion allow stakeholders to summarize data concisely and detect patterns, anomalies, and variability. Understanding distribution shape, including skewness and kurtosis, ensures that analyses are robust and appropriate for the dataset.

In the **AI-enhanced era**, descriptive statistics are integrated with automated profiling, anomaly detection, and visual analytics. AI tools can generate frequency tables, histograms, and dashboards almost instantly, highlighting unusual patterns and suggesting optimal measures for interpretation. However, while AI automates calculations and visualization, **human understanding remains essential** to contextualize results, interpret outputs correctly, and make informed decisions.

By combining classical statistical principles with AI-assisted insights, analysts can explore larger datasets, detect subtle trends, and communicate actionable findings effectively. Mastery of these concepts ensures that data-driven decisions are reliable, interpretable, and relevant for both current data and potential future applications.

2.13 References

[1] DataKitchen. (2025). The 2026 Open Source Data Profiling Software Landscape. https://datakitchen.io/the-2026-open-source-data-profiling-software-landscape/

[2] Nile Secure. (2025). Anomaly Detection Using AI & Machine Learning. https://nilesecure.com/ai-networking/anomaly-detection-ai

[3] Domo. (2025). 8 Best AI Tools for Data Visualization. https://www.domo.com/learn/article/ai-data-visualization-tools

Chapter 3

Obtaining and Exploring Data

3.1 Learning Outcomes

3-1. Identify and describe common modern data sources, including databases, files, web-based sources, real-time data streams, and manually collected data, and explain how AI tools support data discovery and access.

3-2. Recognize and work with different data file types—such as CSV, proprietary formats, and unstructured data—using AI-enhanced tools for format detection, conversion, and preprocessing.

3-3. Diagnose common data quality issues, including missing values, inconsistent formatting, duplicates, and anomalies, and explain how AI tools assist in data cleaning and validation.

3-4. Explore and evaluate datasets using automated profiling, visualization, and pattern detection tools while applying human judgment, domain knowledge, and ethical considerations.

3.2 Introduction

In data analytics, the quality of your insights depends heavily on the quality, structure, and understanding of the data you work with. Before any modeling, visualization, or advanced analysis can occur, analysts must first locate appropriate data, assess its condition, and explore its underlying patterns. This process—often referred to as data acquisition and exploration—is one of the most critical stages of the data analytics lifecycle.

In today's AI-enhanced environment, obtaining and exploring data looks very different from how it did even a decade ago. Data is no longer confined to local files or static databases. Instead, analysts routinely work with cloud databases, real-time data streams, unstructured text, proprietary formats, and datasets pulled from multiple internal and external sources. At the same time, artificial intelligence tools have dramatically reduced the technical barriers to accessing, cleaning, and understanding data.

This chapter introduces the modern landscape of data acquisition and exploration, with a strong emphasis on practical tools and real-world workflows. You will learn how AI tools assist with discovering data sources, connecting to databases, converting file formats, cleaning messy data, and exploring patterns visually and statistically. While automation plays an increasingly important role, this chapter also emphasizes the continued importance of human judgment, domain expertise, and ethical responsibility in working with data.

3.3 Data Sources in the AI Era

Data can originate from diverse origins, and the landscape has exploded with new possibilities thanks to AI and automation. In the past, prior to the rise of cloud computing and widespread internet connectivity, computers operated largely in isolation. Data was stored locally on floppy disks or hard drives, and if data exchange was necessary, it was commonly facilitated by physical mailing disks between locations.

In contemporary times, data acquisition often involves linking to a database, but AI has made this process much more user-friendly than ever before. This connection could entail retrieving data either through internet access or within a company's internal network. In the latter scenario, you might establish a connection to another computer within the company via an internal network, bypassing the internet entirely, to access a backend database that contains the information you need.

When establishing a connection to a database, the standard protocol employed is Open Database Connectivity (ODBC), offering a uniform method for connecting to and engaging with databases regardless of their specific type or vendor. Structured Query Language (SQL) serves as the primary means to query data, facilitating tasks such as selecting specific data from tables, filtering records based on criteria, and combining information from multiple sources.

3.3.1 Modern AI-Powered Data Discovery

Here's where AI gets really helpful for everyday users. Tools like ChatGPT, GitHub Copilot, or even Microsoft Excel's new AI features can now generate SQL queries from plain English descriptions, making database access much more accessible to non-technical users. For example, in Excel, you can literally type "show me all sales from last month where the amount was over $1000" in the formula bar, and it will write the SQL code for you automatically. In Google Sheets, the "Help me organize" feature does something similar, translating natural language requests into appropriate database queries.

One of the biggest changes AI has brought is in data discovery, which involves finding data sources you didn't even know existed within your organization or in public repositories. Traditional data catalogs were like old library card systems, requiring you to know exactly what you were looking for before you could find it. AI-powered data catalogs are more like having a smart librarian who can understand what you're trying to accomplish and suggest relevant datasets that might help you achieve your analytical goals.

For example, if you're working on a customer analysis project, tools like Tableau's Ask Data feature or Microsoft Power BI's Q&A can automatically suggest combining your sales data with demographic data from public sources, weather data that could affect purchasing patterns, or social media sentiment data about your products. These connections often wouldn't occur to human analysts working in isolation, but AI can spot patterns and relationships across vast numbers of data sources that might prove valuable for your specific analysis.

Even free tools like Google Sheets now have AI features that can automatically detect data types and suggest appropriate charts or analyses. When you upload a dataset, Google Sheets might pop up a message saying "this dataset contains personally identifiable information" or "this data appears to be financial transaction records" without you having to manually examine every column and row in the file.

3.3.2 Real-Time and Streaming Data

AI has also made it much easier to work with real-time data streams, which represent information that flows continuously rather than being collected in discrete batches. In the past, analyzing data from sources like website clicks, sensor readings, or social media posts required specialized technical skills and custom programming. Now, AI-powered platforms can automatically process these streams, detect anomalies, and alert you to interesting patterns as they happen in real-time.

For instance, an e-commerce company might use AI to monitor their website traffic in real-time, automatically detecting when there's an unusual spike in visitors from a particular region or when customers are abandoning their shopping carts at higher than normal rates. The AI doesn't just collect this data passively but interprets it actively and suggests what actions to take based on the patterns it identifies.

3.3.3 Web Scraping and Legal Considerations

Alternatively, you may opt to extract data from the internet through web scraping, albeit with accompanying considerations and constraints that must be carefully evaluated. The legal ambiguity surrounding web scraping underscores the necessity to comprehend the legal and ethical ramifications before engaging in such activities. AI tools can now help navigate these complexities by automatically checking robots.txt files, respecting rate limits, and ensuring compliance with data protection regulations like GDPR or CCPA.

3.3.4 Manual Data Entry and Automation

Conversely, manual data entry may still be necessary, particularly in instances involving research or data collection during site visits where automated systems cannot reach. However, this manual process can be laborious and time-consuming, often prone to human error and inconsistency. AI-powered tools like optical character recognition (OCR) and natural language processing can now automate much of this work, converting physical documents, handwritten notes, and even audio recordings into structured data that can be analyzed using standard tools.

3.4 File Types and AI-Enhanced Processing

When it comes to file types, data can be stored in a variety of formats, and AI has dramatically expanded our ability to work with different file types automatically without requiring extensive technical knowledge. If your goal is to analyze data, strive to obtain CSV (comma-separated values) files whenever feasible, as they tend to be the most universally compatible for reading and writing across different software systems, including R, Python, and Excel. However, AI systems can now automatically convert between different file formats, making this less of a constraint than it used to be for most analysts.

3.4.1 Smart File Format Detection

Here's something really practical that demonstrates the power of modern AI tools. Tools like Tableau Prep, Power BI, or even free options like OpenRefine can automatically detect what type of file you're working with and how it's structured, even when the file extension is wrong or missing entirely. For example, when you drag a file into Tableau Prep, it might tell you "this appears to be a CSV file with pipe delimiters, containing financial data with dates in European format." It then shows you a preview and suggests the best way to import the data, often identifying potential problems before they cause issues in your analysis.

This capability is incredibly helpful when you're dealing with data from multiple sources that use different conventions and formatting standards. Instead of spending time figuring out whether dates are in MM/DD/YYYY or DD/MM/YYYY format, these tools can detect the pattern automatically and show you options to standardize everything consistently. In Tableau Prep, you'll see a little lightbulb icon that suggests these fixes, making the process much more intuitive than manual inspection and correction.

3.4.2 Proprietary Formats and Conversion

Proprietary file formats, such as those utilized by SAS and SPSS, are prevalent in high-end software requiring expensive licenses that many organizations cannot afford. While SAS is widely utilized in enterprise environments, it's advisable to avoid receiving data in SAS formats if you lack access to the respective software, as this can create significant barriers to analysis. However, AI-powered data conversion tools can now automatically translate between different proprietary formats, reducing the need for expensive software licenses just to access data that should be universally readable.

Even with programming code available to manage these formats, ensuring correct formatting and data integrity can pose significant challenges that require specialized knowledge. Therefore, opting for a straightforward file type like CSV is generally the preferable choice for most analytical work, but AI systems can now handle format conversion automatically, making this less of a concern than it was in the past.

Table 3.1: Comparison of Structured vs. Unstructured Data

Category	Structured Data	Unstructured Data
Format	Organized, tabular	Free-form, no fixed structure
Examples	Spreadsheets, SQL DBs	Emails, images, videos
Storage	Relational databases	Data lakes, NoSQL, cloud storage
Processing	Easy analysis (SQL)	Requires AI, NLP, data mining

Category	Structured Data	Unstructured Data

One of the most exciting developments in recent years is how AI has made unstructured data accessible to regular analysts who don't have extensive programming backgrounds. In the past, if you had a folder full of customer service emails or product reviews, you'd need specialized programming skills to extract useful information from these text-based sources. Now, AI tools can automatically process these text files and create structured datasets showing things like customer sentiment, common complaint categories, or frequently mentioned product features.

For example, you might upload 1000 customer service chat logs to a tool like MonkeyLearn, which has a free tier available for small projects, and it could automatically create a spreadsheet showing the date, customer sentiment (positive, negative, or neutral), main issue category (billing, technical, shipping), and resolution status for each interaction. You literally upload a CSV file, select "sentiment analysis" from the menu, and download the results. This kind of analysis used to require weeks of manual coding or expensive consulting services from specialized firms.

The key advantage of modern AI-enhanced file processing is that you no longer need to worry as much about format compatibility or technical conversion issues. AI systems can automatically detect file types, convert between formats, and even repair corrupted files in many cases. This allows you to focus more on the analytical questions you want to answer rather than the technical details of data format management, which can be a significant time-saver for analysts at all skill levels.

3.5 Problems with Imported Data and AI Solutions

Importing data can pose numerous challenges, particularly when dealing with messy datasets that haven't been carefully curated, but AI has provided powerful new tools for automatically detecting and resolving many of these issues that previously required extensive manual work. This issue frequently arises when data has been manually entered by humans, such as in surveys featuring open-ended responses where consistency wasn't enforced. When respondents have the freedom to input data as they see fit, inconsistencies like variations in capitalization and spelling can abound throughout the dataset. Examples include "Dog" versus "dog" versus "dogs" or "New York" versus "NY" versus "new york."

3.5.1 AI-Powered Data Cleaning

Here's where AI really shines for everyday analysts who need to clean data efficiently. Tools like OpenRefine, which is completely free, Tableau Prep, or Excel's Data Types feature can automatically detect and fix common data quality issues that used to take hours to identify and correct manually. For example, in OpenRefine, if you have a customer database where some people entered their state as "NY," others as "New York," and others as "new york," you can click on the column header, select "Facet > Text facet," and OpenRefine will show you all the variations present in that column. Then you can click "Cluster" and it will automatically group similar entries together, letting you standardize them with one click rather than editing each record individually.

The same principle applies to duplicate detection, which can be particularly challenging when records aren't identical but represent the same entity. In Excel, the new "Data Types" feature can identify that "John Smith, 123 Main St" and "J. Smith, 123 Main Street" are probably the same person, even though the records aren't identical in their text. You'll see a small icon next to the cell that you can click to see suggested matches, along with confidence scores that help you decide whether the matches are likely to be correct.

3.5.2 Data Wrangling Fundamentals

Similar to renovating a cluttered house, cleaning and organizing your data are essential steps to render it functional for analysis. This process remains critical even when dealing with initially disorganized data, as you must make do with what you have rather than starting from scratch. Data wrangling entails transforming raw data into a format suitable for analysis, and the extent of wrangling required varies significantly depending on the circumstances and the original data collection methods.

While medical and government data collection systems tend to be well-structured due to regulatory requirements and standardized procedures, other fields present different challenges. Survey data with free-text responses, in particular, often demands substantial cleaning and organization before analysis can commence effectively. The good news is that modern tools can help automate much of this work, reducing the time and effort required while improving consistency and accuracy.

3.5.3 Intelligent Data Validation

Another challenge in dealing with data arises when it becomes incomprehensible to the analyst, which differs significantly from simply being messy or disorganized. Incomprehensible data may be impeccably organized but exist within a subject area unfamiliar to the analyst. For instance, deciphering medical coding, such as ICD-9 codes, can prove daunting without prior familiarity with healthcare terminology and classification systems. There's no shame in seeking guidance from experts to gain a clearer understanding of the data you're working with.

Modern tools can help bridge this knowledge gap in practical ways. As mentioned earlier, Excel's Data Types feature can automatically provide context for coded data, explaining what various codes mean and providing additional information that helps with interpretation. Tools like Tableau can flag unusual codes that might need expert review, identifying entries that appear infrequently or seem out of place compared to the rest of the dataset.

3.5.4 Collaboration with Domain Experts

As an analyst, it's often necessary to collaborate closely with domain experts who understand the subject matter behind the data. For instance, in a project involving neurological assessments for stroke victims, meeting with the overseeing physician might be essential to interpret the data on swallowing assessments, cognitive function scores, or motor skill evaluations. The automated profiling and quality assessment features of modern tools can help prepare for these conversations by identifying which aspects of the data need clarification or seem unusual.

3.5.5 Common Data Quality Issues

AI tools excel at identifying and addressing several categories of data quality problems that commonly plague imported datasets. Missing values often follow patterns that suggest systematic problems with data collection or entry processes, and AI can identify these patterns automatically while suggesting appropriate handling methods. The system might recommend removing records with missing data, imputing values based on other variables, or flagging cases for manual review depending on the nature and extent of the missing information.

Inconsistent formatting presents another frequent challenge, particularly with dates, phone numbers, and addresses that often appear in multiple formats within the same dataset. AI systems can standardize these automatically while flagging ambiguous cases that require human judgment to resolve correctly. For example, a date like "01/02/03" could be interpreted multiple ways, and the system will flag these for clarification rather than making potentially incorrect assumptions.

Advanced algorithms can identify potential duplicate records even when they aren't identical, considering variations in spelling, abbreviations, and data entry errors that would be extremely difficult to catch through manual review. These systems use sophisticated matching techniques that consider phonetic similarity, common abbreviations, and typical data entry mistakes.

Outliers and anomalies in data can represent either errors that need correction or genuinely interesting cases that warrant further investigation. AI tools can automatically flag unusual values and provide context about why they might be problematic, helping analysts decide whether to investigate further, treat them as errors, or consider them as legitimate extreme values that provide important insights.

3.6 Data Exploration Strategies

Once data has been cleaned and organized properly, the exploration phase begins in earnest. This involves understanding the structure of your data, identifying patterns and relationships, and uncovering potential insights before conducting formal statistical analysis. Modern AI-powered tools have transformed this process from a largely manual endeavor into an interactive dialogue between analyst and system.

3.6.1 Automated Data Profiling

AI-powered data profiling tools can automatically generate comprehensive summaries of your datasets that would take considerable time to produce manually. These tools examine each variable systematically to detect data types and validate whether the content matches expectations based on column names and initial data inspection. They identify missing value patterns that might indicate systematic problems with data collection procedures or entry processes.

For numerical variables, these tools provide detailed statistical summaries including measures of central tendency like mean and median, measures of dispersion such as standard deviation and range, and information about distribution shape including skewness and kurtosis. Categorical variables receive frequency distributions showing the most and least common values, along with counts and percentages for each category.

Perhaps most valuably, these tools can detect correlations between variables that might not be immediately obvious to human analysts working with large datasets. They can identify seasonal trends in time-series data, cyclical behaviors that repeat over specific intervals, or unexpected relationships between seemingly unrelated variables that might suggest interesting avenues for further investigation.

3.6.2 Visual Exploration and Pattern Recognition

Modern visualization tools provide automated suggestions based on the characteristics of your specific data rather than requiring you to manually select chart types and formatting options. When you upload a dataset to tools like Tableau or Power BI, the system analyzes the variable types, distributions, and relationships to suggest appropriate chart types and highlight interesting patterns that merit closer examination.

These suggestions often reveal aspects of the data that might be overlooked in manual exploration, particularly when dealing with datasets containing many variables or complex relationships. The tools can automatically create dashboard-style summaries that provide an overview of key patterns and relationships, serving as a starting point for more detailed investigation.

The interactive nature of modern data exploration tools allows analysts to quickly test hypotheses and drill down into interesting patterns without getting bogged down in technical details. Rather than spending time creating individual charts and tables manually, analysts can focus on asking questions and interpreting results while the tools handle the technical aspects of visualization and statistical summary.

3.6.3 Balancing Automation with Human Insight

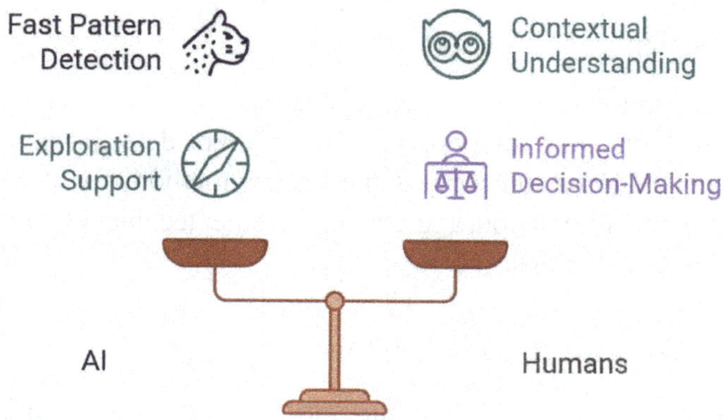

Effective data exploration requires balancing automated assistance with human curiosity and domain knowledge. While AI tools excel at identifying statistical patterns and anomalies in large datasets, human analysts bring contextual understanding and can ask questions that go beyond what the data explicitly shows. They can recognize when patterns might be artifacts of data collection methods rather than genuine phenomena, and they can generate hypotheses based on domain knowledge that might not be apparent from the data alone.

The most successful data exploration combines the computational power of AI with human insight and creativity. AI tools can process vast amounts of data quickly and identify patterns that would be impossible to detect manually, while human analysts provide the context, skepticism, and creative thinking necessary to turn these patterns into meaningful insights and actionable recommendations.

This collaborative approach between human analysts and AI tools represents the future of data exploration, where technology handles the computational heavy lifting while humans focus on interpretation, hypothesis generation, and strategic thinking about what the findings mean for decision-making and action planning.

3.7 Advanced Data Integration Techniques

Modern data analysis often requires combining information from multiple sources, each with its own format, structure, and quality characteristics. AI has revolutionized this process by providing intelligent tools that can automatically identify relationships between datasets and suggest optimal integration strategies.

Traditional data integration required extensive manual work to map fields between different sources, resolve naming conflicts, and handle inconsistencies in data representation. AI-powered integration tools can now automatically detect when fields in different datasets likely represent the same information, even when they have different names or formats. For example, a tool might recognize that "Customer_ID" in one dataset corresponds to "CustNum" in another, or that "DOB" and "Birth_Date" contain the same type of information.

These tools also excel at handling temporal alignment issues that arise when combining datasets collected at different time intervals or with different date formats. AI can automatically detect time patterns and suggest appropriate methods for aligning data temporally, whether through interpolation, aggregation, or other techniques that preserve the integrity of temporal relationships.

3.7.1 Entity Resolution and Record Linkage

One of the most challenging aspects of data integration involves determining when records from different sources refer to the same real-world entity. This process, known as entity resolution or record linkage, traditionally required extensive manual review and custom programming. AI-powered tools can now perform this matching automatically using sophisticated algorithms that consider multiple types of evidence.

These systems can identify potential matches even when records contain errors, abbreviations, or alternative representations of the same information. They use techniques like fuzzy matching, phonetic similarity, and machine learning models trained on patterns of data variation to achieve high accuracy in matching records across different sources.

The tools typically provide confidence scores for potential matches, allowing analysts to focus their manual review efforts on cases where the automated matching is less certain. This dramatically reduces the time required for data integration while improving accuracy compared to purely manual approaches.

3.8 Data Quality Assessment and Monitoring

Ensuring data quality is an ongoing process that extends beyond initial cleaning and preparation. AI tools have made it possible to implement continuous monitoring systems that can detect quality issues as they arise and alert analysts to potential problems before they affect analysis results.

3.8.1 Automated Quality Metrics

Modern data quality tools can automatically calculate and track various metrics that indicate the health of your datasets over time. These include completeness measures that track the percentage of missing values in each field, consistency metrics that identify when the same information is represented differently across records, and accuracy indicators that flag values that seem implausible or inconsistent with expected patterns.

These tools can establish baseline quality metrics for your datasets and then monitor for deviations that might indicate new problems with data collection or processing systems. For example, if the percentage of missing values in a particular field suddenly increases, this might indicate a problem with the data source or collection process that needs immediate attention.

3.8.2 Anomaly Detection and Alert Systems

AI-powered anomaly detection systems can identify unusual patterns in your data that might indicate quality problems or interesting phenomena that warrant investigation. These systems learn the normal patterns in your data and then flag deviations that exceed expected variation levels.

The sophistication of these systems allows them to distinguish between different types of anomalies. Some might represent data quality problems that need correction, while others might indicate genuine changes in the underlying phenomena being measured. The systems can be configured to send alerts when certain types of anomalies are detected, allowing for rapid response to data quality issues.

3.9 Ethical Considerations in Data Collection and Use

As data collection and analysis capabilities have expanded dramatically with AI tools, ethical considerations have become increasingly important for analysts at all levels. Understanding these issues is crucial for responsible data practice and avoiding potential legal and ethical problems.

3.9.1 Privacy and Consent

The ease with which AI tools can collect and analyze personal information raises important questions about privacy and consent. Analysts must understand the legal and ethical requirements for handling personal data, including regulations like GDPR in Europe and various state privacy laws in the United States.

Modern AI tools often include features designed to help with privacy compliance, such as automatic detection of personally identifiable information (PII) and suggestions for anonymization or pseudonymization techniques. However, the responsibility for ensuring ethical use ultimately rests with the analyst and their organization.

3.9.2 Bias and Fairness

AI tools can inadvertently perpetuate or amplify biases present in training data or collection processes. Analysts need to be aware of these potential issues and take steps to identify and mitigate bias in their data and analysis processes.

This includes understanding how data collection methods might introduce systematic biases, recognizing when datasets might not be representative of the populations they're intended to represent, and being aware of how analytical choices might affect different groups differently.

3.9.3 Transparency and Accountability

The increasing sophistication of AI tools can make it tempting to treat them as "black boxes" that produce results without requiring understanding of the underlying processes. However, responsible data analysis requires maintaining transparency about methods used and being able to explain and justify analytical choices.

This means understanding the limitations of the tools being used, documenting analytical processes clearly, and being prepared to explain results and methods to stakeholders who may not have technical backgrounds. It also involves being honest about uncertainty and limitations in data and analysis results.

3.10 Key Terms

Data Acquisition – The process of obtaining data from various sources for analysis.

Data Exploration – The practice of examining datasets to understand structure, patterns, and anomalies before formal analysis.

Structured Data – Data stored in organized formats like spreadsheets or relational databases.

Unstructured Data – Data without a fixed schema, such as emails, images, audio, and text documents.

Open Database Connectivity (ODBC) – A standardized protocol for connecting to databases, enabling queries across different database systems.

SQL (Structured Query Language) – A programming language used to query and manipulate relational databases.

AI-Powered Data Discovery – Tools that help find relevant datasets, including hidden internal or external sources, using AI and automation.

Real-Time / Streaming Data – Continuously generated data from sources like sensors, website clicks, or social media.

Web Scraping – Extracting data from websites, often requiring legal and ethical considerations.

Optical Character Recognition (OCR) – Technology that converts images or scanned text into machine-readable formats.

CSV (Comma-Separated Values) – A simple file format for tabular data, widely compatible across software.

Proprietary File Formats – Software-specific data formats like SAS or SPSS that may require special tools to access.

Data Wrangling – Transforming raw data into a clean, usable format for analysis.

Data Cleaning / Data Validation – Identifying and correcting errors, inconsistencies, duplicates, and missing values in datasets.

Automated Data Profiling – Using AI tools to summarize datasets with statistics, distributions, correlations, and anomaly detection.

Entity Resolution / Record Linkage – Identifying when different records refer to the same real-world entity.

Anomaly Detection – Using AI to find unusual or unexpected patterns in data.

Ethical Data Use – Considering privacy, consent, bias, fairness, transparency, and accountability in data collection and analysis.

AI-Enhanced File Processing – Tools that detect file types, convert formats, and handle corrupted or unstructured data automatically.

Domain Expertise – Knowledge of the subject area that helps interpret complex or unfamiliar data.

3.11 Review Questions

1. What are the main types of data sources in modern analytics, and how has AI changed access to these sources?

2. Explain the difference between structured and unstructured data and provide examples of each.

3. What role does SQL play in accessing and querying databases? How can AI assist non-technical users in generating SQL queries?

4. How do AI-powered tools improve the discovery of relevant datasets within an organization or public repositories?
5. Describe some of the ethical and legal considerations when using web scraping or real-time data streams.
6. Why are CSV files generally preferred for analysis, and how can AI tools help when working with proprietary or unusual file formats?
7. What are common data quality issues that occur with imported datasets? How can AI help detect and fix them?
8. Explain the concept of data wrangling and why it is important in the analytics process.
9. How can AI-powered tools assist with entity resolution or record linkage when combining multiple datasets?
10. What is automated data profiling, and how does it support effective data exploration?
11. Give examples of how AI visualization tools can help detect patterns or anomalies that might be overlooked manually.
12. Why is balancing AI automation with human insight essential during data exploration?
13. How can AI tools assist in continuous monitoring of data quality over time?
14. Discuss the importance of domain expertise in interpreting datasets that may be unfamiliar or highly specialized.
15. How should analysts handle privacy, consent, and bias considerations when collecting and analyzing data with AI tools?

3.12 Lab 3: Obtaining and Exploring Data

In this lab, you will practice acquiring, exploring, and cleaning real-world datasets. You will learn how to work with data from different sources, including structured tables, JSON from APIs, and common file formats such as CSV and Excel. The lab guides you through loading, examining, and comparing these datasets, as well as identifying and resolving common data quality issues, including missing values, inconsistent formatting, and duplicate records. You will also standardize data, handle missing values, and remove duplicates to create a clean dataset ready for analysis. Throughout the lab, you will develop practical skills in preparing data for analysis, understanding how different sources and formats affect your workflow, and interpreting patterns and insights from your data.

3.12.1 Demonstration

First, let's import the essential libraries we'll use throughout this lab:

```
import pandas as pd
import numpy as np
import matplotlib.pyplot as plt
import json
from pathlib import Path

# Display settings for better output
pd.set_option('display.max_columns', None)
pd.set_option('display.width', None)
pd.set_option('display.max_rows', 10)
```

3.12.1.1 Step 1: Understanding Data Sources

In analytics when we obtain data we no longer just work with local files - we connect to databases, APIs, web sources, and real-time streams. Let's explore these different approaches with simple examples.

```
print("DEMONSTRATION 1: MODERN DATA ACQUISITION")
print("=" * 45)

# Create sample datasets representing different data sources
print("Creating sample data from different sources...")

# Simulate database-style structured data
print("\nDATABASE-STYLE DATA (Structured):")
database_data = {
    'employee_id': [f'EMP{str(i).zfill(3)}' for i in range(1, 11)],
    'department': ['Sales', 'Support', 'Engineering', 'HR',
       'Marketing', 'Sales', 'Support', 'Engineering', 'HR',
       'Marketing'],
    'quarterly_sales': [85.2, 92.1, 78.5, 88.9, 91.3,
                        76.8, 89.4, 82.7, 87.1, 90.6],
    'satisfaction': [8.5, 7.2, 9.1, 6.8, 8.9,
                     7.5, 8.3, 8.7, 7.9, 8.1],
    'years_experience': [5, 8, 3, 12, 7, 4, 9, 6, 11, 5]
}

df_database = pd.DataFrame(database_data)
print("Database connection simulated - 10 employee records")
print(f"Columns: {list(df_database.columns)}")
print("\nFirst 3 rows:")
```

```
print(df_database.head(3))
```

Output:

```
DEMONSTRATION 1: MODERN DATA ACQUISITION
==================================================
Creating sample data from different sources...

DATABASE-STYLE DATA (Structured):
Database connection simulated - 10 employee records
Columns: ['employee_id', 'department', 'quarterly_sales',
  'satisfaction', 'years_experience']

First 3 rows:
employee_id   department  quarterly_sales  satisfaction  years_exp
EMP001         Sales               85.2           8.5              5
EMP002       Support               92.1           7.2              8
EMP003   Engineering               78.5           9.1              3
```

Notice how this structured data is organized in rows and columns, just like a spreadsheet. Each row represents one employee, and each column represents a different attribute about that employee.

Next lets simulate data coming from an API in JSON format, which is a common way that data is delivered from web services. The variable api_data is a Python dictionary containing a key 'customers' that maps to a list of customer records. Each record is itself a dictionary with fields like id, name, age, monthly_spend, and location.

Since JSON data is nested (a list of dictionaries inside another dictionary), it isn't immediately usable for analysis. The pd.json_normalize() function converts this nested JSON structure into a flat, tabular DataFrame where each customer is a row and each attribute is a column. This makes it easy to perform standard data analysis tasks, such as calculations, filtering, and plotting.

The last lines of the code print a message confirming the data was processed, and show the first three rows so you can see the flattened table. In other words, this demonstrates how API-style JSON data can be transformed into a format suitable for analysis in Python.

```
# Simulate API-style JSON data
print("\nAPI-STYLE DATA (JSON Structure):")
api_data = {
    'customers': [
        {'id': 1, 'name': 'Customer_1', 'age': 34,
        'monthly_spend': 156.78, 'location': 'NY'},
        {'id': 2, 'name': 'Customer_2', 'age': 28,
```

```
        'monthly_spend': 203.45, 'location': 'CA'},
        {'id': 3, 'name': 'Customer_3', 'age': 45,
        'monthly_spend': 89.23, 'location': 'TX'},
        {'id': 4, 'name': 'Customer_4', 'age': 52,
        'monthly_spend': 178.90, 'location': 'FL'},
        {'id': 5, 'name': 'Customer_5', 'age': 29,
        'monthly_spend': 234.56, 'location': 'WA'}
    ]
}

# Convert JSON-style data to DataFrame
df_api = pd.json_normalize(api_data['customers'])
print("API data processed - 5 customer records")
print("JSON structure flattened to tabular format")
print("\nFirst 3 rows:")
print(df_api.head(3))
```

Output:

```
API-STYLE DATA (JSON Structure):
API data processed - 5 customer records
JSON structure flattened to tabular format

First 3 rows:
   id        name  age  monthly_spend location
0   1  Customer_1   34         156.78       NY
1   2  Customer_2   28         203.45       CA
2   3  Customer_3   45          89.23       TX
```

Different data sources provide information in different formats, but we can typically convert them all into the familiar table structure for analysis.

3.12.1.2 Step 2: File Format Handling

This part of the lab shows how to work with different file formats commonly used in data analysis. First, it creates a folder called sample_data and saves the same dataset in different formats:

- **CSV** – the most universal, plain-text format that works with almost any program
- **JSON** – a structured format often used by APIs and web services

After saving the files, the code demonstrates how to load each format back into Python so you can analyze the data. Real-world data comes in many forms and knowing how to read and process multiple file types is an essential skill for data work.

```
print("\nDEMONSTRATION 2: FILE FORMAT HANDLING")
print("=" * 40)

# Create directory for our sample files
Path("sample_data").mkdir(exist_ok=True)

# Save data in different formats
print("Creating sample files in multiple formats...")

# CSV format (most universal, as textbook recommends)
df_database.to_csv('sample_data/employees.csv', index=False)
print("Created employees.csv (recommended format)")

# JSON format (common for API data)
with open('sample_data/customers.json', 'w') as f:
    json.dump(api_data, f, indent=2)
print("Created customers.json (API-style format)")
```

Now let's practice loading these different file formats back.

```
print("\nLoading different file formats:")

# Load CSV file
print("\nLoading CSV file:")
df_from_csv = pd.read_csv('sample_data/employees.csv')
print(f"CSV loaded: {df_from_csv.shape[0]} rows x
↪ {df_from_csv.shape[1]} columns")

# Load JSON file
print("\nLoading JSON file:")
with open('sample_data/customers.json', 'r') as f:
    json_data = json.load(f)
df_from_json = pd.json_normalize(json_data['customers'])
print(f"JSON loaded: {df_from_json.shape[0]} rows x
↪ {df_from_json.shape[1]} columns")

print("\nAll files loaded successfully!")
```

3.12.1.3 Step 3: Data Quality Assessment and Cleaning

In this demonstration, you will explore the concept of data quality and why it is critical for any analysis. Real-world datasets often contain errors, inconsistencies, missing values, or duplicate records that can distort results and lead to incorrect conclusions. You will learn how to recognize common data quality issues, understand their potential impact, and prepare datasets for reliable analysis. This demonstration emphasizes the importance of ensuring that data is accurate, consistent, and complete before drawing insights or making decisions.

```
# Create messy data that simulates real-world problems
messy_customer_data = {
    'customer_id': [1, 2, 3, 4, 5, 6, 7, 8],
    'name': ['John Smith', 'jane doe', 'MIKE JOHNSON', 'Sarah Wilson',
             'john smith', 'Jane Doe', 'Mike Johnson', 'sarah wilson'],
    'state': ['NY', 'New York', 'ny', 'California', 'NY',
             'new york', 'CA', 'calif'],
    'email': ['john@email.com', 'jane@email.com', 'mike@email.com',
              None, 'john@email.com', 'jane@email.com',
              'mike@email.com', 'sarah@email.com'],
    'purchase_amount': [100.50, 250.75, None, 89.99, 100.50, 250.75,
              89.99, 89.99]
}

df_messy = pd.DataFrame(messy_customer_data)
```

This dataset contains several common real-world problems that often appear in business data. Names are inconsistently capitalized, for example, “John Smith” versus “john smith,” which can cause mismatches in analysis. State entries vary in format, such as “NY,” “New York,” and “ny,” making it difficult to group or filter data accurately. Some values are missing entirely, such as blank email addresses or purchase amounts, and there are potential duplicate records where the same customer appears more than once. These issues highlight the importance of carefully assessing and cleaning data before performing any analysis.

Sample of messy data:

```
customer_id  name           state       email              purchase_amount
-----------  -------------  ----------  -----------------  ---------------
1            John Smith     NY          john@email.com              100.50
2            jane doe       New York    jane@email.com              250.75
3            MIKE JOHNSON   ny          mike@email.com                 NaN
4            Sarah Wilson   California  NaN                          89.99
5            john smith     NY          john@email.com              100.50
6            Jane Doe       new york    jane@email.com              250.75
7            Mike Johnson   CA          mike@email.com               89.99
8            sarah wilson   calif       sarah@email.com             89.99
```

This part of the lab focuses on assessing and cleaning data to make it reliable for analysis. It begins by identifying quality issues within the dataset. One of the first checks is for missing values, where each column is examined to see how many entries are absent and what percentage of the dataset they represent. Missing data can lead to errors or bias in analysis if it is not properly addressed. The code also looks for duplicate records by counting exact duplicate rows, which can distort summaries such as totals or averages if they are left in the dataset.

In addition to missing values and duplicates, the lab examines inconsistencies in text data. For example, the state column contains multiple formats for the same state, such as "NY," "New York," and "ny," which can create confusion when grouping or filtering the data. By identifying these inconsistencies, students can see where standardization is necessary to ensure the dataset is accurate and consistent. This initial assessment sets the stage for cleaning the data so that subsequent analysis produces valid and reliable results.

```
# Check for missing values
print("Missing value analysis:")
missing_summary = df_messy.isnull().sum()
for col, missing_count in missing_summary.items():
    if missing_count > 0:
        pct = (missing_count / len(df_messy)) * 100
        print(f"  {col}: {missing_count} missing ({pct:.1f}%)")
    else:
        print(f"  {col}: No missing values")
```

Output:

```
Missing value analysis:
  customer_id: No missing values
  name: No missing values
  state: No missing values
  email: 1 missing (12.5%)
  purchase_amount: 1 missing (12.5%)
```

```
# Check for duplicates
print(f"\nDuplicate analysis:")
exact_duplicates = df_messy.duplicated().sum()
print(f"  Exact duplicates: {exact_duplicates}")
```

Output:

```
Duplicate analysis:
  Exact duplicates: 0
```

```
# Check for inconsistencies
print("\nConsistency analysis:")

# Explicitly include both object and string types to avoid
# future warnings
```

```
for col in df_messy.select_dtypes(include=['object',
    'string']).columns:
    unique_count = df_messy[col].nunique()
    print(f"  {col}: {unique_count} unique values")

    # Example: highlight states that may need standardization
    if col == 'state' and unique_count > 5:
        sample_values = list(df_messy[col].dropna().unique())
        print(f"    Sample values: {sample_values}")
        print("    May need standardization")
```

Output:

```
Consistency analysis:
  name: 8 unique values
  state: 7 unique values
    Sample values: ['NY', 'New York', 'ny', 'California',
      'new york', 'CA', 'calif']
    May need standardization
  email: 4 unique values
```

After identifying the problems, the code proceeds to clean the data to ensure it is consistent and reliable. A backup copy is made of the data before cleaning (in case anything goes wrong). The first step is standardizing text, where customer names are converted to title case—for example, "john smith" becomes "John Smith"—and state entries are mapped to consistent abbreviations. This standardization ensures that all text data follows a uniform format, which is essential for accurate analysis and grouping. The next step addresses missing values by filling in any missing purchase amounts with the median value of the column. Using the median provides a reasonable estimate without being overly influenced by extreme values, preserving the integrity of the dataset. Finally, duplicate rows are removed to prevent inflated counts or biased calculations. Eliminating duplicates ensures that each record represents a unique observation, allowing subsequent analysis to produce valid results.

```
# Create a copy for cleaning
df_clean = df_messy.copy()

print("Step 1: Standardizing text data")
# Standardize names to title case
df_clean['name'] = df_clean['name'].str.title().str.strip()
print("  Names standardized to title case")

# Standardize states
state_mapping = {
```

```
    'ny': 'NY',
    'new york': 'NY',
    'california': 'CA',
    'calif': 'CA'
}
df_clean['state']
  = df_clean['state'].str.lower().map(state_mapping).fillna(df_clean[
  ↪  'state'].str.upper())
print("  States standardized using mapping")

print("\nStep 2: Handling missing values")
# Fill missing purchase amounts with median
median_amount = df_clean['purchase_amount'].median()
missing_count = df_clean['purchase_amount'].isnull().sum()
df_clean['purchase_amount'].fillna(median_amount, inplace=True)
print(f"  Filled {missing_count} missing purchase amounts with median:
 ↪  ${median_amount}")

print("\nStep 3: Removing duplicates")
initial_rows = len(df_clean)
df_clean = df_clean.drop_duplicates()
removed_rows = initial_rows - len(df_clean)
print(f"  Removed {removed_rows} duplicate rows")
```

Finally, the code summarizes the cleaning process, showing the number of rows before and after cleaning, and displays a sample of the dataset before and after changes. This demonstrates the importance of cleaning for accurate, reliable analysis: without addressing missing values, duplicates, and inconsistencies, any insights drawn from the data could be misleading.

```
print(f"\nCLEANING SUMMARY:")
print(f"Original rows: {len(df_messy)}")
print(f"Cleaned rows: {len(df_clean)}")
print(f"Rows removed: {len(df_messy) - len(df_clean)}")

print("\nBefore cleaning:")
print(df_messy.head(3))
print("\nAfter cleaning:")
print(df_clean.head(3))
```

Output:

```
CLEANING SUMMARY:
Original rows: 8
```

```
Cleaned rows: 8
Rows removed: 0

Before cleaning:

customer_id  name          state      email             purchase_amount
-----------  ------------  ---------  ---------------   ---------------
1            John Smith    NY         john@email.com             100.50
2            jane doe      New York   jane@email.com             250.75
3            MIKE JOHNSON  ny         mike@email.com                NaN


After cleaning:

customer_id  name          state  email             purchase_amount
-----------  ------------  -----  ---------------   ---------------
1            John Smith    NY     john@email.com             100.50
2            Jane Doe      NY     jane@email.com             250.75
3            Mike Johnson  NY     mike@email.com                NaN
```

3.12.2 Practice

In this exercise, you will work with three different datasets: structured product data, API-style customer orders, and messy customer service records. The goal is to practice inspecting data, handling different file formats, and cleaning inconsistent or missing information. Use Python and pandas to answer all questions.

```python
import pandas as pd
import numpy as np
import json
from pathlib import Path

pd.set_option('display.max_columns', None)
pd.set_option('display.width', None)

# ---------------------------------------------------------
# DATASET 1: Structured "database-style" product data
# ---------------------------------------------------------
product_data = {
    'product_id': [f"P{str(i).zfill(3)}" for i in range(1, 11)],
    'category': ['Home', 'Electronics', 'Clothing',
          'Home', 'Sports',  'Electronics', 'Clothing',
          'Sports', 'Home', 'Clothing'],
    'units_sold': [120, 85, 60, 140, 95, 110, 75, 88, 132, 70],
```

```
    'rating': [4.2, 4.7, 3.9, 4.5, 4.1, 4.8, 3.8, 4.0, 4.6, 3.7]
}

df_products = pd.DataFrame(product_data)
print("Structured product data:")
print(df_products.head(), "\n")

# ----------------------------------------------------
# DATASET 2: API-style JSON customer orders
# ----------------------------------------------------
api_orders = {
    "orders": [
        {"order_id": 1, "customer": "Alicia",
        "total": 89.50, "state": "NY"},
        {"order_id": 2, "customer": "Ben",
        "total": 120.00, "state": "CA"},
        {"order_id": 3, "customer": "Carla",
        "total": 45.25, "state": "TX"},
        {"order_id": 4, "customer": "Derek",
        "total": 200.10, "state": "WA"},
        {"order_id": 5, "customer": "Alicia",
        "total": 99.99, "state": "ny"}
    ]
}

df_orders = pd.json_normalize(api_orders["orders"])
print("API-style order data:")
print(df_orders.head(), "\n")

# ----------------------------------------------------
# DATASET 3: Messy customer service data
# ----------------------------------------------------
messy_service = {
    'cust_id': range(1, 9),
    'name': ['john doe', 'JOHN DOE', 'Jane Smith', 'jane smith ',
    'ALAN', 'alan', None, 'Eve'],
    'state': ['ca', 'CA', 'California', 'calif', 'NV',
    'nv', 'nevada', None],
    'email': ['john@example.com', 'john@example.com',
    'jane@example.com', None,'alan@example.com',
    'alan@example.com', 'alan@example.com',
    'eve@example.com'],
    'issue_cost': [50.25, 50.25, None, 75.00, 20.00,
```

```
        None, 20.00, 20.00]
}

df_service = pd.DataFrame(messy_service)
print("Messy service dataset:")
print(df_service.head())
```

3.12.2.1 Lab 3 Questions

1. Print the number of rows and columns in the `df_products` dataset. List all the column names included in this dataset.

2. Display the first 3 rows of `df_products`. Describe what each row represents.

3. Load and inspect the `df_orders` DataFrame. How many orders were placed? How many unique customers appear?

4. Save `df_products` as a CSV file named `products.csv` and then load it back into a new DataFrame. Does the shape of the new DataFrame match the original? Explain.

5. Save the `api_orders` dictionary as a JSON file named `orders.json`. Load it back and flatten it into a DataFrame. Does this loaded DataFrame match the original `df_orders`? Explain.

6. Using `df_service`, identify which columns contain missing values and how many missing values exist in each column.

7. Using `df_service`, check for any exact duplicate rows. Are there any? If so, how many?

8. List the unique values in the `name` column of `df_service`. Identify which values clearly need standardization.

9. List the unique values in the `state` column of `df_service`. Identify which values represent the same state but are formatted differently.

10. Clean the `df_service` dataset by performing the following tasks:

    - Standardize names to title case and remove extra whitespace
    - Map all California variants to "CA" and Nevada variants to "NV"
    - Fill missing `issue_cost` values with the median
    - Remove duplicate rows

    After cleaning, report how many rows were removed, how many missing values were filled, and provide a preview of the cleaned DataFrame.

3.13 Conclusion

The landscape of data acquisition and exploration has been fundamentally transformed by AI tools that automate many previously manual and time-consuming tasks. From intelligent data discovery and format conversion to automated cleaning and pattern recognition, these tools enable analysts to focus on higher-level analytical questions rather than technical data management challenges.

However, this technological advancement comes with increased responsibility for understanding the capabilities and limitations of these tools. Success in modern data analysis requires balancing automated AI assistance with human judgment, domain knowledge, and critical thinking about data quality and interpretation. The tools handle much of the technical heavy lifting, but analysts remain essential for asking the right questions, providing context for findings, and drawing meaningful conclusions from the data.

Understanding which tools are available and how to leverage them effectively remains crucial for modern analysts. Equally important is maintaining awareness of data quality issues, ethical considerations in data collection and use, and the ongoing importance of domain expertise in interpreting results. AI tools can identify patterns and anomalies, but human judgment remains essential for determining what these findings mean in practical contexts and how they should influence decision-making.

As AI continues to evolve, these capabilities will become even more sophisticated and accessible to analysts at all skill levels. However, the fundamental principles of careful data handling, quality assessment, and thoughtful interpretation will remain central to producing reliable and actionable insights from data analysis projects. The future belongs to analysts who can effectively combine the power of AI tools with strong analytical thinking and ethical practice.

Chapter 4

Data Preprocessing

4.1 Learning Outcomes

4-1. Explain the purpose and steps of data preprocessing in data mining.
4-2. Identify and address common data quality issues such as inconsistencies, missing values, and duplicates.
4-3. Apply data cleaning, modification, and restructuring techniques to prepare datasets for analysis.
4-4. Normalize quantitative data using z-scores and understand the impact of scaling on analysis.
4-5. Reduce dimensionality using principal component analysis (PCA) and interpret PCA results including scores, loadings, and explained variance.

4.2 Introduction

Data preprocessing is the essential step of preparing your data for mining. This involves tasks of cleaning, modifying, and restructuring data. This chapter will focus on key aspects and introduce important preprocessing techniques commonly used in data mining, such as principal component analysis.

While the fundamentals of data preprocessing remain the same, AI tools have made many of these tasks more accessible and efficient. You'll still need to understand what's happening behind the scenes, but modern tools can help automate routine tasks and catch issues you might miss manually.

4.3 Data Cleaning

Data cleaning involves identifying and rectifying discrepancies in your dataset, such as inaccuracies and inconsistencies. Several common issues must be addressed before data analysis, and modern AI-powered tools can help detect many of these automatically.

Data type inconsistencies occur when entries do not match the expected format. For example, if respondents are asked to provide their age as a number but some enter it as text, numeric fields are mixed with character data. Modern tools like Excel's Data Types feature and Google Sheets can automatically detect these inconsistencies and suggest corrections.

Data range problems arise when entries fall outside expected limits. For instance, someone might enter the year as 2,300 instead of 2023 or an age as 2010 instead of 21. These errors are often the result of human mistakes. Examining minimum and maximum values or analyzing frequency distributions can reveal outliers and anomalies. Today's data profiling tools can automatically flag unusual values for review.

Data uniqueness is important to ensure that each entry is distinct. Duplicate records, such as repeated sales transactions, can compromise data integrity. Unique identifiers for each record help prevent this, and relational databases enforce uniqueness with key constraints. Modern duplicate detection tools use fuzzy matching to identify variations like "John Smith" and "J. Smith." In Excel's Data Types feature, a small icon next to potential matches lets you review suggested duplicates with a single click.

Spelling and capitalization errors are common in manual data entry and create inconsistencies. Standardizing text formats, such as converting all entries to uppercase, helps correct these issues. Free tools like Open Refine allow you to select a column, apply a text facet, and use the cluster function to automatically group similar entries such as "NY," "New York," and "new york" for one-click standardization.

Set membership ensures that categorical responses adhere to predefined options. For example, college year responses should be limited to freshman, sophomore, junior, or senior to avoid entries like "second year." Modern data validation tools can automatically check for values outside these expected categories.

4.3.1 Format and Consistency Issues

Pattern issues occur when data formats, such as phone numbers or zip codes, do not follow standard conventions. These inconsistencies can complicate analysis and must be standardized. Modern tools like Tableau Prep use smart pattern recognition to automatically flag format inconsistencies with red exclamation marks, and clicking the marks reveals suggested corrections.

Cross-field issues arise when multiple fields need to align logically. For example, a person's age should match their birthdate, and a product's price should correspond to its category. Ensuring that data such as years in college aligns with a respondent's academic status helps prevent inconsistencies. Contemporary data validation tools can automatically check these relationships and flag potential problems.

4.3.2 Missing and Incomplete Information

Missing data can create significant challenges, especially when it occurs systematically. Although some data mining algorithms can handle missing values, it is important to assess the extent and nature of the missing information. AI tools can help detect patterns in missing data, revealing whether gaps are random or indicate systematic issues.

Incomplete data differs from missing data in that entries are partially filled but lack critical information, such as an address missing the state. Modern data completion tools can sometimes suggest likely values based on other available information, helping to fill these gaps.

Random characters or extra spaces in text data can disrupt analysis and lead to inaccurate results. Cleaning these elements is essential, and automated text processing tools can efficiently identify and remove such anomalies, ensuring that the dataset is ready for analysis.

4.4 Data Modification

Data modification, a secondary step after cleaning, involves altering clean data fields in some way to prepare them for analysis. After ensuring cleanliness, modifying data becomes essential for refining its representation, aiding in more effective analysis. Let's delve into data modification scenarios.

4.4.1 Variable Naming and Format Changes

When preparing to merge datasets, if both contain a column labeled X but representing different variables, one must be renamed to avoid confusion. Changing variable names is often crucial for clarity, especially if initial labels are unclear or redundant. Always preserve the original data and document modifications to maintain integrity. Modern data preparation tools can help track these changes automatically, creating an audit trail of modifications.

In another instance, modifying data involves altering the structure of the data values. This might entail adjusting phone numbers to exclude area codes, assuming they're already standardized, because they need to be in a specific format. Reformatting zip codes is a typical example, simplifying data management by converting nine-digit codes to five digits for consistency and ease of analysis. This isn't cleaning; rather, it's optimizing data while ensuring uniformity.

4.4.2 Field Operations

Another common data modification task is joining or splitting fields. Joining fields combines separate data elements, like merging first and last names into a full name column. Conversely, splitting fields divides combined data into separate components, such as extracting first and last names from a single field. In Excel, you can use the "Text to Columns" feature or the newer "Split Column" option in Power Query, which automatically detects common delimiters like spaces or commas and suggests appropriate splits.

4.4.3 Grouping and Binning

Additionally, grouping and binning data are common data modifications, involves categorizing data into intervals or groups for better interpretation. Particularly with quantitative data, grouping is essential. This entails categorizing continuous variables into intervals for better analysis, enabling techniques like frequency distributions and graphical representations. Many software tools offer automated binning functionality - for example, in Tableau, you can right-click a continuous field and select "Create Bins," where the software suggests optimal bin sizes based on your data distribution.

Grouping effectively converts quantitative data into categorical variables, facilitating analysis. For instance, salary data can be binned into categories like "greater than" or "less than or equal to" a certain threshold. Retaining the original data ensures flexibility and reproducibility in analysis.

Another way to group salary data is by creating a binary variable, such as indicating whether a salary is above or below a certain threshold. Often creating ranges or groups is essential for generating histograms or charts, which can be easily done in Excel or other software. Custom categories can also be manually created if needed. This process is crucial for many data mining techniques and software tools.

Categorical data, although not continuous, may also benefit from grouping. For instance, pet data collected with various specific breeds could be grouped into broader categories like "cat" or "dog," or further refined into groups like "large dog" or "small dog" for simplicity and clarity.

4.5 Data Restructuring

Beyond cleaning and modifying individual data points, restructuring the entire dataset is the next step. This involves operations on the entire data table, such as converting data types, summarizing data or subsetting the data.

4.5.1 Data Format Structure Transformations

A data table itself is a data type and can be changed (restructured). In R, for example, converting a regular data frame to a Tibble using the Tidy verse package is a common restructuring task. The Tibble has different properties from the original data frame. Similarly, in Excel, where data is typically organized into sheets, you can convert them into table formats, altering the data structure's properties.

Converting data from long to wide format and vice versa is a data restructuring common practice, especially when dealing with time columns. In the long format, years may be stacked vertically (e.g., 1990, 2000, 2010), whereas in the wide format, each year occupies its own column. This transformation is often necessary for analytics tools like SPSS, which require specific data formats for some types of analysis. Modern data preparation tools like Tableau Prep can handle these transformations with simple drag-and-drop operations.

4.5.2 Data Aggregation and Integration

Aggregate data creation is another important aspect of data restructuring. This involves summarizing data into a pivot table-like format, aggregating information such as averages or counts. For example, instead of having individual student records, you might create an aggregated database showing the count of students in each class level (freshman, sophomore, etc.). This simplifies the database while retaining essential information for analysis and is often used for presentation and analytical graphs which need summarized data for interpretation.

Typically, data mining will use non-aggregated data although one of the things data mining can do is find groups (clusters) in data which can be used for the aggregation structure.

Another aspect of data restructuring involves integrating data from other sources, a process commonly done through joins. For instance, you might join additional variables, such as population numbers for towns based on zip codes in your dataset. This is often necessary to enrich the existing data with supplementary information. AI-powered data integration tools can now suggest potential joins and help identify matching fields across different datasets.

4.5.3 Data Subsetting

Creating a smaller or sub-set dataset is another restructuring approach, distinct from aggregation. Instead of using all available columns, you select only the relevant ones, forming a more focused analytical file. While this was once crucial due to computational limitations, modern technology makes it less necessary, though still beneficial for efficiency. For instance, you could subset data on people for individuals over 65 years old. This allows you to work with a refined dataset tailored to your analysis needs.

4.6 Normalizing Data

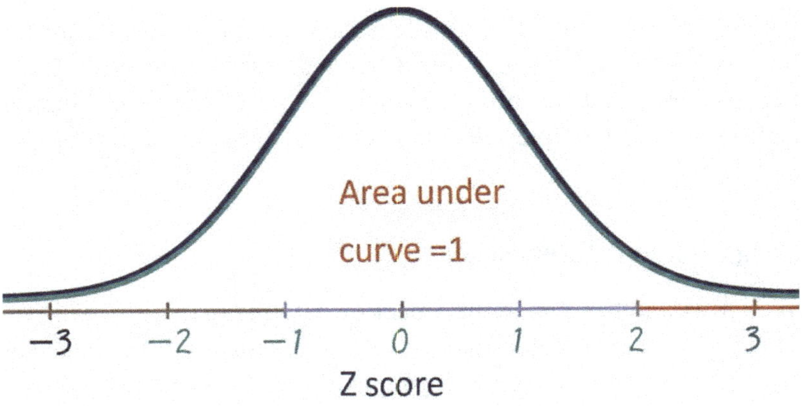

Normalization involves transforming data to adhere to a standard distribution, typically the standard normal distribution but there are other methods. In the standard normal distribution, the mean is zero and the standard deviation is one.

Crucially, this standardization creates "z-scores," which represent the number of standard deviations a data point is from the mean of that data. Converting data to z-scores makes it independent of measurement units, allowing for fair comparisons across different scales. For example, whether measuring height in inches or centimeters, converting to z-scores yields comparable results. This scale-independent metric enhances the reliability and interpretability of data mining analyses.

To compute a z-score, subtract the mean (denoted by μ, representing the population mean) from each data point and then divide by the standard deviation (denoted by σ). This yields a z-score, indicating how many standard deviations a data point is from the mean. A z-score of one signifies one standard deviation above the mean, while a z-score of zero corresponds to the mean itself.

$$z = \frac{x - \mu}{\sigma}$$

$$z = \frac{85 - 75}{10}$$

$$z = 1$$

Let's say we have a test score of 85. The average score (mean) of the class is 75, and the standard deviation is 10. Calculate the z score as 85-75 divided by 10. So, the Z-score is 1. This means that the test score of 85 is 1 standard deviation above the mean.

Most software simplifies this process with automatic z-score calculation. In Excel, you can use the STANDARDIZE function, while statistical packages like R or Python handle this with built-in functions. However, it's essential to understand when to apply standardization. In data mining, where fair comparisons are vital for metrics such as distance, normalized data is preferred. Conversely, for descriptive statistics or summaries, retaining original units may be preferable.

Normalization applies only to quantitative data, not categorical data, and is fundamental in data mining to mitigate the influence of measurement scales.

4.7 Reducing Dimensionality

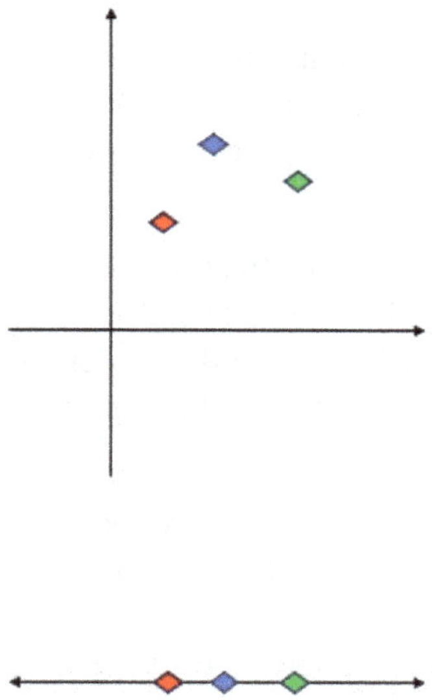

Let's touch on the Curse of Dimensionality. Essentially, when dealing with datasets with many variables, things get complicated. To put it simply, the more variables you have, the more complex your data becomes. While what constitutes "small" or "big" is subjective, having over 20 variables can start to make things feel hefty. And it's not uncommon to encounter datasets with many more variables than that.

The Curse of Dimensionality manifests as the volume of the data space exponentially increases with each additional variable. This leads to a sparse distribution of data points, making analysis, visualization, and modeling challenging.

Let's break it down further. In one dimension, like plotting age on a number line, it's straightforward. Move to two dimensions, and you're into XY coordinate territory, still manageable. But beyond three dimensions, things get tricky. Our brains are wired to comprehend and interact with three-dimensional space. Trying to visualize data in four or more dimensions becomes a mental gymnastics exercise. After all, our world is three-dimensional, and grasping concepts beyond that is tough.

So, what does the Curse of Dimensionality really mean? Essentially, when we're dealing with data in higher dimensions, our ability to analyze and model it accurately starts to falter. Our brains struggle to intuitively grasp and comprehend data in these higher-dimensional spaces. As a result, interpreting and explaining the results of models and analyses becomes challenging.

Enter dimension reduction, the antidote to this curse. The goal here is to decrease the number of dimensions in our dataset. But it's not as simple as just cherry-picking a couple of variables out of many. Instead, it involves creating new derived variables that capture the essence of the original ones, condensing the dataset into a more manageable size.

Let's visualize this concept. Imagine we have data plotted in a two-dimensional graph. By carefully selecting a single dimension, we can still capture much of the information present in the original two dimensions. This reduction from a higher to a lower dimension is at the heart of dimensionality reduction.

So, how do we actually reduce dimensions? The mathematical intricacies involve concepts like eigenvalues and decompositions, typically covered in higher mathematics courses like linear algebra. But a commonly used technique for dimension reduction is principal component analysis (PCA) which can be understood at a practical level without too much math.

Dimension reduction isn't merely about discarding variables; it's a more nuanced process. It's particularly prevalent in fields dealing with extensive datasets, such as bioinformatics. In these domains, datasets often exhibit high dimensionality, characterized by numerous variables rather than just many observations. So, it's not solely about the sample size (n), but also about the sheer volume of variables.

Modern statistical software has made dimensionality reduction more accessible, with tools that can automatically suggest optimal numbers of components to retain and provide clearer interpretations of what the reduced dimensions represent.

4.8 Principal Components Analysis

Principal components analysis (PCA) is a key technique for reducing dimensionality. Through PCA, we transform the original n-dimensional data into a lower-dimensional space (K dimensions). This is achieved by creating new variables known as principal components. These components serve as amalgamations of the original variables, capturing their essence in a more condensed form.

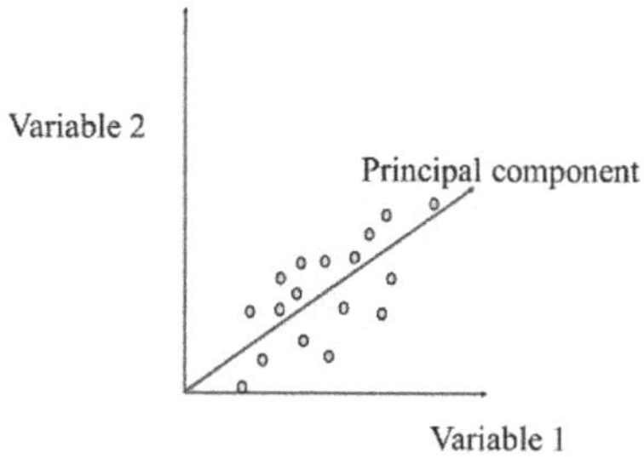

Consider this illustration: imagine we have two-dimensional data represented by variables X and Y. The scatter plot of this data reveals points scattered across. Now, the line drawn through the plot isn't a regression line; rather, it represents a principal component. By combining the weights of the original variables, we create this principal component, effectively reducing the data from two dimensions to one along this component. Visually, it's akin to rotating the axes, condensing the information into a single dimension.

In essence, principal components serve as meta-variables, summarizing the underlying patterns of the original data in a more manageable form. Through PCA, we navigate the complexities of high-dimensional datasets, simplifying them for easier interpretation and analysis.

Now, let's dive into a real-world dataset: the cheese tasting dataset which collects data on acid levels and a taste rating on cheese. Here, we have 20 cases of cheese samples, each evaluated across four variables: acidity, sulfuric acid, lactic acid, and taste. While there are only four variables, we still need six plots to explore the two-by-two relationships adequately.

Table 4.1: Original Data — First 10 Rows

Case	Acetic	H2S	Lactic	Taste
1	4.543	3.135	0.86	12.3
2	5.159	5.043	1.53	20.9
3	5.366	5.438	1.57	39.0
4	5.759	7.496	1.81	47.9
5	4.663	3.807	0.99	5.6
6	5.697	7.601	1.09	25.9
7	5.892	8.726	1.29	37.3
8	6.078	7.966	1.78	21.9
9	4.898	3.850	1.29	18.1
10	5.242	4.174	1.58	21.0

For example, when we examine the relationship between acetic acid and sulfuric acid, a linear pattern emerges.

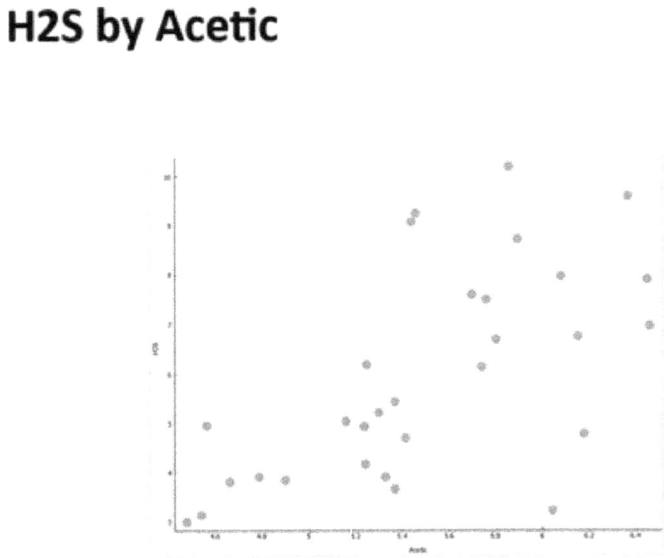

Each plot offers unique insights into the interaction between these variables, revealing their collective impact on the taste of the cheese. Across all the bivariate relationships, if we continued looking at bivariate plots common linear patterns are evident. Although it's impossible to represent four-dimensional data on a single plot, analyzing the two-by-two relationships uncovers intriguing patterns. While the scatter plots do not show perfect correlations, discernible linear trends suggest potential redundancy among the variables.

Indeed, the variables seem to convey similar information about taste, indicating redundancy and collinearity. Given this redundancy, principal components analysis (PCA) emerges as a promising tool for dimension reduction. PCA aims to distill the essence of the original variables into a smaller set of meta-variables, or principal components, thus reducing dimensionality while preserving essential information. In our case, with four(N) original variables, we could derive one, two, three, or four (possible values of K) principal components as the number of principal components maximizes at the number of original variables (four in this case).

4.8.1 Scree Plot

So, when it comes to determining the number of principal components (K) to retain, we aim for a balance between capturing information and reducing dimensionality. Technically, we could perform principal components analysis (PCA) up to the number of original variables, but with four informative variables, we typically aim for one, two, or three principal components. But how do we decide? The key lies in examining a scree plot, a graphical representation of the proportion of variability captured by each principal component. In simpler terms, it shows how much information each component holds.

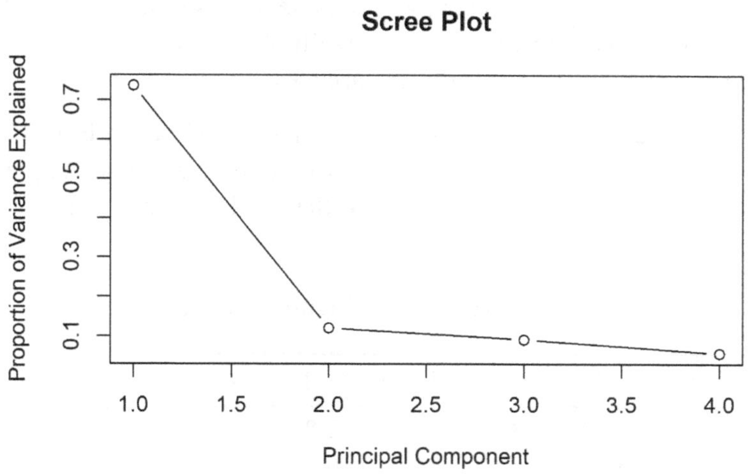

Here's how it works: The orange curve in the scree plot represents the proportion of variability captured by each principal component. For instance, if the first principal component captures 70% of the variability, that's quite substantial. However, we don't stop there. We examine where the curve "elbows," indicating diminishing returns in terms of information captured.

In our example, the curve starts to level off after the first two components, with the third component adding only a marginal increase in variability capture. So, by retaining the first two principal components, which collectively capture around 85% of the variability, we strike a balance between reducing dimensionality and retaining essential information.

Technically, you could extend the analysis to three principal components, but remember our goal is to reduce dimensionality. Going from four original variables to three principal components doesn't offer significant reduction. And if we retain all four principal components, we're essentially keeping the same number of components as variables, which defeats the purpose of dimensionality reduction. So, two principal components seem to be the optimum choice.

Modern software tools can now provide more intelligent guidance on this decision. Some AI-enhanced PCA tools can automatically suggest the optimal number of components based on various criteria, though understanding the scree plot interpretation remains valuable for making informed decisions.

4.8.2 Principal Component Variables

Principal components are new variables derived from linear combinations of the original variables. In the case of the cheese data, we'll generate two new variables, PC1 and PC2, which will capture the essence of the original variables.

Computing the actual values of the principal component variables is rather complex. Fortunately, software tools can handle the calculations for us, saving us from the manual labor of performing complex linear algebra. So now, we'll obtain two new derived variables that capture the essence of the original four variables.

Looking at the table, the first columns represent the original data, while the last two columns are our new variables, PC1 and PC2. Each row corresponds to a cheese sample, with its associated values for the original variables and the newly derived principal components.

Table 4.2: PCA Scores — First 10 Rows (2 Significant Digits)

Case	Acetic	H2S	Lactic	Taste	PC1	PC2
1	4.54	3.14	0.86	12	-2.81	-0.62
2	5.16	5.04	1.53	21	-0.46	-0.34
3	5.37	5.44	1.57	39	0.44	-0.61
4	5.76	7.50	1.81	48	1.94	-0.56
5	4.66	3.81	0.99	5.6	-2.55	-0.35
6	5.70	7.60	1.09	26	0.024	0.21
7	5.89	8.73	1.29	37	1.15	-0.004
8	6.08	7.97	1.78	22	1.44	0.64
9	4.90	3.85	1.29	18	-1.45	-0.46
10	5.24	4.17	1.58	21	-0.52	-0.15

It is important to note that the principal components were computed from normalized data (vs original data on measurement scale – note the table shows original measurement scale). It's essential to note that using non-normalized values would yield completely different results. If original scale variables are used values with larger scales would distort the results.

This ensures consistency and accuracy in the dimension reduction process (the principal components remain the same if the measurement scale is changed since they are based on normalized data). These new variables, PC1 and PC2, are crucial. With them, we can effectively discard the original four variables and still work with meaningful data. For instance, we can perform cluster analysis directly on these principal components. This approach simplifies visualization and analysis, especially when dealing with high-dimensional data.

4.8.3 Weights

So, where do these values of the principal component variables come from?

Coefficients, often referred to as weights, play a crucial role in understanding principal components.

These weights are extracted from the software, usually presented in a table format. Think of them like the coefficients in the equation of a line, but with a twist. From the software, you'll obtain these coefficients, which essentially tell you how much each original variable contributes to the principal component.

4.8.4 PCA Loadings

Table 4.3: PCA Loadings and Variance Explained (2 Significant Digits)

Component	Acetic	H2S	Lactic	Taste	Variance Explained
PC1	0.47	0.52	0.50	0.51	0.74
PC2	0.85	-0.20	-0.095	-0.48	0.12

For example, let's take Principal Component 1 (PC1). We have four original variables: acetic acid, sulfuric acid, lactic acid, and taste. Each of these variables is associated with a weight, indicating its influence on PC1. So, if we have weights of 0.46, 0.51, 0.50, and 0.51 respectively for these variables, the calculation for PC1 becomes:

PC1=0.46*acetic +0.51*h2s + 0.50*lactic + 0.51*taste

By plugging in the respective weights and values of the normalized data, you could calculate values of PC1 and PC2 using very simple algebra.

4.8.5 Interpretation of Principal Components

Now, instead of thinking about the cheese data in terms of the original four variables, we can consider it in terms of the two principal component variables. Although we sacrificed a bit of information, capturing 85% of the data information, we simplified our analysis by working with fewer variables. This simplification is crucial, especially when dealing with large datasets with numerous variables.

Throughout this course, we primarily use original data. However, keep in mind that many analyses can also be conducted on principal components. Since principal components encapsulate the essence of the variables, they are incredibly useful for various analyses like clustering. Thus, understanding and utilizing principal components effectively can significantly enhance data analysis processes.

Interpreting the weights assigned to each variable may require some domain expertise. In the case of the cheese data, the weights seem relatively straightforward. For example, the first principal component evenly weighs all cheese tasting information, while the second heavily emphasizes acetic acid, contrasting with taste. While this interpretation might not always be straightforward, understanding the patterns in the weights can provide valuable insights.

This is where AI-enhanced tools are starting to make a difference. Some modern PCA software can provide natural language interpretations of what each principal component represents, helping bridge the gap between mathematical output and practical understanding. However, these interpretations should always be validated with domain expertise.

Don't hesitate to consult with experts familiar with the data when analyzing principal components. While they may lack analytical skills, their knowledge of the data's context can help interpret the results effectively. Ultimately, leveraging principal components can enhance data analysis processes, providing deeper insights into complex datasets.

So, the gist of principal components is this: they're a handy tool for dealing with large datasets. Imagine you're faced with a dataset containing hundreds of variables. It's just not feasible to work with all of them directly. That's where principal components come in. They allow you to distill the essence of your data into a more manageable number of derived variables. In practical terms, this means taking those 100 variables and condensing them down to, say, seven or six derived variables. This reduction in dimensionality makes it much easier to analyze the data effectively.

With modern software, the process is quite straightforward to use principal components. You don't need to crunch numbers manually like in the old days. The software does the heavy lifting for you. They're a valuable tool for making sense of big datasets and extracting meaningful insights. And the best part? They're not as hard to use as you might think. So, next time you're faced with a mountain of data, remember the power of principal components. They just might be your new best friend in data analysis.

Modern AI-enhanced PCA tools are making this process even more accessible, with features like automatic component interpretation, optimal component number suggestion, and integration with downstream analysis tools. While the mathematical foundations remain the same, these enhancements make PCA more practical for everyday data analysis tasks.

4.9 Key Terms

Data Preprocessing: Preparing raw data for analysis through cleaning, modification, and restructuring.

Data Cleaning: Detecting and correcting errors and inconsistencies in datasets.

Normalization: Transforming quantitative data to a standard scale, often using z-scores.

Z-Score: A measure of how many standard deviations a value is from the mean.

Dimensionality Reduction: Techniques to reduce the number of variables in a dataset while retaining essential information.

Curse of Dimensionality: The phenomenon where high-dimensional data becomes sparse, complicating analysis and visualization.

Principal Component Analysis (PCA): A method to transform original variables into principal components to reduce dimensionality.

PCA Scores: Values of principal components for individual cases.

PCA Loadings: Weights showing the contribution of each original variable to a principal component.

4.10 Review Questions

1. Explain the purpose of data preprocessing and its main steps.
2. What is the difference between missing and incomplete data?
3. Why is normalization important in data mining, and how do z-scores help?
4. What is the curse of dimensionality, and how does PCA help overcome it?
5. How are PCA scores different from PCA loadings?
6. Explain how you would decide how many principal components to retain.

4.11 Lab 4: Data Preprocessing

In this lab, you will master two fundamental techniques for preparing data for mining: standardization and Principal Component Analysis (PCA). You will learn why standardization is essential when working with variables measured on different scales, how to apply z-score standardization both manually and using automated tools, and how to implement PCA to reduce dimensionality while preserving the most important information in your data. The lab guides you through interpreting PCA results, including explained variance ratios and component loadings, and translating these technical outputs into meaningful business insights.

4.11.1 Demonstration

First, let's import the essential libraries we'll use throughout this lab:

```
import pandas as pd
import numpy as np
import matplotlib.pyplot as plt
from sklearn.preprocessing import StandardScaler
from sklearn.decomposition import PCA
```

```
# Display settings for better output
pd.set_option('display.max_columns', None)
pd.set_option('display.width', None)
pd.set_option('display.max_rows', 10)

# Set random seed for reproducible results
np.random.seed(42)
```

4.11.1.1 Step 1: Understanding the Scale Problem

The core problem is simple: when you have variables measured in different units - like comparing employee salaries ($50,000) to performance ratings (4.2 out of 5) - the computer thinks salary is 10,000 times more important just because it's a bigger number. Standardization fixes this by converting all variables to the same scale, so a $10,000 salary difference and a 1-point rating difference are treated as equally important. Once your data is standardized, PCA helps you find the most meaningful patterns by combining related variables into "principal components" that explain the maximum amount of variation in your data. You'll learn both the mathematical foundations and practical applications of these essential data science techniques.

```
print("DEMONSTRATION 1: THE SCALE PROBLEM")
print("=" * 40)

# Create sample datasets representing different measurement scales
print("Creating sample data with different scales...")

# Product performance data with mixed scales
product_data = {
    'units_sold': [120, 250, 180, 300, 220, 260, 150, 275],
    'price_dollars': [12.99, 9.99, 11.49, 8.99, 10.99, 9.49, 13.49,
     ↪ 8.49],
    'advertising_spend': [5000, 12000, 8000, 15000, 10000, 13000, 6000,
     ↪ 14000],
    'customer_rating': [4.2, 3.8, 4.0, 3.6, 4.1, 3.9, 4.3, 3.7]
}

df_products = pd.DataFrame(product_data)
print("Product performance dataset created")
print(f"Shape: {df_products.shape[0]} rows x {df_products.shape[1]}
 ↪ columns")
print("\nFirst 3 rows:")
print(df_products.head(3))
```

Output:

```
First 3 rows:
   units_sold  price_dollars  advertising_spend  customer_rating
0         120          12.99               5000              4.2
1         250           9.99              12000              3.8
2         180          11.49               8000              4.0
```

Let's examine the scale differences more systematically:

```
# Analyze the scale differences
print("\nSCALE ANALYSIS:")
print("=" * 20)

scale_analysis = df_products.describe()
print("Descriptive statistics:")
print(scale_analysis.round(2))

print("\nScale comparison:")
for col in df_products.columns:
    mean_val = df_products[col].mean()
    std_val = df_products[col].std()
    min_val = df_products[col].min()
    max_val = df_products[col].max()
    range_val = max_val - min_val

    print(f"{col}:")
    print(f"  Range: {min_val:.2f} to {max_val:.2f} (span:
     ↪ {range_val:.2f})")
    print(f"  Mean: {mean_val:.2f}, Std: {std_val:.2f}")
    print()
```

Output:

```
Scale comparison:

units_sold:
  Range: 120.00 to 300.00 (span: 180.00)
  Mean: 219.38, Std: 63.72
price_dollars:
  Range: 8.49 to 13.49 (span: 5.00)
  Mean: 10.74, Std: 1.83
```

```
advertising_spend:
  Range: 5000.00 to 15000.00 (span: 10000.00)
  Mean: 10375.00, Std: 3739.27
customer_rating:
  Range: 3.60 to 4.30 (span: 0.70)
  Mean: 3.95, Std: 0.24
```

Units sold ranges from 120 to 300 with a mean of 219.38 and a standard deviation of 63.72, indicating moderate variability in sales volume. Price ranges from 8.49 to 13.49 with a mean of 10.74 and a standard deviation of 1.83, showing relatively small variation compared to other variables. Advertising spend ranges from 5,000 to 15,000 with a mean of 10,375 and a large standard deviation of 3,739.27, making it the most widely spread variable. Customer rating ranges from 3.60 to 4.30 with a mean of 3.95 and a small standard deviation of 0.24, indicating very tight clustering of ratings.

The scale differences are substantial: advertising spend operates in the thousands, units sold in the hundreds, price around tens, and customer rating on a 1–5 scale. Without standardization, advertising spend would dominate any distance-based analysis because of its large numerical magnitude rather than its actual importance.

4.11.1.2 Step 2: Manual Z-Score Standardization

Manual z-scores tie directly to the standard normal distribution, which is a theoretical distribution with mean 0 and standard deviation 1. When we compute a z-score, we are expressing a raw value in terms of how many standard deviations it lies above or below the mean, effectively mapping it onto this standard normal scale. This matters statistically because the standard normal distribution has well-known properties: about 68% of values fall within ±1 standard deviation, 95% within ±2, and 99.7% within ±3. By converting values like units_sold or advertising_spend into z-scores, we can interpret them using these probabilities—for example, identifying whether an observation is typical or unusually high or low. In this sense, z-scores are not just about rescaling; they allow us to compare values across different variables using a common probabilistic framework and to assess how extreme or typical observations are relative to their distributions.

The Z-Score Formula:

$$z = \frac{x - \mu}{\sigma}$$

Where:

- z = standardized value (z-score)
- x = original value
- μ = mean of the variable
- σ = standard deviation of the variable

Let's explore how this works on our un-standardized data.

```
print("DEMONSTRATION 2: MANUAL Z-SCORE STANDARDIZATION")
print("=" * 50)

print("Z-Score Formula: z = (x - μ) / σ")
print("Where:")
print("  z = standardized value (z-score)")
print("  x = original value")
print("  μ = mean of the variable")
print("  σ = standard deviation of the variable")

# Manual calculation for units_sold
print(f"\nManual z-score calculation for 'units_sold':")
print("-" * 45)

mean_units = df_products['units_sold'].mean()
std_units = df_products['units_sold'].std()

print(f"Step 1: Calculate mean (μ) = {mean_units:.2f}")
print(f"Step 2: Calculate std (σ) = {std_units:.2f}")
print(f"Step 3: Apply formula z = (x - {mean_units:.2f}) /
 ↪ {std_units:.2f}")
```

Now we have all the values we have to use in the formula.

Output:

```
Step 1: Calculate mean (μ) = 219.38

Step 2: Calculate std (σ) = 63.72

Step 3: Apply formula z = (x - 219.38) / 63.72
```

```
# Calculate z-scores manually
df_products['units_sold_z_manual'] = (df_products['units_sold'] -
 ↪ mean_units) / std_units

print("\nOriginal vs. Standardized Values:")
comparison = df_products[['units_sold', 'units_sold_z_manual']].copy()
comparison.columns = ['Original', 'Z-Score']
print(comparison.round(3))
```

This compares the original scale and the standardized z score scale for units sold.

Output:

```
   Original  Z-Score
0       120   -1.560
1       250    0.481
2       180   -0.618
3       300    1.265
4       220    0.010
5       260    0.638
6       150   -1.089
7       275    0.873
```

```
# Verify standardization properties
manual_mean = df_products['units_sold_z_manual'].mean()
manual_std = df_products['units_sold_z_manual'].std()

print(f"\nVerification:")
print(f"Standardized mean: {manual_mean:.10f} (should be ≈ 0)")
print(f"Standardized std: {manual_std:.10f} (should be ≈ 1)")
```

Output:

```
Verification:

Standardized mean: 0.0000000000 (should be ≈ 0)

Standardized std: 1.0000000000 (should be ≈ 1)
```

Perfect! The manual z-score calculation produces a variable with mean = 0 and standard deviation = 1, exactly as expected.

4.11.1.3 Step 3: Automated Standardization

The StandardScaler function from the scikit-learn library is an automated tool that performs z-score standardization on your data. Instead of manually computing the mean and standard deviation for each variable, it does this internally: during the .fit() step, it calculates and stores the mean and standard deviation for each feature, and during the .transform() step, it applies the z-score formula to convert every value into its standardized form. The result is a dataset where each feature has a mean of 0 and a standard deviation of 1. This is important in practice because it ensures consistency, reduces the chance of calculation errors, and is easily reusable—for example, the same scaling parameters learned from training data can be applied to new data. In statistical terms, StandardScaler is simply automating the process of mapping your variables onto the standard normal scale, making them directly comparable and suitable for methods that depend on distance or variance.

```
print("DEMONSTRATION 3: AUTOMATED STANDARDIZATION")
print("=" * 45)
```

```
# Initialize the StandardScaler
scaler = StandardScaler()
print("StandardScaler initialized")

# Fit and transform all variables
print("Applying StandardScaler to all variables...")
X_scaled = scaler.fit_transform(df_products[['units_sold',
 ↪  'price_dollars',
                                              'advertising_spend',
                                              ↪  'customer_rating']])

# Create DataFrame with standardized values
df_scaled = pd.DataFrame(
    X_scaled,
    columns=['units_sold', 'price_dollars', 'advertising_spend',
 ↪  'customer_rating'],
    index=df_products.index
)

print("Standardization complete!")
print("\nStandardized Dataset:")
print(df_scaled.round(3))
```

Output:

```
Standardized Dataset:
   units_sold  price_dollars  advertising_spend  customer_rating
0      -1.667          1.313             -1.537            1.091
1       0.514         -0.438              0.465           -0.655
2      -0.661          0.438             -0.679            0.218
3       1.353         -1.021              1.322           -1.528
4       0.010          0.146             -0.107            0.655
5       0.682         -0.729              0.750           -0.218
6      -1.164          1.605             -1.251            1.528
7       0.933         -1.313              1.036           -1.091
```

```
print("\nVerification - All variables should have:")
print("Mean ≈ 0 and Standard Deviation ≈ 1")
print("\nMeans:")
means = df_scaled.mean()
for col, mean_val in means.items():
    print(f"  {col}: {mean_val:.10f}")
```

```
print("\nStandard Deviations:")
stds = df_scaled.std()
for col, std_val in stds.items():
    print(f"  {col}: {std_val:.10f}")
```

Output:

```
Means:
  units_sold: -0.0000000000
  price_dollars: 0.0000000000
  advertising_spend: 0.0000000000
  customer_rating: -0.0000000000

Standard Deviations:
  units_sold: 1.0690449676
  price_dollars: 1.0690449676
  advertising_spend: 1.0690449676
  customer_rating: 1.0690449676
```

Excellent! Now all variables are on the same scale, making them directly comparable for analysis techniques like PCA.

4.11.1.4 Step 4: Principal Component Analysis

Principal Component Analysis (PCA) is a technique used to simplify complex datasets by reducing the number of variables while keeping as much important information as possible. In many real-world datasets, variables are related to each other—for example, higher advertising spend may be associated with higher units sold. PCA takes advantage of these relationships by combining variables into a smaller set of new variables called *principal components*. These components summarize the original data without simply throwing information away.

The key idea behind PCA is variance, which in statistics measures how much the data varies or spreads out. PCA looks for directions in the data where this variation is the greatest, because those directions contain the most information. Instead of analyzing each original variable separately, PCA creates new axes (principal components) that capture these patterns of variation. The first principal component captures the most variance, the second captures the next most (while being independent of the first), and so on.

You can think of PCA as re-expressing your data in a smarter way. Rather than viewing the data from the original perspective (your original variables), PCA rotates the data to find better angles that reveal the underlying structure more clearly. This is especially useful when you have many variables, because it allows you to reduce dimensionality, remove redundancy, and make patterns easier to visualize and analyze without losing the essence of the data.

This code is taking your cleaned and standardized dataset and trying to simplify it without losing important information. Principal components should always be done on standardized data. Instead of working with all the original variables (like units sold, price, advertising, and rating), it uses PCA to create new variables that summarize the same patterns in a more efficient way.

```
print("DEMONSTRATION 4: PRINCIPAL COMPONENT ANALYSIS")
print("=" * 50)

# Apply PCA to standardized data
print("Applying PCA to standardized data...")
pca = PCA()
X_pca = pca.fit_transform(df_scaled)

print(f"Original data shape: {df_scaled.shape}")
print(f"PCA-transformed data shape: {X_pca.shape}")
print("PCA transformation complete!")
```

First, the line pca = PCA() creates a PCA model, and pca.fit_transform(df_scaled) actually does the work. It looks at your standardized data and finds new directions (called principal components) that capture the most variation in the data. The result, X_pca, is a transformed version of your dataset where each column is now one of these new components instead of the original variables. The shape print statements are just confirming that you still have the same number of rows (observations), but now the columns represent these new summarized features.

Next, the code looks at explained variance, which tells you how much information each principal component keeps. For example, if PC1 explains 70% of the variance, that means it captures most of the important patterns in the data by itself. The loop prints each component's individual contribution and the cumulative total, so you can see how quickly you are capturing most of the information.

```
# Analyze explained variance
print("\nEXPLAINED VARIANCE ANALYSIS:")
print("=" * 35)

explained_variance = pca.explained_variance_ratio_
cumulative_variance = np.cumsum(explained_variance)

print("Individual and Cumulative Explained Variance:")
for i, (var, cum_var) in enumerate(zip(explained_variance,
 ↪  cumulative_variance)):
```

```
    print(f"PC{i+1}: {var:.3f} ({var*100:.1f}%) | Cumulative:
    ↪ {cum_var:.3f} ({cum_var*100:.1f}%)")
```

Output:

```
Individual and Cumulative Explained Variance:
PC1: 0.964 (96.4%) | Cumulative: 0.964 (96.4%)
PC2: 0.026 (2.6%) | Cumulative: 0.990 (99.0%)
PC3: 0.009 (0.9%) | Cumulative: 1.000 (100.0%)
PC4: 0.000 (0.0%) | Cumulative: 1.000 (100.0%)
```

Finally, the last part answers a practical question: *how many components do you actually need?* The code checks how many principal components are required to keep 80%, 90%, or 95% of the total information. This is the whole point of PCA for beginners—you can reduce your dataset from many variables down to just a few while still keeping most of what matters.

```
# Determine components needed for different variance thresholds
components_80 = np.argmax(cumulative_variance >= 0.8) + 1
components_90 = np.argmax(cumulative_variance >= 0.9) + 1
components_95 = np.argmax(cumulative_variance >= 0.95) + 1

print(f"\nComponents needed for:")
print(f"  80% variance: {components_80}")
print(f"  90% variance: {components_90}")
print(f"  95% variance: {components_95}")
```

Output:

```
Components needed for:

80% variance: 1

90% variance: 1

95% variance: 1
```

This tells us that the first principal component captures over 95% of the total variance in our data. We could reduce our 4-dimensional dataset to 1 dimension while retaining almost all the information! If we include the second principal component we capture over 99% of the total variance (from explained variance analysis above).

4.11.1.5 Step 5: Understanding PCA Loadings

In PCA, loadings tell us how much each original variable contributes to each principal component. They are like weights that describe the influence of each variable on the new components, similar to coefficients in a regression model. Understanding loadings is key to interpreting what each principal component actually represents.

```
print("DEMONSTRATION 5: PCA LOADINGS ANALYSIS")
print("=" * 40)

# Create loadings DataFrame
loadings = pd.DataFrame(
    pca.components_.T,
    columns=[f'PC{i+1}' for i in range(len(df_products.columns))],
    index=['units_sold', 'price_dollars', 'advertising_spend',
 ↪  'customer_rating']
)

print("Component Loadings Matrix:")
print("(Shows how each variable contributes to each component)")
print(loadings.round(3))
```

Output:

```
Component Loadings Matrix:

(Shows how each variable contributes to each component)

PC1 PC2 PC3 PC4

units_sold 0.502 0.457 0.419 -0.604

price_dollars -0.502 -0.009 0.849 0.165

advertising_spend 0.506 0.336 0.152 0.780

customer_rating -0.490 0.824 -0.285 0.018
```

This table shows exactly how each original variable contributes to each principal component. Rows are the original variables—units sold, price, advertising spend, and customer rating—and columns are the new components created by PCA (PC1, PC2, etc.). Each number indicates the strength and direction of a variable's contribution. A positive value means the variable increases the component score, while a negative value means it decreases the score.

Next, we focus on interpreting the first two principal components:

```
# Interpret the first two components
print("\nCOMPONENT INTERPRETATION:")
print("=" * 30)
```

```
print("PC1 - Highest absolute loadings:")
pc1_loadings = loadings['PC1'].abs().sort_values(ascending=False)
for var in pc1_loadings.index:
    original_loading = loadings.loc[var, 'PC1']
    contribution = "positive" if original_loading > 0 else "negative"
    print(f"  {var}: {original_loading:.3f} ({contribution}
     ↪ contribution)")

print("\nPC2 - Highest absolute loadings:")
pc2_loadings = loadings['PC2'].abs().sort_values(ascending=False)
for var in pc2_loadings.index:
    original_loading = loadings.loc[var, 'PC2']
    contribution = "positive" if original_loading > 0 else "negative"
    print(f"  {var}: {original_loading:.3f} ({contribution}
     ↪ contribution)")
```

Output:

```
PC1 - Highest absolute loadings
advertising_spend: 0.506 (positive contribution)
price_dollars: -0.502 (negative contribution)
units_sold: 0.502 (positive contribution)
customer_rating: -0.490 (negative contribution)


PC2 - Highest absolute loadings
customer_rating: 0.824 (positive contribution)
units_sold: 0.457 (positive contribution)
advertising_spend: 0.336 (positive contribution)
price_dollars: -0.009 (negative contribution)
```

From these results, we can see that PC1 reflects overall product performance: products that sell well and have high advertising spend tend to have higher PC1 scores, while higher price and lower customer rating reduce the score. PC2, on the other hand, emphasizes customer satisfaction: products with higher ratings contribute most to PC2, with moderate influence from sales and advertising, and almost no effect from price.

By examining the loadings this way, we can interpret what each principal component actually measures, turning abstract PCA math into concrete insights about the relationships among our original variables. PC1 summarizes overall success across multiple metrics, while PC2 highlights the trade-off between quality (rating) and other factors.

4.11.2 Practice

In this exercise, you will work with three datasets: store performance data, fitness tracking data, and marketing campaign data. You will practice standardizing variables, applying Principal Component Analysis (PCA), and interpreting the results. The goal is to understand how scaling affects analysis and how PCA can reduce dimensionality while preserving important information.

```
import pandas as pd
import numpy as np
from sklearn.preprocessing import StandardScaler
from sklearn.decomposition import PCA

# Set random seed for reproducible results
np.random.seed(42)

# -----------------------------------------------------
# DATASET 1: Store Performance Data
# -----------------------------------------------------
store_data = {
    'daily_customers': [220, 180, 260, 300, 240,
      210, 280, 195, 230, 270],
    'avg_purchase_value': [32, 28, 35, 40, 37, 30, 38, 29, 33, 36],
    'employees_on_shift': [8, 6, 9, 10, 9, 7, 10, 6, 8, 9],
    'hours_open': [10, 9, 11, 12, 11, 10, 12, 9, 10, 11]
}

df_store = pd.DataFrame(store_data)
print("Store Performance Dataset:")
print(df_store.head())
print()

# -----------------------------------------------------
# DATASET 2: Fitness Tracking Data
# -----------------------------------------------------
fitness_data = {
    'weekly_workouts': [2, 4, 3, 5, 6, 4, 3, 5, 6, 2],
    'avg_workout_minutes': [30, 45, 40, 60, 70, 50, 35, 65, 75, 25],
    'monthly_calories_burned': [4000, 8500, 7000, 11000, 13000,
      9000, 6000, 12000, 14000, 3500],
    'resting_heart_rate': [72, 68, 70, 65, 62, 67, 71, 64, 60, 74]
}

df_fitness = pd.DataFrame(fitness_data)
print("Fitness Tracking Dataset:")
```

```
print(df_fitness.head())
print()

# ---------------------------------------------------------
# DATASET 3: Marketing Campaign Data
# ---------------------------------------------------------
marketing_data = {
    'ad_impressions': [45000, 52000, 38000, 61000, 48000, 55000, 42000,
    ↪
      58000, 47000, 53000, 41000, 59000, 46000, 54000, 43000],
    'click_through_rate': [2.8, 3.2, 2.1, 4.1, 3.0, 3.5, 2.5, 3.8,
      2.9, 3.3, 2.4, 3.9, 2.7, 3.4, 2.6],
    'conversion_rate': [1.5, 2.1, 1.2, 2.8, 1.8, 2.3, 1.4, 2.6,
      1.7, 2.0, 1.3, 2.7, 1.6, 2.2, 1.5],
    'revenue_per_campaign': [18000, 24000, 15000, 28000, 21000, 25000,
      17000, 27000, 19000, 23000, 16000, 26000, 20000, 24000, 18000]
}

df_marketing = pd.DataFrame(marketing_data)
print("Marketing Campaign Dataset:")
print(df_marketing.head())
```

4.11.2.1 Lab 4 Questions

1. Look at the df_store dataset. Identify which variables use different measurement units. For each variable, calculate the range defined as maximum minus minimum.

2. For the daily_customers variable in df_store, calculate the mean and standard deviation. Then apply the z-score formula $z = (x - \mu)/\sigma$and show the calculations for the first three values.

3. After computing the z-scores for daily_customers, verify that the transformed values have a mean close to 0 and a standard deviation close to 1.

4. Use StandardScaler to standardize all columns in df_store. Verify that each standardized column has a mean approximately equal to 0 and a standard deviation approximately equal to 1.

5. Create a table showing the first 5 rows of both the original df_store data and the standardized version side by side. Describe how the values have changed.

6. Explain in your own words why it is important to standardize variables before applying PCA. Describe what could go wrong if PCA is applied to unstandardized data.

7. Standardize all columns in the df_fitness dataset using StandardScaler.
8. Perform PCA on the standardized df_fitness data. How many principal components are created?
9. Create a table showing, for each principal component, the component number, individual explained variance, cumulative explained variance, percentage of variance explained, and cumulative percentage of variance explained.
10. Based on the explained variance results, determine how many principal components are needed to capture at least 80 percent of the variance and how many are needed to capture at least 90 percent.
11. Examine the PCA loadings for df_fitness and write a short interpretation of the first two principal components in clear, business-friendly language.
12. For the df_marketing dataset, calculate the mean and standard deviation for each variable before standardization. Explain why standardization is necessary for this dataset.
13. Perform the full PCA workflow on df_marketing by standardizing the data, applying PCA, analyzing explained variance, and examining component loadings.
14. Interpret the first two principal components for df_marketing. Describe in plain language what each component represents in terms of marketing outcomes.
15. Determine how many principal components are required to explain at least 80 percent, 90 percent, and 95 percent of the variance in df_marketing, and describe what actionable insights this PCA analysis provides for decision-making.

4.12 Conclusion

Data preprocessing is a critical foundation for effective data analysis and mining. Without proper cleaning, modification, and restructuring, datasets can contain errors, inconsistencies, and redundancies that compromise the reliability of results. By addressing issues such as missing values, duplicate records, incorrect formats, and out-of-range entries, analysts ensure that the data accurately reflects the phenomena being studied. Modern AI-powered tools streamline many of these tasks, automatically detecting and suggesting corrections, but a clear understanding of the underlying principles remains essential to maintain control and interpret results correctly.

Beyond cleaning, modifying data enhances its usability and analytical potential. Techniques such as renaming variables, splitting or merging fields, grouping, and binning simplify data interpretation while preserving essential information. Restructuring datasets through aggregation, subsetting, or format transformation prepares data for analysis and ensures compatibility with different software tools. Normalization standardizes quantitative data, enabling fair comparisons across variables with differing scales, which is especially important for distance-based methods or multivariate analyses.

Finally, dimensionality reduction addresses the challenges of high-dimensional datasets. Principal component analysis (PCA) allows complex data to be condensed into fewer, meaningful variables while retaining most of the original information. By understanding how to interpret PCA scores, loadings, and variance explained, analysts can simplify analysis, improve visualization, and enhance model performance. Overall, this chapter emphasizes that preprocessing is not merely a preliminary step, but a crucial process that directly impacts the accuracy, interpretability, and effectiveness of all subsequent data mining and analytical efforts.

Chapter 5

Cluster Analysis

5.1 Learning Outcomes

5-1. Explain the concept of cluster analysis and its role in unsupervised learning, distinguishing between labeled and unlabeled data.

5-2. Compute and interpret distances between data points using Euclidean and alternative distance metrics, including in multidimensional spaces.

5-3. Apply normalization and scaling to data to ensure meaningful clustering results.

5-4. Compare and contrast hierarchical clustering, K-means, and DBSCAN, including their advantages, limitations, and practical applications.

5-5. Determine when to use hybrid or AI-enhanced clustering approaches.

5.2 Introduction

In this chapter, we will begin exploring the techniques of data mining, starting with cluster analysis. Cluster analysis is a technique used to group a set of objects in such a way that objects in the same group (or cluster) are more similar to each other than to those in other groups. While the fundamental principles remain unchanged, modern AI tools have made clustering more accessible and powerful for beginners and experts alike.

5.3 Understanding Unsupervised Learning

Cluster analysis falls under a category of algorithms known as unsupervised learning. This concept originates from machine learning, a field where algorithms learn patterns from data without predefined labels. Today's AI-enhanced clustering tools can automatically suggest optimal parameters and provide intelligent insights about discovered patterns.

5.3.1 Labeled and Unlabeled Data

When dealing with a dataset, it may or may not include labels. Labels can be thought of as tags or identifiers—typically categorical variables with finite values like "yes" or "no." For instance, if we consider whether an object is a tree, the label could be "yes" or "no."

Consider items in a grocery store. Each item can be labeled with a category, like "vegetable," "fruit," or "herb." If we have this category column, our data is labeled. However, if we lack this category column, we have unlabeled data.

Labeled data has a categorical variable serving as a tag or identifier. With labeled data, we perform tasks such as prediction and classification. These methods are referred to as supervised learning because the labels "supervise" the learning process by providing a reference for what each data point represents. For example, knowing that cilantro is an herb and tomato is a vegetable allows us to train a model based on these categories.

Unlabeled data does not contain predefined labels. An example of unlabeled data might include a set of eight binary variables with no clear identification or grouping information. Without labels, it's challenging to group or organize this data effectively.

This chapter will focus on techniques for analyzing unlabeled data, known as unsupervised learning in machine learning parlance. In unsupervised learning, we explore the structure and patterns within the data without predefined categories.

5.3.2 The Purpose and Value of Clustering

When you have novel data without predefined labels, it's challenging to group or organize this data effectively. Clustering techniques can help here. These techniques are examples of unsupervised algorithms—a concept rooted in machine learning and AI. With no categorical variable to classify the data values, the goal is to discover the underlying structure of the data.

Working with unlabeled data is often a precursor to eventually labeling it. It's a crucial first step, which is why we address it at the beginning of our exploration. Unsupervised algorithms help in finding patterns within the data, making it an exploratory technique. Data mining aims to uncover these patterns and relationships before applying other data analysis methods.

Modern AI clustering tools can now provide automated pattern recognition and suggest meaningful cluster interpretations, making this exploratory process more intuitive for beginners.

In unsupervised data mining, there are two primary techniques: clustering and association. This chapter focuses on clustering, while a subsequent chapter will cover association, a different type of unsupervised data mining.

5.4 Mathematical Foundations: Distance and Similarity

Clustering involves grouping data points based on their similarities. This technique uses mathematical distance to measure similarity, helping to uncover the structure of the data by comparing how far apart different values are.

To understand clustering, we first need to learn how to calculate mathematical distance. This concept should be familiar from geometry and mathematics. For instance, the Pythagorean theorem leads to the distance formula, which calculates the distance between two points.

Mathematical distance is a key concept in clustering. It refers to how far apart two points are in space. For example, if you've used a ruler to measure the length of an object, you've measured distance. In geometry, the distance between two points is the shortest line connecting them.

5.4.1 From Basic Distance to Multidimensional Space

In everyday physical space, distance is the shortest measurement between two locations. This is the straightforward measurement between two points, such as the shortest line between a block and an oval.

In algebra, you might have encountered problems where you needed to calculate the distance between two points on a coordinate plane. In the Cartesian (x and y) plane, two points can be plotted and connected with a segment. The length of the segment is the distance between them, which is easy to measure when the segment is vertical or horizontal. For example, the distance between points (1, 1) and (1, 4) is 3, as they share the same x-value and differ by 3 units on the y-axis.

When dealing with points in a two-dimensional space that cannot easily be connected by a vertical or horizontal segment, the distance formula (derived from the Pythagorean theorem) helps calculate how far apart the points are.

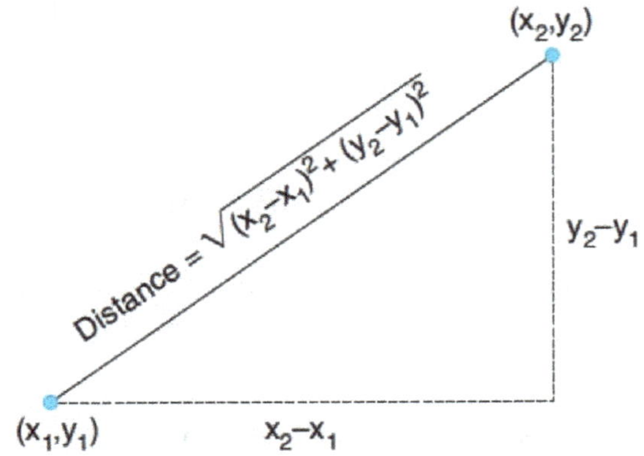

Euclidean distance is the application of the Pythagorean theorem in a coordinate system. The concept of mathematical distance is rooted in the Pythagorean theorem. According to the theorem, in a right triangle with sides a and b, the length of the hypotenuse c is given by: $c^2 = a^2 + b^2$

When we refer to Euclidean distance in data analysis, we're measuring how far apart points are in a multidimensional space. The distance formula derived from the Pythagorean theorem substitutes for the sides the vertical and horizontal lengths of the right triangle as computed on the coordinate plane, with the horizontal side length being the difference of the x coordinates and the vertical side length the difference of the y coordinates.

For example, consider two points (1, 4) and (-4, 1) on a Cartesian plane. Plugging these values into the distance formula:

Distance = $\sqrt{[(1-(-4))^2 + (4-1)^2]} = \sqrt{[25 + 9]} = \sqrt{34} = 5.83$

This formula extends to higher dimensions, allowing us to measure distances in three-dimensional space and beyond. The 2-d Cartesian plane extends to a 3-d plane easily and points can be located with x, y, and z coordinates.

For three-dimensional space, the Euclidean distance formula extends to compute distance between two points in three-dimensional space to include the z-axis:

Distance = $\sqrt{[(x_2-x_1)^2 + (y_2-y_1)^2 + (z_2-z_1)^2]}$

5.4.2 Generalizing Distance to n-Dimensions

Using the basic distance formula, calculating the distance between two points in two-dimensional or three-dimensional space is straightforward. However, we can extend this concept to any number of dimensions. This is crucial in data analysis because data often exists in multidimensional space, with each dimension representing a variable.

While humans can't visualize beyond three dimensions, in data analysis, we routinely work with datasets that have many variables. The number of dimensions in data space corresponds to the number of variables in a dataset. Despite the challenge of visualizing higher dimensions, we can still calculate distances in these spaces using a generalized formula.

In a multidimensional space, we can generalize the distance formula. If we have points P and Q in n-dimensional space, the Euclidean distance between them is:

Distance = $\sqrt{[\Sigma(p_i - q_i)^2]}$ for i = 1 to n

This formula allows us to calculate the distance between any two points regardless of the number of variables (dimensions) they have. This generalization is known as Euclidean distance, and it's the most used distance metric in data analysis.

5.4.3 Alternative Distance Metrics for Different Data Types

While Euclidean distance is widely used, there are other distance metrics suitable for different scenarios. Euclidean distance is used on continuous measurable variables and can be used for discrete variables as well. However, other data types and situations may be more suited to other distance metrics.

Binary data consists of values like 0 and 1, often representing yes/no or true/false responses. This type of data is common in many datasets, such as survey responses where people answer yes or no to various questions. For binary data, the Jaccard distance is often more appropriate than Euclidean distance, as it measures dissimilarity between sets of binary values.

When variables are correlated, the **Mahalanobis distance** may be used instead. This metric accounts for covariance between variables, providing more accurate distance measurements when variables are not independent. Another frequently used metric is the **Minkowski distance**, which is actually a generalization of the Euclidean distance metric.

Modern clustering software can automatically recommend the most appropriate distance metric based on your data characteristics. Tools like Orange, WEKA, or even Excel's clustering add-ins can analyze your data type and suggest optimal distance measures, making the selection process more intuitive for beginners.

These metrics are implemented in data analysis software, so you don't need to calculate them manually. The software will choose the appropriate metric based on your data and analysis requirements.

5.4.4 Practical Application: Employee Data Example

To illustrate distance calculations in clustering, consider a small dataset containing five employees with two variables: Salary and Experience.

Table 5.1: Original Employee Data

Employee	Salary	Experience
1	50000	2
2	60000	5
3	55000	3
4	70000	8
5	65000	6

Each row represents an employee, and each column represents a variable. Using the Euclidean distance formula, we can calculate how far apart each employee is from every other employee in this two-dimensional space.

A **distance matrix** is a convenient way to summarize the distances between all pairs of points. Each row and column represents a point, and the diagonal values are zero since the distance from a point to itself is always zero.

Table 5.2: Euclidean Distance Matrix (Raw Data)

Row	1	2	3	4	5
1	0	10000	5000	20000	15000
2	10000	0	5000	10000	5000
3	5000	5000	0	15000	10000
4	20000	10000	15000	0	5000
5	15000	5000	10000	5000	0

This matrix clearly shows which employees are more similar based on Salary and Experience. For example, employees 2 and 5 have a distance of 5,000, indicating they are relatively close.

5.5 Data Preparation: Normalization and Scaling

Raw data can have different measurement scales, which can distort distance calculations. For instance, Salary is in tens of thousands of dollars, while Experience is measured in years. Without scaling, Salary dominates the distance metric, producing misleading clustering results.

Normalization standardizes each variable so that all measurements contribute equally. Typically, data is scaled to a Z-score, which represents how many standard deviations each value is from the mean:

$Z = (X - \mu) / \sigma$

Where X is the original value, μ is the mean, and σ is the standard deviation.

Table 5.3: Normalized Employee Data

Employee	Salary (Normalized)	Experience (Normalized)
1	-1.3	-1.2
2	0.00	0.08
3	-0.63	-0.75
4	1.3	1.3
5	0.63	0.50

After normalization, all variables are on the same scale, ensuring that distances reflect relative differences rather than absolute magnitudes.

Table 5.4: Euclidean Distance Matrix (Normalized Data)

Row	1	2	3	4	5
1	0.00	1.78	0.76	3.57	2.53
2	1.78	0.00	1.05	1.78	0.76
3	0.76	1.05	0.00	2.83	1.78
4	3.57	1.78	2.83	0.00	1.05
5	2.53	0.76	1.78	1.05	0.00

Notice how the distances have changed after normalization. Now, both Salary and Experience contribute equally to the distance calculation, producing more meaningful measures of similarity. This comparison highlights the importance of normalization. Distances on raw data are heavily influenced by Salary, while distances on normalized data give a balanced representation of both variables. Using normalized distances ensures that clustering algorithms accurately identify similar employees based on both variables.

5.6 Clustering Methodology Overview

Cluster analysis is fundamentally about grouping unlabeled data based on similarity. Essentially, we're letting the data tell its own story, revealing patterns and structures that might not be immediately obvious. The first step in any clustering project is deciding which variables to include. While it's tempting to include every available variable, this can actually obscure meaningful patterns—especially with large datasets.

For small datasets with just a few variables, including all of them may be fine, but in larger datasets with dozens or hundreds of variables, focusing on a subset—say five or six key variables—often yields better, more interpretable results. When selecting variables, prioritize those that capture the essence of the data. For example, if you're analyzing customer behavior, age, spending habits, and purchase frequency might reveal useful clusters. Avoid irrelevant variables like ID numbers or administrative codes—they won't add insight and may even dilute your clustering results.

Clustering relies on mathematical distance metrics to measure similarity between observations. Euclidean distance is the most common, but there are alternatives tailored to specific data types, such as binary or categorical data. These distance calculations form the backbone of clustering, determining which points are close enough to belong together.

5.6.1 Real-World Applications of Clustering

The applications of clustering are wide-ranging and span virtually every industry. In retail, clustering can uncover buying patterns, such as groups of products that customers tend to purchase together, guiding marketing campaigns and product bundles. In finance, clustering can identify stocks with similar behavior, helping investors understand market trends and manage risk. In biology, it might group genes with similar expression patterns, leading to discoveries in genomics and disease research.

Modern AI-powered tools take clustering a step further by automatically interpreting clusters. Rather than just listing "Cluster 1" or "Cluster 2," these tools can provide descriptive labels based on the underlying data, such as "Budget-conscious shoppers" or "Premium product enthusiasts," making the results immediately actionable.

5.6.2 Primary Clustering Methodologies

There are several primary clustering methodologies to consider, each with its own strengths:

- **Hierarchical clustering** builds a tree of nested clusters, revealing relationships at multiple levels
- **K-means clustering** partitions data into a fixed number of clusters, optimizing for compact, evenly sized groups
- **DBSCAN (density-based clustering)** identifies clusters based on data density, capturing irregularly shaped clusters and detecting outliers

Choosing the right method depends on your data structure, objectives, and desired insights, but the underlying principle remains the same: clustering helps you uncover hidden patterns and make sense of complex data.

5.7 Hierarchical Clustering

Hierarchical clustering, also known as agglomerative clustering, starts with each data point as its own cluster. As the algorithm progresses, it merges similar clusters together, creating a hierarchical structure that reveals relationships at multiple levels.

5.7.1 The Agglomerative Process

To illustrate hierarchical clustering, consider an example with six data points labeled A, B, C, D, E, and F, each with X and Y coordinates. These points are initially plotted on a graph, with each point constituting its own cluster.

Table 5.5: Original Points

Point	X	Y
a	1	2
b	2	2
c	3	8
d	4	9
e	5	4
f	6	7

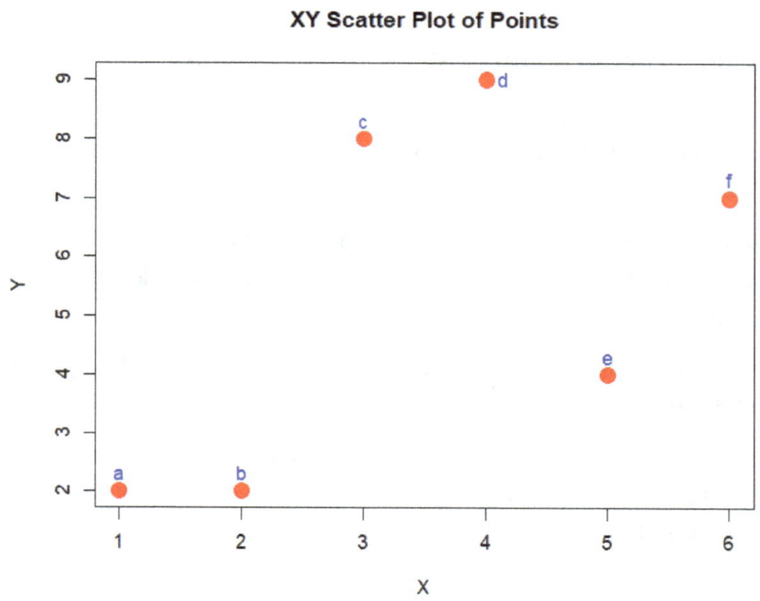

The process begins by calculating the distance matrix, a crucial step in hierarchical clustering. This matrix depicts the distances between all pairs of points. Although the data in this example is not standardized, it is on the same measurement scale of the coordinate axis. Note that in real-world applications, it's advisable to work with standardized data to ensure accurate clustering results.

5.7.2 Euclidean Distance Matrix

Table 5.6: Distance Matrix for Points a–f (2 Significant Digits)

point	a	b	c	d	e	f
a	0.00	0.53	2.22	2.78	2.23	3.13
b	0.53	0.00	2.02	2.51	1.73	2.69
c	2.22	2.02	0.00	0.63	1.68	1.64
d	2.78	2.51	0.63	0.00	1.71	1.25
e	2.23	1.73	1.68	1.71	0.00	1.11
f	3.13	2.69	1.64	1.25	1.11	0.00

In hierarchical clustering, the first step involves identifying the closest points—those with the smallest distances between them. In our example, points A to B and C to D have relatively small distances compared to the others, so they form clusters. At this stage, each point starts as its own cluster, and the closest pairs are merged to form new clusters. In this case, A and B form one cluster, while C and D form another, leaving E and F as individual clusters.

5.7.3 Linkage Methods: Determining Inter-Cluster Distance

As clusters are formed, we need to calculate distances between clusters as well as individual points. This introduces the concept of **linkage**—the method used to determine the distance between clusters.

Single linkage seeks to minimize the distance between the closest points of two clusters. In our example, single linkage would consider the distance between the closest points of the AB cluster and the CD cluster.

Complete linkage, on the other hand, measures the distance between the furthest points of two clusters. This method tends to create more compact, evenly sized clusters.

Average linkage is generally recommended because this method tends to provide more reliable results in hierarchical clustering. It calculates the average distance between all points in one cluster and all points in another cluster. It's considered a sensible choice for most scenarios.

Ward's method is another important approach that minimizes the within-cluster sum of squares. Although it's widely used, this method can be complex and may require a deeper understanding to implement effectively. Ward's method tends to create clusters of similar sizes and is particularly effective when clusters are expected to be roughly spherical.

Modern clustering software often provides intelligent recommendations for linkage methods based on your data characteristics. Tools like Orange or WEKA can analyze your data distribution and suggest the most appropriate linkage method, making the decision process easier for beginners.

5.7.4 The Iterative Merging Process

Returning to our example, after the first two clusters are formed, the algorithm continues by finding the next smallest distance. Using single linkage, if the next smallest distance is from point F to the CD cluster, then point F is joined (agglomerated) to the cluster containing C and D.

This process continues systematically. The algorithm identifies the next closest pair or cluster and merges them. Point E might then be clustered with its closest cluster, creating progressively larger groupings. This iterative process continues until we have one big cluster containing all points, marking the completion of our hierarchical clustering.

5.7.5 Dendrograms: Visualizing the Clustering Hierarchy

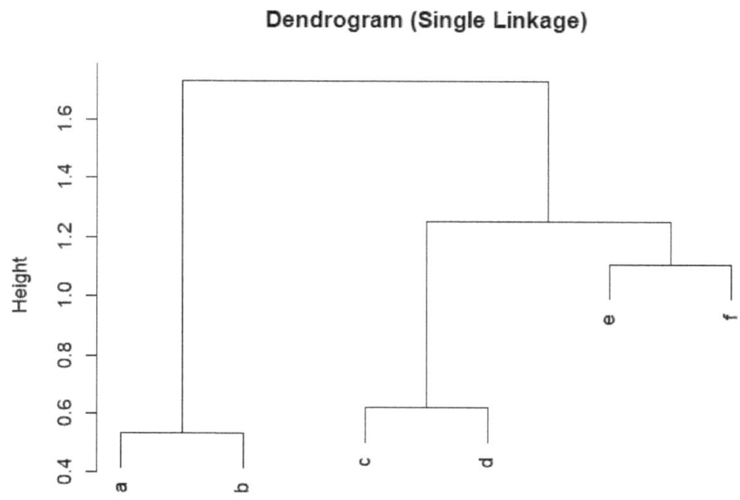

To visualize the hierarchical clustering process, we use a tool called a **dendrogram**. This graphical representation helps us understand hierarchical clustering better than simple illustrations. Each step of the merging process is illustrated in the dendrogram, showing the initial clusters and the subsequent merging of points until we have one unified cluster.

Dendrograms can be particularly useful for identifying patterns or groupings within your data, such as different product categories or customer segments. In the dendrogram, the vertical axis measures the distances between clusters, highlighting the proximity of different data points. The horizontal axis shows the individual data points or clusters being merged.

Reading a dendrogram requires understanding that the height at which two clusters merge indicates their distance or dissimilarity. Clusters that merge at lower heights are more similar than those that merge at higher heights. By "cutting" the dendrogram at different heights, you can obtain different numbers of clusters.

Modern tools can now provide automated interpretation of dendrograms, suggesting optimal cut points and describing what each cluster represents in business terms. This makes hierarchical clustering much more accessible to beginners who might find traditional dendrograms difficult to interpret.

5.7.6 Advantages and Limitations of Hierarchical Clustering

Hierarchical clustering offers several significant advantages that make it valuable for exploratory data analysis. You don't need to specify the number of clusters in advance, which is particularly useful when you're exploring data structure for the first time. It provides a complete hierarchy of clusters, allowing you to examine relationships at multiple levels of granularity. Results are deterministic—the same input data will always produce the same clustering result. The method works well with any distance measure, providing flexibility in how similarity is calculated.

However, hierarchical clustering also has important limitations to consider. The method can be computationally expensive for large datasets, with time complexity of $O(n^3)$ making it impractical for very large datasets. It is sensitive to outliers, which can significantly affect the clustering structure. The algorithm has difficulty handling very large datasets due to memory and computational requirements. Once a merge is made during the clustering process, it cannot be undone, which means early mistakes in merging can propagate through the entire clustering process.

Despite some visually appealing outcomes, there are instances where hierarchical clustering results might seem odd or uninformative. This is partly because the method is exploratory—there's no definitive right or wrong outcome. Additionally, due to its computational demands, hierarchical clustering could strain older computer systems, although this is less of an issue with modern technology.

5.8 K-Means Clustering: Partitioning Data into Distinct Groups

While hierarchical clustering merges clusters to build a tree structure, K-means clustering takes a fundamentally different approach. It divides data into distinct, independent clusters by partitioning the data space into regions, each represented by a cluster center called a centroid.

5.8.1 The K-Means Algorithm Process

The K-means algorithm follows a systematic iterative process. The first step is selecting K, the number of clusters you want to create. This is a critical decision that significantly affects the results. Centroids are then randomly placed in the data space—these serve as initial cluster centers.

Each data point is assigned to the nearest centroid based on distance calculations (typically Euclidean distance). After all points are assigned, centroids are recalculated as the mean (average) position of all points in their cluster. This iterative process continues—reassigning points to the nearest centroid and recalculating centroid positions—until the centroids stabilize and cluster memberships no longer change significantly.

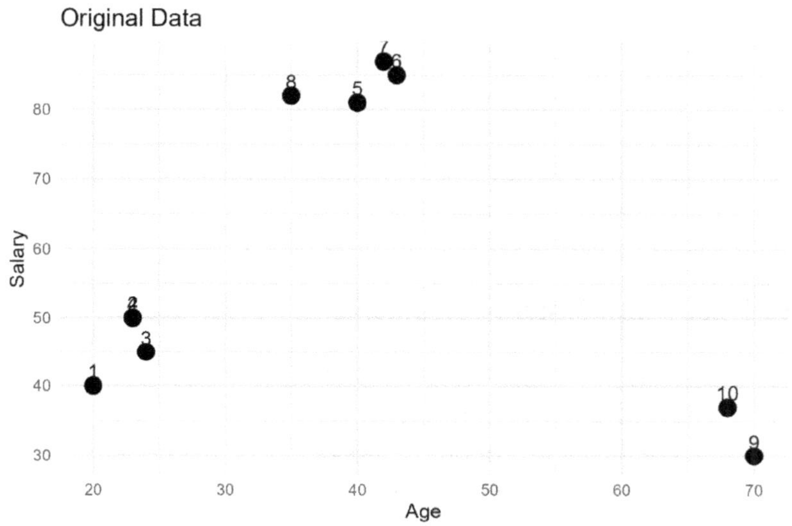

Imagine an unlabeled dataset with age and salary information for employees (data shown in table in next section). By plotting the data, you may notice three natural groupings based on career stage: early career (young, lower salary), mid-career (middle-aged, moderate salary), and senior career (older, higher salary). K-means starts by randomly placing three centroids in the data space, then iteratively assigns points and recalculates centroids until the clusters become stable. This dynamic adjustment ensures the final clusters best represent the structure of the data.

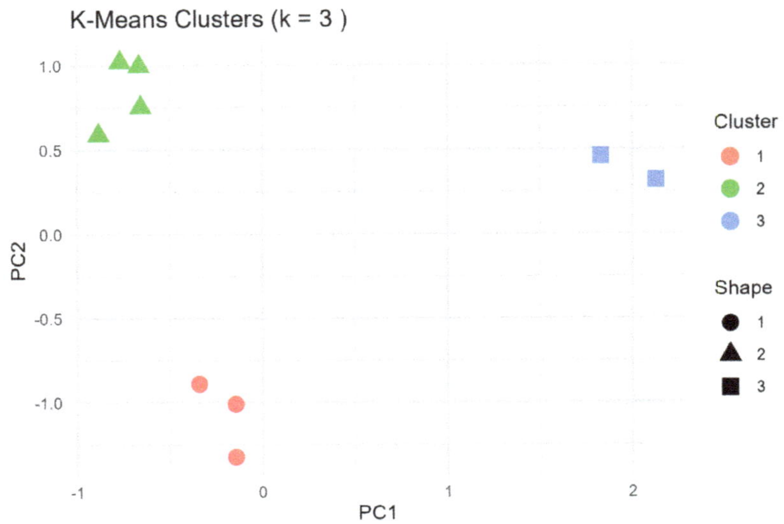

5.8.2 Annotated Data with Cluster Assignments

Table 5.7: Clustered Points Data

Point	Age	Salary	Cluster
1	20	40	1
2	23	50	1
3	24	45	1
4	23	50	1
5	40	81	2
6	43	85	2
7	42	87	2
8	35	82	2
9	70	30	3
10	68	37	3

5.8.3 Determining the Optimal Number of Clusters (K)

Choosing the right K is critical for meaningful clustering results. Several methods help guide this important decision:

The Elbow Method is one of the most popular approaches. Plot the within-cluster sum of squares (WCSS) for different values of K (e.g., 1–10). WCSS measures how tightly grouped the points are within each cluster. As K increases, WCSS generally decreases because smaller clusters have less internal variation. The optimal K is often found at the "elbow"—the point where adding another cluster produces minimal improvement in WCSS. This appears as a bend or elbow in the plot.

Silhouette Analysis provides another valuable approach. This method measures how well each point fits its assigned cluster compared to neighboring clusters. Silhouette scores range from -1 to 1. Scores near 1 indicate that points are well-matched to their own cluster and poorly matched to neighboring clusters. Scores around 0 suggest that points are on the border between clusters. Negative scores indicate that points might be assigned to the wrong cluster. The K that maximizes the average silhouette score across all points is often ideal.

5.8.4 Silhouette Scores (k = 2 to 6)

Table 5.8: Silhouette Scores for Different k

k	Silhouette
2	0.61
3	0.85
4	0.69
5	0.53
6	0.35

Practical Guidelines can also help. A simple heuristic suggests using K = √(n/2), where n is the number of data points. However, this should be combined with domain knowledge and business context. Always consider whether the resulting clusters make practical sense for your specific application.

Modern AI tools can combine multiple validation methods and provide automated recommendations for optimal K values. These tools analyze various metrics simultaneously and suggest K values that balance statistical optimality with practical interpretability.

5.8.5 Advantages and Limitations of K-Means

K-means clustering offers several significant advantages that make it popular for many applications. It is computationally efficient and scalable, making it suitable for large datasets. The algorithm is relatively easy to implement and understand, with a straightforward iterative process. K-means works particularly well when clusters are roughly spherical (round) and similar in size. The method is less sensitive to outliers than hierarchical clustering, though outliers can still affect results.

However, K-means also has important limitations. The most significant is the requirement to specify K in advance, which can be challenging when you don't know the natural number of clusters in your data. The algorithm is sensitive to initial centroid placement, though techniques like K-means++ help mitigate this issue by choosing initial centroids more intelligently. K-means assumes that clusters are spherical and of similar size, which may not match real-world data patterns. The algorithm can be sensitive to outliers, and it may converge to local optima rather than finding the globally optimal solution.

Modern AI and software tools enhance K-means by providing intelligent suggestions for optimal K values, offering robust initialization methods like K-means++, and providing interactive exploration of cluster assignments. These enhancements make K-means both practical and accessible for real-world data mining tasks while helping users understand the impact of different parameter choices.

5.9 DBSCAN: Density-Based Clustering for Complex Patterns

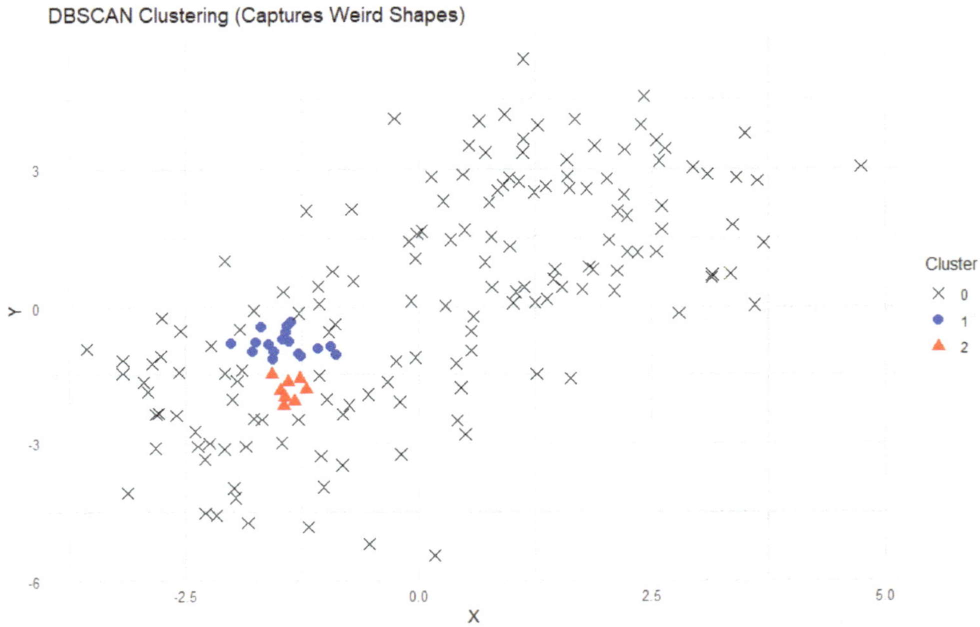

{width-60% fig-alt="Sample DB scan clustering where clusters are not of simple shapes" fig-cap="DB Clustering"}

DBSCAN (Density-Based Spatial Clustering of Applications with Noise) represents a fundamentally different approach to clustering. Unlike hierarchical clustering and K-means, which are based on distance to centroids or linkage criteria, DBSCAN groups together points that are closely packed while marking points in low-density regions as outliers.

5.9.1 Core Concepts and Definitions

DBSCAN introduces several key concepts that make it unique among clustering algorithms. Understanding these concepts is essential for effectively applying the algorithm.

A point is considered a **core point** if it has at least a minimum number of points (MinPts) within a specified distance (ε, epsilon) of itself, including the point itself. Core points form the foundation of clusters and represent areas of high density in the data.

Border points are those that are not core points themselves but fall within the neighborhood (ε distance) of a core point. These points are on the edge of clusters and are assigned to the cluster of the nearest core point.

Noise points (also called outliers) are those that are neither core points nor border points. These points are isolated and don't belong to any cluster. This is one of DBSCAN's key advantages—it can automatically identify and handle outliers rather than forcing them into clusters.

The concept of **density-connected points** is also important: two points are density-connected if there is a chain of core points connecting them, where each consecutive pair is within distance ε of each other. This allows DBSCAN to form clusters of arbitrary shapes, not just spherical ones.

5.9.2 Parameter Selection and Tuning

DBSCAN requires two main parameters that significantly affect the clustering results.

Epsilon (ε) represents the maximum distance between two points for them to be considered neighbors. This parameter defines the radius of the neighborhood around each point. A smaller ε creates tighter, more numerous clusters, while a larger ε creates looser, fewer clusters.

MinPts (Minimum Points) is the minimum number of points required to form a dense region (cluster). This includes the point itself. A common rule of thumb is to set MinPts equal to 2 times the number of dimensions in your data, but this can be adjusted based on your specific dataset and requirements.

Choosing appropriate values for these parameters is crucial for DBSCAN's success. Modern clustering tools can help determine optimal ε and MinPts values through techniques like the k-distance graph, which plots the distance to the k-th nearest neighbor for each point, or through automated parameter tuning that tests multiple combinations.

5.9.3 The DBSCAN Algorithm in Action

The DBSCAN algorithm follows a systematic approach that builds clusters by expanding from core points.

First, for each point in the dataset, the algorithm determines if it's a core point by counting how many neighbors (including itself) are within distance ε. If this count meets or exceeds MinPts, the point is classified as a core point.

Next, starting with an arbitrary unvisited core point, the algorithm finds all points that are density-reachable from it. This involves following chains of core points and including their border points, forming one complete cluster. This process is repeated for all unvisited core points, creating additional clusters.

Border points are then assigned to the cluster of the nearest core point. If a border point is within ε distance of multiple core points from different clusters, it's typically assigned to the cluster of the first core point encountered.

Finally, points that are not core points and not within ε distance of any core point are marked as noise or outliers.

5.9.4 Practical Example and Applications

Consider a dataset with points that form two distinct dense regions with some scattered outliers between them. Traditional K-means might struggle with this data because the clusters aren't spherical, and it would force the scattered outliers into one of the two clusters, potentially distorting the cluster boundaries.

DBSCAN, however, would identify the two dense regions as separate clusters based on the density of points in those areas. The scattered points between the clusters would be correctly classified as noise/outliers rather than being forced into either cluster. Additionally, DBSCAN would handle the irregular shapes of the clusters naturally, following the actual distribution of the data rather than assuming spherical shapes.

This makes DBSCAN particularly valuable for real-world data that often contains noise and irregularly shaped clusters. Applications include identifying customer segments with unusual purchasing patterns, detecting anomalies in network traffic, or finding clusters of similar genes in biological data where outliers might represent interesting mutations or errors.

5.9.5 Advantages and Limitations of DBSCAN

DBSCAN offers several significant advantages that make it valuable for many clustering applications. It can find clusters of arbitrary shapes, not just spherical ones, making it more flexible than K-means. The algorithm automatically determines the number of clusters based on the data density, eliminating the need to specify this in advance. DBSCAN is robust to outliers by marking them as noise rather than forcing them into clusters, which can lead to more accurate cluster representations. The algorithm does not require cluster centers and can handle clusters of different sizes and densities within the same dataset.

However, DBSCAN also has important limitations. It's sensitive to the choice of ε and MinPts parameters, and poor parameter selection can lead to either too many small clusters or too few large clusters. The algorithm can struggle with clusters of varying densities—if some clusters are much denser than others, the parameters that work well for dense clusters might not work for sparse ones. DBSCAN can be memory intensive for large datasets because it needs to store neighborhood information. The algorithm also has difficulty with high-dimensional data due to the "curse of dimensionality," where distance measures become less meaningful as the number of dimensions increases.

5.9.6 When to Use DBSCAN

DBSCAN is particularly useful in several scenarios. Use it when you expect irregular cluster shapes that wouldn't be well-captured by spherical clusters. It's ideal when your data contains outliers that should be identified rather than forced into clusters. DBSCAN works well when you don't know the number of clusters in advance and want the algorithm to determine this automatically. It's also effective when clusters have similar densities but you want to avoid the spherical cluster assumption of K-means.

Modern software implementations of DBSCAN often include helpful features that make the algorithm more accessible. Many tools can analyze your data and suggest appropriate ε and MinPts values through automated parameter suggestion. Advanced platforms provide interactive visualizations showing how different parameter values affect cluster formation, helping you understand the impact of your choices. Some tools can provide insights into why certain points were classified as noise, helping you understand your data better and potentially identify data quality issues.

5.10 Comparative Analysis of Clustering Methods

Table 5.9: Comparison of Clustering Algorithms

Aspect	Hierarchical	K-Means	DBSCAN
Cluster Shape	Any shape	Spherical	Any shape
Number of Clusters	Determined from dendrogram	Must specify K	Automatic
Outlier Handling	Poor	Poor	Excellent
Computational Complexity	$O(n^3)$	O(nkt)	O(n log n)
Large Datasets	Challenging	Excellent	Good
Parameter Sensitivity	Low	Medium	High
Deterministic Results	Yes	No	Yes
Memory Requirements	High	Low	Medium
Cluster Size Assumptions	None	Similar sizes	None

Each clustering method has distinct strengths and is suited for different types of data and analysis goals. Understanding when to use each method is crucial for successful cluster analysis and meaningful results.

5.10.1 Comprehensive Method Comparison

5.10.2 Decision Framework for Method Selection

Use hierarchical clustering when: - You want to understand the hierarchical structure of your data and see relationships at multiple levels - You have a small to medium-sized dataset (typically fewer than a few thousand points) - You don't know the number of clusters in advance and want to explore different possibilities - You want deterministic results that don't change between runs - The shape of clusters is not a primary concern - You need to present results that show how clusters relate to each other

Use K-means when: - You have a large dataset where computational efficiency is important - You have a good idea of how many clusters to expect based on domain knowledge or previous analysis - Your clusters are roughly spherical and similar in size - You can tolerate some randomness in results due to random initialization - You need a fast, scalable algorithm for production environments - Outliers are not a major concern or have been handled separately

Use DBSCAN when: - Your data contains outliers that should be identified rather than forced into clusters - You expect clusters of irregular, non-spherical shapes - You don't know the number of clusters and want the algorithm to determine this automatically - Clusters may have different densities but you want to avoid spherical assumptions - You want to automatically handle noise in your data - You're working with spatial data or other applications where density-based clustering makes intuitive sense

5.10.3 Hybrid and Advanced Approaches

Modern clustering often involves using multiple methods in combination to leverage the strengths of each approach while mitigating individual limitations.

Sequential application is a common hybrid approach. You might use hierarchical clustering first to get an initial understanding of the data structure and estimate the number of natural clusters. Then apply K-means with the suggested number of clusters to take advantage of its computational efficiency for larger datasets. This approach combines the exploratory power of hierarchical clustering with the scalability of K-means.

Ensemble clustering combines results from multiple algorithms to get more robust clustering solutions. This might involve running several different algorithms on the same data and then using voting or consensus methods to determine final cluster assignments. Ensemble approaches can be particularly valuable when different algorithms suggest different cluster structures, helping you understand the stability and reliability of your clustering results.

AI-enhanced selection represents the cutting edge of clustering methodology. Intelligent tools can analyze your data characteristics—such as size, dimensionality, distribution shape, and presence of outliers—and automatically recommend the most appropriate clustering method. These systems can even suggest optimal parameters and provide explanations for their recommendations, making advanced clustering techniques accessible to users without deep technical expertise.

5.11 Key Terms

Cluster Analysis – A data mining technique used to group objects based on similarity.

Unsupervised Learning – Machine learning approach for analyzing unlabeled data without predefined categories.

Labeled Data – Data with categorical identifiers that allow supervised learning.

Unlabeled Data – Data lacking predefined categories, typically analyzed using clustering.

Distance Metric – A mathematical measure of similarity or dissimilarity between data points (e.g., Euclidean distance).

Normalization / Scaling – Adjusting variables to a common scale so no single variable dominates the clustering process.

Hierarchical Clustering – Clustering method that builds nested clusters and visualizes them using a dendrogram.

Linkage Methods – Approaches for measuring distance between clusters (single, complete, average, Ward's method).

Dendrogram – Tree-like diagram that illustrates hierarchical clustering and inter-cluster distances.

K-Means Clustering – Partition-based clustering algorithm that divides data into K distinct clusters using centroids.

Centroid – The mean position of points in a K-means cluster.

Elbow Method – Technique to determine optimal K by observing where within-cluster variance stops decreasing significantly.

Silhouette Analysis – Method to evaluate how well points fit their assigned cluster versus neighboring clusters.

DBSCAN – Density-based clustering algorithm that identifies dense clusters and labels outliers.

Core Point – In DBSCAN, a point with a minimum number of neighbors within ε distance.

Border Point – Point within ε distance of a core point but not dense enough to be a core itself.

Noise / Outlier – Points not assigned to any cluster in DBSCAN.

Density-Connected Points – Points linked by a chain of core points in DBSCAN.

Hybrid Clustering – Combining multiple clustering methods for improved accuracy and interpretability.

AI-Enhanced Clustering – Modern tools that recommend clustering methods and parameters automaticall

5.12 Review Questions

1. What distinguishes unsupervised learning from supervised learning? Provide examples.
2. How does clustering help analyze unlabeled data?
3. Explain the concept of Euclidean distance and how it is calculated in multidimensional space.
4. Why is normalization important before performing clustering?
5. Describe the main differences between hierarchical clustering, K-means, and DBSCAN.
6. What is a dendrogram, and how do you interpret it to determine clusters?
7. Explain single, complete, average, and Ward's linkage methods in hierarchical clustering.
8. How does K-means determine cluster assignments, and why is the choice of K important?
9. Describe the Elbow Method and Silhouette Analysis for selecting the optimal number of clusters.
10. What are the key parameters of DBSCAN, and how do they affect clustering results?
11. In what scenarios would DBSCAN be preferable to K-means?
12. Identify advantages and limitations of hierarchical clustering for large datasets.
13. How can hybrid clustering approaches improve clustering outcomes?
14. Explain how modern AI tools enhance clustering analysis and interpretation.
15. Consider a dataset of customer purchasing patterns. Which clustering method would you choose and why?

5.13 Lab 5: Cluster Analysis

In this lab, you will explore how to find patterns in data when there are no predefined categories (aka labels) or "correct answers" provided. Instead of predicting an outcome, your goal is to group similar observations together based on their characteristics. You will apply three clustering methods—hierarchical clustering, K-means, and DBSCAN—to see how each approach forms groups from the same dataset. By the end of the lab, you will understand how clustering helps uncover hidden patterns and how these groupings can be used to better understand data in real-world situations.

5.13.1 Demonstration

First setup to run the code by installing essential libraries.

```
# Essential libraries for cluster analysis
import pandas as pd
import numpy as np
import matplotlib.pyplot as plt
import seaborn as sns
from sklearn.cluster import KMeans, AgglomerativeClustering, DBSCAN
from sklearn.preprocessing import StandardScaler
from sklearn.metrics import silhouette_score
from scipy.cluster.hierarchy import dendrogram, linkage
from scipy.spatial.distance import pdist, squareform
import warnings
warnings.filterwarnings('ignore')

# Set up plotting style
plt.style.use('default')
sns.set_palette("husl")
```

5.13.1.1 Step 1: Understanding Distance and Similarity

To group data, we first need a clear way to decide what makes two observations similar. In clustering, we use distance for this—observations that are close together are grouped, and those that are far apart are separated. This is important because clustering algorithms rely entirely on distance to form groups, so how we measure it directly affects the results we get.

First we need to create some data to work with.

```
# Create a simple employee dataset for demonstration
employee_data = {
    'Employee': [1, 2, 3, 4, 5],
    'Salary': [50000, 60000, 55000, 70000, 65000],
```

```
    'Experience': [2, 5, 3, 8, 6]
}

df_employees = pd.DataFrame(employee_data)
print("Employee Dataset:")
print(df_employees)
```

Output:

```
Employee Dataset:
   Employee  Salary  Experience
0         1   50000           2
1         2   60000           5
2         3   55000           3
3         4   70000           8
4         5   65000           6
```

5.13.1.1.1 Calculating Euclidean Distance

When we want to group data points based on how similar they are, we need a way to measure "distance" between them. Euclidean distance is one of the simplest ways to do this. Think of it as the straight-line distance between two points, just like measuring with a ruler—but it works in any number of dimensions, not just on a 2D plane. In clustering, Euclidean distance helps us answer questions like: Which employees have similar salaries and experience? or Which products have similar characteristics? The smaller the distance, the more similar the points are.

```
# Function to calculate Euclidean distance between two points
def euclidean_distance(point1, point2):
    """
    Calculate Euclidean distance between two data points
    This is the foundation of most clustering algorithms
    """
    return np.sqrt(np.sum((point1 - point2) ** 2))

# Example: Distance between Employee 1 and Employee 2
emp1 = df_employees.iloc[0][['Salary', 'Experience']].values
emp2 = df_employees.iloc[1][['Salary', 'Experience']].values

distance = euclidean_distance(emp1, emp2)
print(f"Distance between Employee 1 and 2: {distance:.2f}")
print("This means Employee 1 and 2 are relatively similar in salary and
 ↪ experience")
```

Output:

```
Distance between Employee 1 and 2: 10000.00
This means Employee 1 and 2 are relatively similar in salary and experience
```

5.13.1.1.2 Creating a Distance Matrix

Once we can measure the distance between two points, it's useful to see the distances for every pair of points in our dataset. This is called a distance matrix. Think of it as a map of similarities: the smaller the distance between two points, the more alike they are. In clustering, the distance matrix helps us see the overall structure of our data and identify which points naturally group together.

```
# Create distance matrix for all employees
from scipy.spatial.distance import pdist, squareform

# Extract numerical features
features = df_employees[['Salary', 'Experience']].values

# Calculate pairwise distances
distances = pdist(features, metric='euclidean')
distance_matrix = squareform(distances)

# Create a DataFrame for better visualization
distance_df = pd.DataFrame(distance_matrix,
                          index=df_employees['Employee'],
                          columns=df_employees['Employee'])

print("Distance Matrix (Raw Data):")
print(distance_df.round(0))
```

Output:

```
Distance Matrix (Raw Data):
Employee        1        2        3        4        5
Employee
1             0.0  10000.0   5000.0  20000.0  15000.0
2         10000.0      0.0   5000.0  10000.0   5000.0
3          5000.0   5000.0      0.0  15000.0  10000.0
4         20000.0  10000.0  15000.0      0.0   5000.0
5         15000.0   5000.0  10000.0   5000.0      0.0
```

This output shows the pairwise Euclidean distances between employees based on Salary and Experience, where smaller values indicate more similar employees. It provides a complete view of how close or far apart all employees are, which is used as the foundation for clustering.

5.13.1.1.3 Importance of Data Normalization

When we calculate distances between data points, variables with larger scales can dominate the calculation. For example, consider an employee dataset:

- Salary ranges from 50,000 to 70,000 (thousands)
- Experience ranges from 2 to 8 years (single digits)

If we use the raw data, differences in salary will outweigh differences in experience, which can mislead clustering results. To fix this, we use normalization—specifically Z-score standardization—to bring all variables onto the same scale.

```
# Demonstrate the scaling problem
print("\nProblem with Raw Data:")
print("Salary ranges from 50,000 to 70,000 (scale: thousands)")
print("Experience ranges from 2 to 8 (scale: single digits)")
print("Salary differences will dominate the distance calculation!")

# Apply normalization (Z-score standardization)
scaler = StandardScaler()
normalized_features = scaler.fit_transform(features)

# Create normalized DataFrame for visualization
df_normalized = pd.DataFrame(normalized_features,
                             columns=['Salary_Normalized',
 ↪  'Experience_Normalized'])
df_normalized['Employee'] = df_employees['Employee']

print("\nNormalized Data (Z-scores):")
print(df_normalized.round(2))

# Calculate distance matrix with normalized data
normalized_distances = pdist(normalized_features, metric='euclidean')
normalized_distance_matrix = squareform(normalized_distances)

normalized_distance_df = pd.DataFrame(normalized_distance_matrix,
                                      index=df_employees['Employee'],
                                      columns=df_employees['Employee'])

print("Distance Matrix (Normalized Data):")
print(normalized_distance_df.round(2))
print("\nNotice how the distances are now more balanced!")
```

Output:

```
Problem with Raw Data:
```

```
Salary ranges from 50,000 to 70,000 (scale: thousands)
Experience ranges from 2 to 8 (scale: single digits)
Salary differences will dominate the distance calculation!

Normalized Data (Z-scores):
   Salary_Normalized  Experience_Normalized  Employee
0              -1.41                  -1.41         1
1               0.00                   0.00         2
2              -0.71                  -0.71         3
3               1.41                   1.41         4
4               0.71                   0.71         5

Distance Matrix (Normalized Data):
Employee      1     2     3     4     5
Employee
1          0.00  1.99  0.85  3.99  2.83
2          1.99  0.00  1.17  1.99  0.85
3          0.85  1.17  0.00  3.16  1.99
4          3.99  1.99  3.16  0.00  1.17
5          2.83  0.85  1.99  1.17  0.00
```

Comparing the two outputs, the raw distance matrix is dominated by Salary differences, so large numbers overshadow smaller differences in Experience. After standardization, the normalized distance matrix shows more balanced distances where both Salary and Experience contribute equally, giving a fairer view of employee similarity for clustering.

5.13.1.2 Step 2: Hierarchical Clustering

5.13.1.2.1 Understanding the Agglomeration Process

Hierarchical clustering is a way to group similar data points step by step. It starts by treating each point as its own cluster. Then, it merges the closest clusters repeatedly until all points are combined into a single large cluster. Think of it like making a family tree of customers based on how similar they are. The dendrogram (tree diagram) shows these relationships visually.

First let's expand the data to be more practical for a real demonstration.

```
# Create a larger dataset for better demonstration
np.random.seed(42)
customer_data = {
    'CustomerID': range(1, 21),
    'Age': np.random.normal(35, 10, 20).astype(int),
    'Annual_Spending': np.random.normal(5000, 2000, 20).astype(int),
    'Purchase_Frequency': np.random.poisson(12, 20)
}
```

```
df_customers = pd.DataFrame(customer_data)
df_customers = df_customers[(df_customers['Age'] > 18) &
↪ (df_customers['Annual_Spending'] > 0)]
print("Customer Dataset (first 10 rows):")
print(df_customers.head(10))
```

Output:

```
Customer Dataset (first 10 rows):
   CustomerID  Age  Annual_Spending  Purchase_Frequency
0           1   39             7931                   6
1           2   33             4548                   4
2           3   41             5135                  11
3           4   50             2150                  16
4           5   32             3911                  10
5           6   32             5221                   8
6           7   50             2698                  15
7           8   42             5751                  14
8           9   30             3798                  15
9          10   40             4416                  10
```

5.13.1.2.2 Performing Hierarchical Clustering

Before clustering, it's important to normalize the data so no single variable dominates the distance calculation.

```
# Prepare data for clustering
features = df_customers[['Age', 'Annual_Spending',
↪ 'Purchase_Frequency']].values

# Normalize the data (essential for clustering!)
scaler = StandardScaler()
normalized_features = scaler.fit_transform(features)

# Perform hierarchical clustering using different linkage methods
linkage_matrix = linkage(normalized_features, method='average')

# Create and display dendrogram
plt.figure(figsize=(12, 6))
dendrogram(linkage_matrix, labels=df_customers['CustomerID'].values)
plt.title('Hierarchical Clustering Dendrogram\n(Average Linkage
↪ Method)')
plt.xlabel('Customer ID')
```

```
plt.ylabel('Distance')
plt.xticks(rotation=45)
plt.tight_layout()
plt.show()

print("Dendrogram Interpretation:")
print("- The height of each merge shows the distance between clusters")
print("- Lower merges indicate more similar customers")
print("- You can 'cut' the tree at different heights to get different
↪  numbers of clusters")
```

Output:

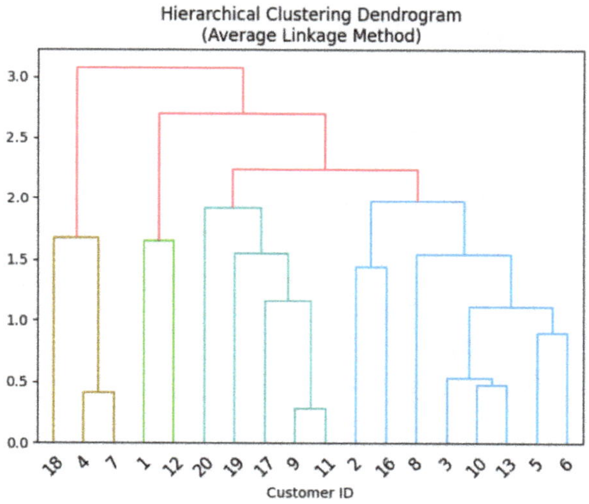


```
Dendrogram Interpretation:
- The height of each merge shows the distance between clusters
- Lower merges indicate more similar customers
- You can 'cut' the tree at different heights to get different
numbers of clusters
```

The dendrogram shows that several customers form very tight, highly similar groups at low distances, particularly on the right side (e.g., customers 3, 10, 13, 5, and 6), where merges occur close to the bottom—indicating these customers have very similar behavior or characteristics. In contrast, customers on the far left (such as 18, 4, and 7) merge at much higher distances, suggesting they are more distinct from the rest of the dataset. A noticeable jump in merge height occurs around the 2.5–3.0 range, which suggests a natural point to "cut" the dendrogram. If cut around this level, the data would form roughly 3 main clusters: one small, distinct group on the left, a moderate cluster in the middle, and a larger, more homogeneous cluster on the right. This implies there is one clearly different segment of customers and two broader groups with varying degrees of internal similarity.

5.13.1.2.3 Extracting Clusters from Hierarchical Clustering

We can now assign each customer to a cluster and analyze their characteristics.

```
# Extract 3 clusters from hierarchical clustering
hierarchical_clusters = AgglomerativeClustering(n_clusters=3,
↪ linkage='average')
cluster_labels = hierarchical_clusters.fit_predict(normalized_features)

# Add cluster labels to original data
df_customers['Hierarchical_Cluster'] = cluster_labels

# Analyze the clusters
print("Hierarchical Clustering Results:")
for cluster in range(3):
    cluster_data = df_customers[df_customers['Hierarchical_Cluster']
↪   == cluster]
    print(f"\nCluster {cluster + 1} ({len(cluster_data)} customers):")
    print(f"  Average Age: {cluster_data['Age'].mean():.1f}")
    print(f"  Average Spending:
     ↪ ${cluster_data['Annual_Spending'].mean():.0f}")
    print(f"  Average Purchase Frequency:
     ↪ {cluster_data['Purchase_Frequency'].mean():.1f}")
```

Output:

```
Hierarchical Clustering Results:

Cluster 1 (13 customers):
  Average Age: 31.9
  Average Spending: $4405
  Average Purchase Frequency: 10.9

Cluster 2 (3 customers):
  Average Age: 46.0
  Average Spending: $1976
  Average Purchase Frequency: 15.3

Cluster 3 (2 customers):
  Average Age: 34.5
  Average Spending: $8318
  Average Purchase Frequency: 8.0
```

Cluster 1 consists of 13 customers who are, on average, 32 years old. They spend around $4,400 annually and make about 11 purchases, representing the largest and most typical customer group. Cluster 2 includes 3 older customers, averaging 46 years of age, who spend less—around $2,000 per year—but purchase more frequently, about 15 times annually. Cluster 3 has 2 customers who are about 35 years old and spend the most, roughly $8,300 per year, but make fewer purchases, around 8 times annually. These clusters highlight distinct customer behaviors: moderate spenders, frequent low spenders, and high value but infrequent shoppers.

Hierarchical clustering lets us see the natural groupings in our data and understand which customers behave similarly. It's particularly useful when you don't know the number of clusters in advance and want to explore the overall structure of your dataset.

5.13.1.3 Step 3: K-Means Clustering

5.13.1.3.1 Understanding the K-Means Process

K-Means clustering is a method used to group data into a predefined number of clusters by identifying central points, called centroids, that minimize the distance between each data point and its assigned cluster. The objective is to ensure that data points within the same cluster are as similar as possible, while clusters themselves remain distinct from one another. Before applying K-Means, it is important to determine an appropriate number of clusters (K) for the data. One common approach is the Elbow Method, which evaluates the within-cluster sum of squares (WCSS), a measure of how tightly grouped the points are within each cluster. By plotting WCSS against different values of K, we look for a point where the rate of decrease sharply slows—forming an "elbow" shape on the graph. This point suggests a good balance between minimizing variation within clusters and avoiding unnecessary complexity, providing a reasonable estimate for the optimal number of clusters.

```
# Demonstrate K-means with the same customer data
# First, we need to determine the optimal number of clusters

# Method 1: Elbow Method
wcss = []  # Within-cluster sum of squares
k_range = range(1, 11)

for k in k_range:
    kmeans = KMeans(n_clusters=k, random_state=42, n_init=10)
    kmeans.fit(normalized_features)
    wcss.append(kmeans.inertia_)

# Plot the elbow curve
plt.figure(figsize=(10, 6))
plt.plot(k_range, wcss, 'bo-')
```

```
plt.title('Elbow Method for Optimal K')
plt.xlabel('Number of Clusters (K)')
plt.ylabel('Within-Cluster Sum of Squares (WCSS)')
plt.grid(True, alpha=0.3)
plt.show()

print("Elbow Method Interpretation:")
print("- Look for the 'elbow' point where WCSS stops decreasing
↪ rapidly")
print("- This suggests the optimal number of clusters")
```

Output:

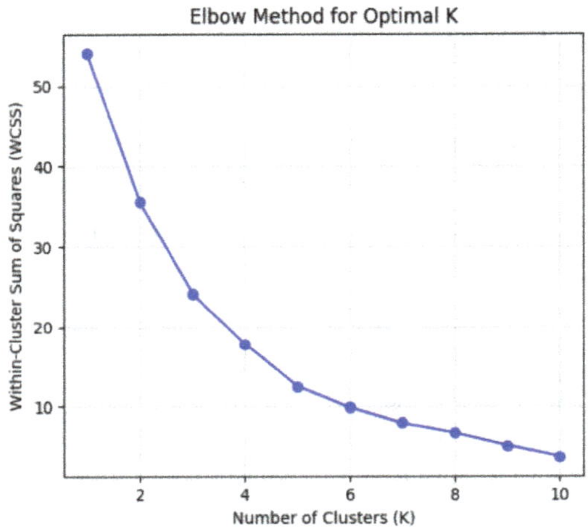


```
Elbow Method Interpretation:
- Look for the 'elbow' point where WCSS stops decreasing rapidly
- This suggests the optimal number of clusters
```

Interpretation: The "elbow" indicates where adding more clusters stops improving the grouping significantly. For this data the elbow is arguably at 3 or 4 or 5 clusters.

5.13.1.3.2 Silhouette Analysis for K Selection

Silhouette analysis measures how well each data point fits within its assigned cluster by comparing its similarity to points in its own cluster versus those in other clusters. A higher silhouette score indicates that a point is much closer to its own cluster than to neighboring clusters, suggesting good clustering structure. To determine the optimal number of clusters, we calculate the average silhouette score for different values of K and select the value with the highest score. This approach helps ensure that clusters are both well-separated and internally cohesive.

```
# Method 2: Silhouette Analysis
silhouette_scores = []

for k in range(2, 11):  # Silhouette score requires at least 2 clusters
    kmeans = KMeans(n_clusters=k, random_state=42, n_init=10)
    cluster_labels = kmeans.fit_predict(normalized_features)
    silhouette_avg = silhouette_score(normalized_features,
 ↪  cluster_labels)
    silhouette_scores.append(silhouette_avg)

# Plot silhouette scores
plt.figure(figsize=(10, 6))
plt.plot(range(2, 11), silhouette_scores, 'ro-')
plt.title('Silhouette Analysis for Optimal K')
plt.xlabel('Number of Clusters (K)')
plt.ylabel('Average Silhouette Score')
plt.grid(True, alpha=0.3)
plt.show()

# Find optimal K
optimal_k = range(2, 11)[np.argmax(silhouette_scores)]
print(f"Optimal K based on Silhouette Score: {optimal_k}")
print(f"Best Silhouette Score: {max(silhouette_scores):.3f}")
```

Output:

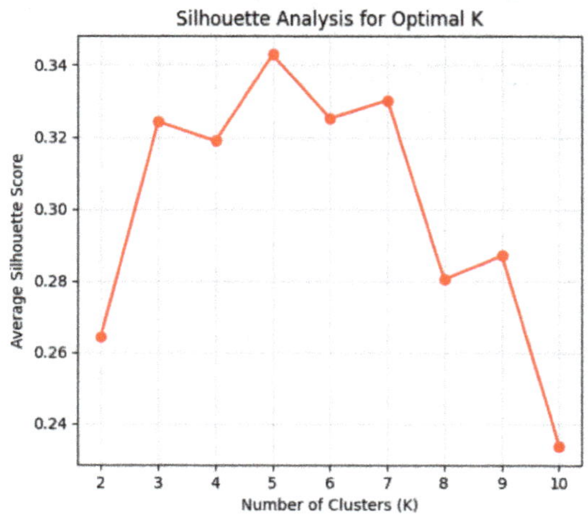


```
Optimal K based on Silhouette Score: 5
Best Silhouette Score: 0.343
```

Interpretation: The K with the highest silhouette score represents the best separation between clusters. Here that is k=5.

5.13.1.3.3 Implementing K-Means Clustering

In this example, we apply K-Means to our customer dataset to identify groups with similar age, annual spending, and purchase frequency. We will use k=5 based on silhouette scores.

```
# Perform K-means with optimal K
kmeans = KMeans(n_clusters=optimal_k, random_state=42, n_init=10)
kmeans_labels = kmeans.fit_predict(normalized_features)

# Add K-means results to dataframe
df_customers['KMeans_Cluster'] = kmeans_labels

# Analyze K-means clusters
print(f"K-Means Clustering Results (K={optimal_k}):")
for cluster in range(optimal_k):
    cluster_data = df_customers[df_customers['KMeans_Cluster'] ==
 ↪  cluster]
    print(f"\nCluster {cluster + 1} ({len(cluster_data)} customers):")
    print(f"  Average Age: {cluster_data['Age'].mean():.1f}")
    print(f"  Average Spending:
     ↪  ${cluster_data['Annual_Spending'].mean():.0f}")
    print(f"  Average Purchase Frequency:
     ↪  {cluster_data['Purchase_Frequency'].mean():.1f}")

# Display cluster centers in original scale
cluster_centers_original =
 ↪  scaler.inverse_transform(kmeans.cluster_centers_)
centers_df = pd.DataFrame(cluster_centers_original,
                          columns=['Age', 'Annual_Spending',
 ↪  'Purchase_Frequency'])
print("\nCluster Centers (Original Scale):")
print(centers_df.round(1))
```

Output:

```
K-Means Clustering Results (K=5):

Cluster 1 (3 customers):
  Average Age: 46.0
  Average Spending: $1976
  Average Purchase Frequency: 15.3
```

```
Cluster 2 (5 customers):
  Average Age: 29.2
  Average Spending: $4326
  Average Purchase Frequency: 7.8

Cluster 3 (4 customers):
  Average Age: 27.2
  Average Spending: $3838
  Average Purchase Frequency: 14.5

Cluster 4 (4 customers):
  Average Age: 40.0
  Average Spending: $5069
  Average Purchase Frequency: 11.2

Cluster 5 (2 customers):
  Average Age: 34.5
  Average Spending: $8318
  Average Purchase Frequency: 8.0

Cluster Centers (Original Scale):
    Age  Annual_Spending  Purchase_Frequency
0  46.0           1976.0                15.3
1  29.2           4326.2                 7.8
2  27.2           3838.5                14.5
3  40.0           5068.8                11.2
4  34.5           8317.5                 8.0
```

The K-Means clustering results reveal five distinct customer groups, each with unique purchasing behaviors and demographic characteristics. The first cluster consists of three older customers, with an average age of 46, who spend the least overall (about $1,976) but make purchases most frequently, averaging 15 transactions. The second cluster includes five young adults, around age 29, who demonstrate moderate spending levels (approximately $4,326) but shop less often, with an average of 8 purchases. The third cluster is made up of four younger customers, averaging 27 years old, who also spend moderately (about $3,838) but purchase more frequently, similar to Cluster 1, with around 15 transactions. The fourth cluster contains four middle-aged customers, with an average age of 40, who exhibit slightly higher spending (around $5,069) and a moderate purchase frequency of about 11 transactions. Finally, the fifth cluster, though the smallest with only two customers, represents the highest-value segment, with an average age of 35 and significantly higher spending (approximately $8,318), despite a lower purchase frequency of 8 transactions.

Overall, these clusters highlight clear differences in customer behavior, ranging from frequent low spenders to high-value but less frequent shoppers. Understanding these segments allows businesses to tailor marketing strategies, such as offering loyalty rewards to frequent shoppers or targeted promotions to encourage repeat purchases among high-spending but infrequent customers, ultimately helping to optimize pricing, improve customer engagement, and increase overall revenue.

5.13.1.4 Step 4: DBSCAN Clustering

Density-based clustering, or DBSCAN, is a method that groups points that are close together while identifying points that are far from any dense region as outliers. To demonstrate this, we will create a dataset with three distinct clusters and a few outliers, which makes it easy to see how DBSCAN separates clusters from noise.

```
import numpy as np
import pandas as pd
from sklearn.preprocessing import StandardScaler
from sklearn.cluster import DBSCAN
import matplotlib.pyplot as plt
from sklearn.datasets import make_blobs

# Step 1: Create synthetic data with 3 clusters and 5 outliers
X, _ = make_blobs(n_samples=50, centers=[[0,0], [5,5], [10,0]],
↪ cluster_std=0.8, random_state=42)

# Add random points as outliers
noise = np.random.uniform(low=-2, high=12, size=(5,2))
X = np.vstack([X, noise])
```

In this step, we generate 50 points around three centers using make_blobs, which creates tight groups of points. We then add five random points outside these clusters to act as outliers. This combination gives us both clearly defined clusters and points that do not belong to any cluster, making DBSCAN's behavior easy to observe.

```
# Step 2: Normalize the data
scaler = StandardScaler()
X_scaled = scaler.fit_transform(X)
```

Normalization is important because DBSCAN uses distance to determine whether points belong to the same cluster. Features on different scales could distort these distances. By standardizing the data, we ensure that all features contribute equally to the distance calculation.

```
# Step 3: Test different eps values
eps_values = [0.3, 0.5, 0.8, 1.0]
min_samples = 3
```

```
print("DBSCAN Parameter Testing:")
for eps in eps_values:
    dbscan = DBSCAN(eps=eps, min_samples=min_samples)
    labels = dbscan.fit_predict(X_scaled)

    n_clusters = len(set(labels)) - (1 if -1 in labels else 0)
    n_noise = list(labels).count(-1)

    print(f"eps={eps}: {n_clusters} clusters, {n_noise} noise points")
```

Output:

```
DBSCAN Parameter Testing:
eps=0.3: 3 clusters, 5 noise points
eps=0.5: 3 clusters, 3 noise points
eps=0.8: 3 clusters, 3 noise points
eps=1.0: 3 clusters, 3 noise points
```

Here, we experiment with different eps values to see how they affect the number of clusters and outliers. A smaller eps will detect fewer clusters and more noise, while a larger eps may merge clusters together. The min_samples parameter ensures that at least three points are needed to form a dense region.

```
# Step 4: Run DBSCAN with chosen eps
optimal_eps = 0.5
dbscan = DBSCAN(eps=optimal_eps, min_samples=min_samples)
labels = dbscan.fit_predict(X_scaled)
```

After testing, we select eps=0.5 as a good balance for this dataset. Running DBSCAN assigns a label to each point. Points labeled -1 are considered noise, while other labels indicate which cluster each point belongs to.

```
# Step 5: Create a DataFrame with results
df_demo = pd.DataFrame(X_scaled, columns=['Feature1', 'Feature2'])
df_demo['DBSCAN_Cluster'] = labels
print("\nDBSCAN Clustering Results:")
print(df_demo.head(6))
```

Output:

```
DBSCAN Clustering Results:
    Feature1  Feature2  DBSCAN_Cluster
0   0.146463  0.698113               0
1  -1.329907 -0.642206               1
2  -0.270408  1.084466               0
```

```
3  -1.400390 -1.057317          1
4  -1.177492 -1.193843          1
5   1.155874 -0.575115          2
```

By storing the results in a DataFrame, we can see the cluster assignment for each point. This makes it easy to check which points are in clusters and which are outliers.

```
# Step 6: Visualize clusters
plt.figure(figsize=(8,6))
plt.scatter(X_scaled[:,0], X_scaled[:,1], c=labels, cmap='rainbow',
 ↪  s=50)
plt.title(f"DBSCAN Clustering Example (eps={optimal_eps},
 ↪  min_samples={min_samples})")
plt.xlabel("Feature 1 (scaled)")
plt.ylabel("Feature 2 (scaled)")
plt.show()
```

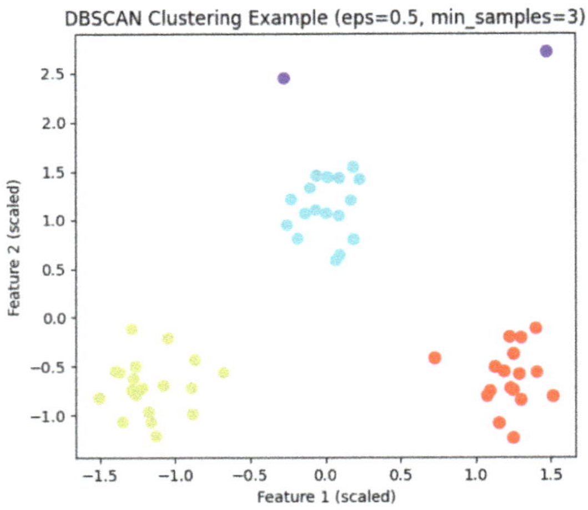

Finally, we visualize the clusters in a scatter plot. Each cluster appears in a different color, and outliers are labeled separately. This plot provides a clear visual representation of how DBSCAN groups points based on density and highlights which points are considered unusual.

After running DBSCAN on this dataset, we can interpret the results by looking at both the clusters and the outliers. The algorithm identifies three main clusters, which correspond to the groups we originally generated with make_blobs. Each cluster contains points that are close together in space, meaning their feature values are similar. For example, one cluster might consist of points near [0,0], another near [5,5], and the third near [10,0]. These clusters show how DBSCAN groups dense areas of points automatically, without needing to specify the number of clusters in advance.

In addition to the clusters, DBSCAN labels several points as outliers (also called noise).

These are points that are far from any dense region and do not fit well into any cluster. In our dataset, these outliers were intentionally added as random points outside the clusters. The algorithm marks them with the label -1. Outliers are important because they highlight unusual data points that might require further investigation. In a real-world scenario, these could represent exceptional customers, rare events, or errors in the data.

By examining the cluster assignments and the scatter plot, beginners can see that DBSCAN effectively separates dense groups while clearly identifying points that do not belong to any cluster. This makes it a powerful tool for understanding complex datasets where the number of clusters is not known ahead of time and where noise or unusual points exist.

5.13.2 Practice

This practice exercise uses a single customer dataset to explore distance calculations and clustering techniques. You will apply Euclidean distance, hierarchical clustering, and K-Means methods to identify meaningful customer segments.

```
np.random.seed(42)

# Create 3 clear customer groups
cluster1 = np.random.normal(loc=[3000, 8, 120], scale=[400, 2, 20],
 ↪  size=(7, 3))
cluster2 = np.random.normal(loc=[6000, 12, 220], scale=[500, 2, 25],
 ↪  size=(7, 3))
cluster3 = np.random.normal(loc=[9000, 6, 350], scale=[600, 2, 30],
 ↪  size=(6, 3))

data = np.vstack([cluster1, cluster2, cluster3])

df = pd.DataFrame(data, columns=[
'Annual_Spending',
'Purchase_Frequency',
'Avg_Order_Value'
]).astype(int)

df['CustomerID'] = range(1, len(df) + 1)

# Reorder columns
df = df[['CustomerID', 'Annual_Spending', 'Purchase_Frequency',
 ↪  'Avg_Order_Value']]

print(df.head(10))
```

5.13.2.1 Lab 5 Questions

1. Using the dataset `df`, calculate the Euclidean distance between Customer 1 and Customer 2 using all numerical features (excluding CustomerID).
2. Using `df`, calculate the Euclidean distance between Customer 1 and Customer 5.
3. Using `df`, create a full distance matrix for all customers based on Annual_Spending, Purchase_Frequency, and Avg_Order_Value.
4. Based on the distance matrix from `df`, identify the two most similar customers.
5. Normalize the dataset `df` (excluding CustomerID) using standard scaling.
6. Recalculate the distance matrix using the normalized version of `df` and compare it to the original. What changed?
7. Using the normalized `df`, perform hierarchical clustering with average linkage.
8. Create a dendrogram using the hierarchical clustering results from `df`.
9. Based on the dendrogram of `df`, determine a reasonable number of clusters and justify your choice.
10. Cut the dendrogram to form 3 clusters and assign cluster labels to each customer in `df`.
11. For the clusters created from `df`, calculate the average Annual_Spending, Purchase_Frequency, and Avg_Order_Value for each cluster.
12. Using the normalized `df`, apply the elbow method to determine the optimal number of clusters (K).
13. Using the same `df`, compute silhouette scores for different values of K and identify the best K.
14. Run K-Means clustering on `df` using your chosen K and assign cluster labels.
15. Based on the K-Means results from `df`, describe each customer segment in terms of spending, frequency, and order value.

5.14 Conclusion

Cluster analysis remains one of the most valuable and accessible techniques in data mining, providing insights into data structure that can inform business strategy, scientific discovery, and decision-making across countless domains. While the fundamental algorithms haven't changed dramatically over the years, modern AI-enhanced tools have made clustering more intuitive and powerful for beginners and experts alike.

The key to successful clustering lies in understanding your data, choosing the appropriate method for your specific situation, and properly interpreting the results within your domain context. Whether you're using hierarchical clustering to understand data structure and relationships, K-means for efficient large-scale analysis, or DBSCAN to handle irregular shapes and outliers, each method offers unique insights into your data's underlying patterns.

As AI continues to evolve, clustering tools are becoming more intelligent, offering automated parameter selection, smart interpretation of results, and seamless integration with business intelligence platforms. However, the fundamental understanding of how these algorithms work remains crucial for making informed decisions about your analysis and ensuring that results are meaningful and actionable.

Remember that clustering is an exploratory technique—there's rarely a single "correct" answer. The goal is to uncover meaningful patterns that provide insights into your data and support decision-making. Different algorithms may reveal different aspects of your data's structure, and the most valuable approach often involves trying multiple methods and comparing their results.

Chapter 6

Classification Analysis

6.1 Learning Outcomes

6-1. Explain the concept of classification analysis as a supervised learning method and distinguish it from clustering and regression.

6-2. Describe the classification process, including data preparation, feature selection, training/testing split, model training, and validation.

6-3. Compare and contrast logistic regression, decision trees, and K-nearest neighbors (KNN) in terms of interpretability, accuracy, and applicability.

6-4. Evaluate classification models using performance metrics such as confusion matrices, accuracy, precision, recall, F1-score, ROC curves, and cross-validation.

6-5. Identify practical considerations for algorithm selection and understand when to explore advanced classification methods like neural networks or ensemble approaches.

6.2 Introduction

Classification analysis represents one of the most fundamental and widely used techniques in data mining. Unlike clustering, which works with unlabeled data, classification is a supervised learning method that uses labeled training data to predict categories or classes for new, unseen data. This chapter focuses on three core classification methods that form the foundation of predictive analytics, with hands-on examples using modern AI-enhanced tools.

6.3 Supervised Learning

Classification falls under the umbrella of supervised learning, a branch of machine learning where algorithms learn from labeled training data to make predictions about new data. The fundamental difference between supervised and unsupervised learning lies in the presence of target variables or labels that guide the learning process.

6.3.1 Labeled Data and Target Variables

In supervised learning, we work with datasets that contain both input features (independent variables) and known outcomes (dependent variables or labels). For example, if we're building a model to predict whether an email is spam or not spam, our training data would include email features like sender information, subject line characteristics, and word frequencies, along with the known classification of each email as "spam" or "not spam."

The target variable, also called the response variable or dependent variable, represents what we want to predict. In classification problems, this target variable is categorical, meaning it represents discrete classes or categories rather than continuous numerical values. Common examples include predicting customer churn (yes/no), medical diagnosis (disease/no disease), or product categories (electronics/clothing/books).

Modern AI tools can now automatically detect the type of target variable in your dataset and suggest appropriate classification algorithms. Platforms like Orange, WEKA, or even business intelligence tools like Tableau can analyze your data structure and recommend whether classification or regression techniques are most suitable.

6.3.2 Classification vs. Regression

While both classification and regression are supervised learning techniques, they differ in their target variables. Classification predicts discrete categories or classes, while regression predicts continuous numerical values. For instance, predicting house prices would be a regression problem (continuous values), while predicting house price categories (low/medium/high) would be a classification problem (discrete categories).

Understanding this distinction is crucial because it determines which algorithms and evaluation metrics are appropriate for your analysis. Classification algorithms are specifically designed to handle categorical outcomes and use different mathematical approaches than regression algorithms.

6.3.3 Types of Classification Problems

Classification problems can be categorized based on the number of classes in the target variable. Binary classification involves predicting between two classes, such as spam/not spam, fraud/legitimate, or pass/fail. This is the most common type of classification problem and serves as our primary focus in this chapter.

Multiclass classification involves predicting among three or more classes, such as predicting product categories, customer segments, or medical conditions. The three core algorithms we'll explore can handle both binary and multiclass problems effectively.

6.4 The Classification Process

The classification process follows a systematic approach that ensures reliable and generalizable results. Understanding this process is essential for successful implementation of classification projects.

6.4.1 Data Preparation and Feature Selection

Successful classification begins with proper data preparation. This involves cleaning the data by handling missing values, removing duplicates, and addressing outliers that might skew the results. Feature selection becomes crucial in classification, as irrelevant or redundant features can negatively impact model performance and interpretability.

Modern AI-enhanced tools can automatically suggest relevant features based on statistical analysis and domain knowledge. These tools can identify which variables are most predictive of the target variable and recommend feature transformations that might improve model performance.

Data preprocessing also includes encoding categorical variables into numerical formats that algorithms can process. Techniques like one-hot encoding or label encoding transform categorical features into numerical representations while preserving their meaning.

6.4.2 Training and Testing Data Split

A fundamental principle in supervised learning is the separation of data into training and testing sets. The training set is used to build the model, while the testing set evaluates how well the model performs on unseen data. This separation is crucial for assessing whether the model can generalize beyond the specific data it was trained on.

The typical split ratio is 70-80% for training and 20-30% for testing, though this can vary based on dataset size and specific requirements. For smaller datasets, techniques like cross-validation become more important to ensure robust evaluation.

Stratified sampling ensures that the proportion of each class in the target variable is maintained in both training and testing sets. This is particularly important for imbalanced datasets where some classes are much more frequent than others.

6.4.3 Model Training and Validation

During the training phase, the classification algorithm learns patterns from the training data to create a model that can make predictions. Different algorithms use various mathematical approaches to identify these patterns, from statistical relationships in logistic regression to tree-like decision structures in decision trees.

Validation involves assessing how well the trained model performs on data it hasn't seen before. This step is crucial for detecting overfitting, where a model performs well on training data but poorly on new data. Cross-validation techniques provide more robust validation by testing the model on multiple subsets of the data.

Modern machine learning platforms often include automated validation procedures that can detect overfitting and suggest adjustments to improve model generalization.

6.5 Logistic Regression

Logistic regression serves as an excellent starting point for understanding classification algorithms. Despite its name suggesting regression, logistic regression is actually a classification technique that predicts the probability of class membership.

6.5.1 Understanding Logistic Regression

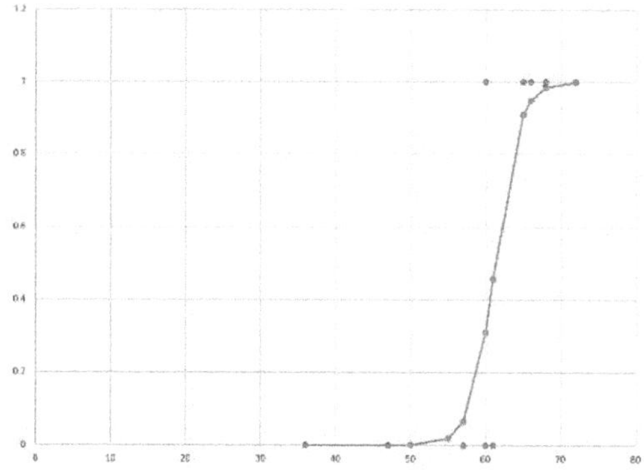

Unlike linear regression, which predicts continuous values, logistic regression predicts probabilities that range between 0 and 1. It accomplishes this through the logistic function (also called the sigmoid function), which transforms any real-valued input into a value between 0 and 1.

The sigmoid function has an S-shaped curve that naturally maps to probability values. When the output is close to 0, it suggests low probability of belonging to the positive class, while values close to 1 indicate high probability. The threshold of 0.5 is commonly used as the decision boundary, though this can be adjusted based on specific requirements.

The mathematical foundation of logistic regression involves the logit function, which is the natural logarithm of the odds ratio. This transformation allows the algorithm to model the relationship between input features and the log-odds of class membership using linear combinations of the features.

6.5.2 How Logistic Regression Works

Logistic regression works by finding the best-fitting line (or hyperplane in higher dimensions) that separates the classes. However, instead of minimizing squared errors like linear regression learned in introductory statistics, it uses maximum likelihood estimation to find the parameters that make the observed data most probable.

The algorithm iteratively adjusts the coefficients for each feature to maximize the likelihood of correctly predicting the training data. This process continues until convergence, where further adjustments don't significantly improve the model's performance.

Each feature in logistic regression receives a coefficient that indicates its importance and direction of influence on the prediction. Positive coefficients increase the probability of the positive class, while negative coefficients decrease it. The magnitude of the coefficient indicates the strength of the relationship.

6.5.3 Advantages and Applications

Logistic regression offers several advantages that make it popular for many classification tasks. It provides probabilistic outputs, which are valuable for understanding prediction confidence and making risk-based decisions. The model is relatively simple to understand and interpret, making it suitable for situations where explainability is important.

The algorithm is computationally efficient and works well with linearly separable data. It doesn't require feature scaling, though it can benefit from it, and it's less prone to overfitting with irrelevant features compared to more complex algorithms.

Common applications include medical diagnosis, where probability estimates are crucial for treatment decisions, marketing response prediction, credit scoring, and any scenario where understanding the likelihood of an outcome is as important as the prediction itself.

6.5.4 Limitations and Considerations

Logistic regression assumes a linear relationship between features and the log-odds of the outcome. This means it may not perform well when the relationship is highly nonlinear. It can also be sensitive to outliers and requires relatively large sample sizes for stable results.

The algorithm assumes independence between features, which may not hold in real-world datasets. When features are highly correlated, the model's interpretability can be compromised, and regularization techniques may be necessary.

Modern implementations of logistic regression often include regularization options (L1 and L2) that help prevent overfitting and handle correlated features. AI-enhanced tools can automatically suggest appropriate regularization parameters based on data characteristics.

6.6 Decision Trees

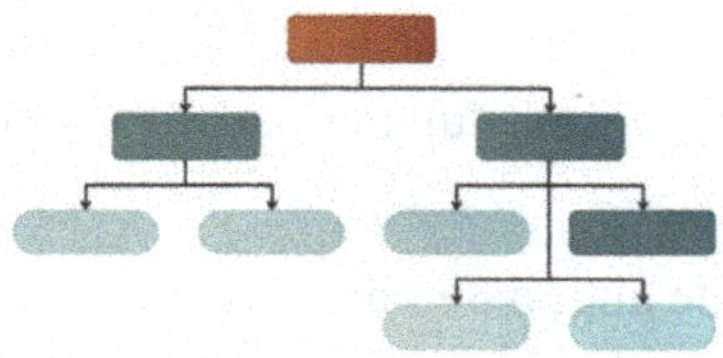

Decision trees represent one of the most intuitive and interpretable classification algorithms. They create a tree-like model of decisions that mirrors human decision-making processes, making them excellent for both prediction and explanation.

6.6.1 Understanding Decision Tree Structure

A decision tree consists of nodes and branches that represent a series of questions about the data. The root node represents the entire dataset, internal nodes represent decision points based on feature values, and leaf nodes represent the final classification decisions.

Each internal node contains a test condition based on a single feature. For example, a node might ask "Is age greater than 30?" or "Is income above $50,000?" Based on the answer, the data flows down different branches to subsequent nodes or final leaf nodes.

The tree structure makes decision trees highly interpretable. You can trace the path from root to leaf to understand exactly why a particular prediction was made. This transparency is valuable in domains where explainability is crucial, such as healthcare or finance.

6.6.2 How Decision Trees Learn

Decision trees learn by recursively splitting the data based on feature values that best separate the classes. The algorithm evaluates different possible splits and chooses the one that results in the purest subsets, meaning subsets where one class dominates.

Common measures for evaluating split quality include Gini impurity and information gain (based on entropy). Gini impurity measures how often a randomly chosen element would be incorrectly classified, while information gain measures the reduction in entropy achieved by the split.

The tree-building process continues until stopping criteria are met, such as reaching a maximum depth, having too few samples in a node, or achieving perfect purity. These stopping criteria help prevent overfitting by avoiding overly complex trees that memorize the training data.

6.6.3 Pruning and Overfitting Prevention

Decision trees are prone to overfitting, especially when they grow very deep and create highly specific rules for the training data. Pruning techniques help address this by removing branches that don't significantly improve performance on validation data.

Pre-pruning (early stopping) prevents overfitting during tree construction by stopping the growth when certain criteria are met. Post-pruning builds a full tree and then removes branches that don't improve validation performance.

Modern decision tree implementations often include automated pruning mechanisms that can optimize tree complexity based on cross-validation results. These tools help balance model complexity with predictive performance.

6.6.4 Advantages and Applications

Decision trees offer several compelling advantages. They're easy to understand and interpret, require minimal data preparation, can handle both numerical and categorical features, and automatically perform feature selection by choosing the most informative features for splits.

The algorithm can capture nonlinear relationships and interactions between features without requiring explicit feature engineering. It's also robust to outliers since splits are based on feature rankings rather than absolute values.

Decision trees are widely used in medical diagnosis, credit approval, customer segmentation, and any domain where understanding the reasoning behind decisions is important. They're also commonly used as base learners in ensemble methods like Random Forests.

6.6.5 Limitations and Considerations

Despite their advantages, decision trees have limitations. They can be unstable, meaning small changes in the data can result in very different trees. They tend to favor features with more levels and can create biased trees if some classes dominate the dataset.

Single decision trees often have lower predictive accuracy compared to more sophisticated algorithms. However, this limitation is often addressed by using ensemble methods that combine multiple trees.

AI-enhanced decision tree tools can automatically optimize parameters like maximum depth, minimum samples per leaf, and splitting criteria. They can also provide visualizations that help users understand tree structure and identify potential improvements.

6.7 K-Nearest Neighbors (KNN)

K-Nearest Neighbors represents a fundamentally different approach to classification. Instead of building an explicit model during training, KNN is a "lazy learning" algorithm that makes predictions based on the similarity of new instances to stored training examples.

6.7.1 Understanding the KNN Concept

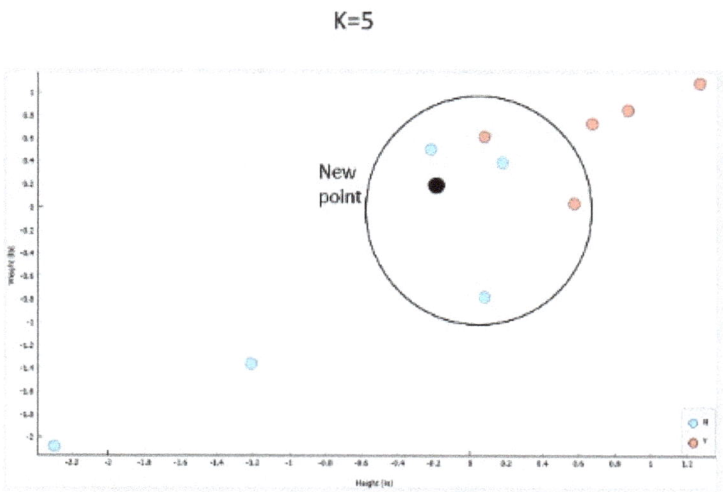

The core idea behind KNN is simple: similar instances should have similar classifications. When making a prediction for a new instance, KNN finds the K most similar instances in the training data and assigns the class that appears most frequently among these neighbors.

The "K" in KNN refers to the number of nearest neighbors to consider. For example, if K=5, the algorithm looks at the 5 most similar training instances and assigns the class that appears most often among these 5 neighbors. The choice of K significantly impacts the algorithm's behavior and performance.

Similarity is typically measured using distance metrics, with Euclidean distance being the most common. However, other distance measures like Manhattan distance or cosine similarity may be more appropriate depending on the data characteristics.

6.7.2 How KNN Makes Predictions

The KNN prediction process involves several steps. First, calculate the distance between the new instance and all training instances. Then, identify the K nearest neighbors based on these distances. For classification, assign the class that appears most frequently among the K neighbors, often called majority voting.

In case of ties, various strategies can be employed, such as reducing K by one, using weighted voting based on distance, or random selection. Weighted voting gives more influence to closer neighbors, which can improve performance in many scenarios.

The algorithm stores all training data and performs calculations at prediction time, which is why it's called "lazy learning." This approach means there's no explicit training phase, but prediction can be computationally expensive for large datasets.

6.7.3 Choosing the Right K Value

Selecting the appropriate K value is crucial for KNN performance. Small K values (like K=1) make the algorithm sensitive to noise and outliers, potentially leading to overfitting. Large K values smooth out the decision boundary but may oversimplify the classification, potentially leading to underfitting.

Common approaches for selecting K include using cross-validation to test different K values and choosing the one with the best performance. The square root of the number of training instances is often used as a starting point, though this rule of thumb should be validated empirically.

Odd values of K are often preferred for binary classification to avoid ties, though weighted voting can handle ties effectively regardless of K value.

6.7.4 Distance Metrics and Feature Scaling

The choice of distance metric significantly impacts KNN performance. Euclidean distance works well for continuous features, while Hamming distance is appropriate for categorical features. For mixed data types, specialized distance measures or feature encoding may be necessary.

Feature scaling is crucial for KNN because the algorithm relies on distance calculations. Features with larger scales can dominate the distance calculation, leading to poor performance. Standardization (z-score normalization) or min-max scaling ensures all features contribute equally to distance calculations.

Modern KNN implementations often include automatic feature scaling and distance metric selection based on data characteristics. Some tools can even suggest optimal preprocessing steps to improve KNN performance.

6.7.5 Advantages and Applications

KNN offers several advantages that make it valuable for many classification tasks. It's simple to understand and implement, makes no assumptions about data distribution, can capture complex decision boundaries, and adapts well to new data without retraining.

The algorithm works well with small datasets and can be effective for both binary and multiclass classification problems. It's particularly useful when the decision boundary is irregular or when local patterns in the data are important.

Common applications include recommendation systems, pattern recognition, image classification, and any scenario where local similarity is a good predictor of class membership.

6.7.6 Limitations and Considerations

KNN has several limitations that should be considered. It can be computationally expensive for large datasets since it requires calculating distances to all training instances for each prediction. The algorithm is sensitive to irrelevant features and the curse of dimensionality, where distance becomes less meaningful in high-dimensional spaces.

KNN doesn't provide probability estimates naturally, though these can be approximated based on the proportion of classes among the K neighbors. The algorithm also requires careful handling of missing values and categorical features.

AI-enhanced KNN implementations often include optimizations like KD-trees or locality-sensitive hashing to speed up neighbor search. They may also provide automated feature selection and dimensionality reduction to improve performance in high-dimensional spaces.

6.8 Advanced Methods Preview

While the three core algorithms covered in this chapter form the foundation of classification analysis, the field continues to evolve with more sophisticated techniques. This section provides a brief preview of advanced methods you may encounter in future studies or professional practice.

6.8.1 Neural Networks: A Glimpse into Deep Learning

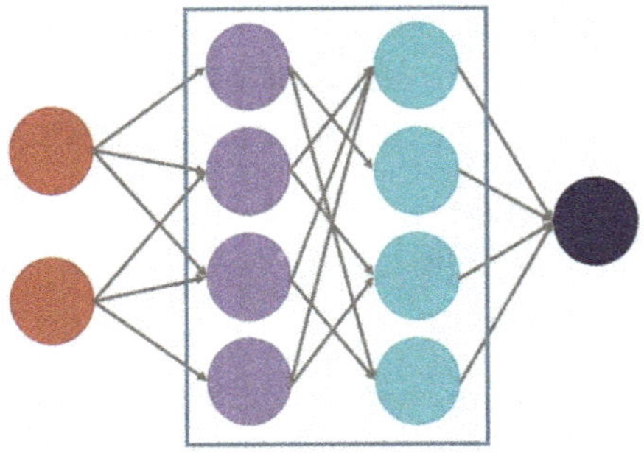

Neural networks represent a powerful class of algorithms inspired by biological brain structures. They consist of interconnected nodes that can learn complex patterns in data. While neural networks require substantial data and computational resources, modern AI platforms like TensorFlow and PyTorch have made them more accessible.

For introductory classification problems, the three core methods we've studied often perform comparably to neural networks while being much easier to understand and implement. Neural networks become particularly valuable for complex data types like images, text, or audio.

6.8.2 Ensemble Methods: Combining Multiple Models

Ensemble methods combine predictions from multiple algorithms to achieve better performance than any single method. Random Forests, for example, combine many decision trees, while boosting methods sequentially improve weak learners.

These techniques often appear in advanced courses and professional practice, but understanding the core algorithms first provides the foundation needed to appreciate how ensembles work.

6.8.3 When to Explore Advanced Methods

Consider exploring advanced methods when the three core algorithms don't meet your performance requirements, when you have very large datasets, when working with complex data types like images or text, or when maximum predictive accuracy is more important than interpretability.

However, always start with the fundamental methods covered in this chapter. They often provide excellent performance while being much easier to understand, implement, and explain to stakeholders.

6.9 Model Evaluation and Performance Metrics

Evaluating classification models requires more sophisticated metrics than simple accuracy, especially when dealing with imbalanced datasets or when different types of errors have different costs. Understanding these evaluation metrics is crucial for selecting the best model and making informed decisions about model performance.

6.9.1 Confusion Matrix

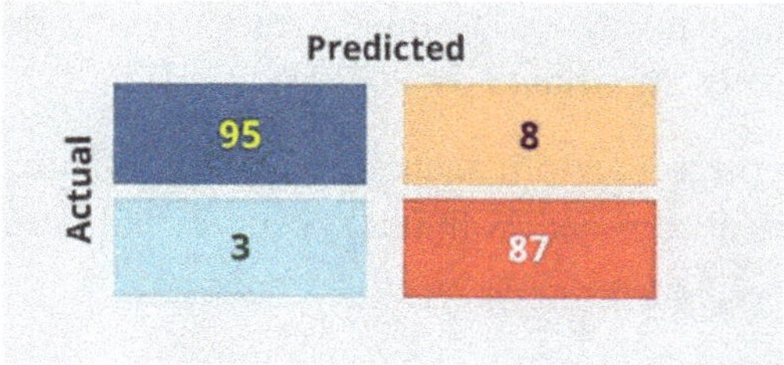

The confusion matrix provides a comprehensive view of classification performance by showing the counts of correct and incorrect predictions for each class. For binary classification, it's a 2x2 table that shows true positives, true negatives, false positives, and false negatives.

True positives (TP) are instances correctly predicted as positive, while true negatives (TN) are instances correctly predicted as negative. False positives (FP) are instances incorrectly predicted as positive (Type I error), and false negatives (FN) are instances incorrectly predicted as negative (Type II error).

The confusion matrix serves as the foundation for calculating other performance metrics and provides insights into which classes the model confuses most often. For multiclass problems, the matrix expands to show predictions for all class combinations.

Modern AI tools automatically generate confusion matrices with visual representations that make it easy to identify patterns in model errors. These visualizations often include percentages and color coding to highlight areas of concern.

6.9.2 Accuracy, Precision, and Recall

Accuracy measures the overall correctness of the model by calculating the proportion of correct predictions out of total predictions. While intuitive, accuracy can be misleading for imbalanced datasets where a model might achieve high accuracy by simply predicting the majority class.

Precision measures the proportion of positive predictions that are actually correct, calculated as TP/(TP+FP). High precision means the model makes few false positive errors, which is important when false positives are costly.

Recall (also called sensitivity) measures the proportion of actual positive instances that are correctly identified, calculated as TP/(TP+FN). High recall means the model captures most positive instances, which is important when false negatives are costly.

The trade-off between precision and recall is fundamental in classification. Improving one often comes at the expense of the other, and the optimal balance depends on the specific application and cost of different error types.

6.9.3 F1-Score and Other Composite Metrics

The F1-score provides a single metric that balances precision and recall by calculating their harmonic mean. It's particularly useful when you need a single metric to compare models or when precision and recall are equally important.

The F1-score ranges from 0 to 1, with 1 being perfect performance. It's more informative than accuracy for imbalanced datasets because it considers both false positives and false negatives.

Variations of the F1-score include F-beta scores, which allow you to weight precision or recall more heavily based on application requirements. For example, F2-score weights recall twice as much as precision, while F0.5-score weights precision twice as much as recall.

6.9.4 ROC Curves and AUC

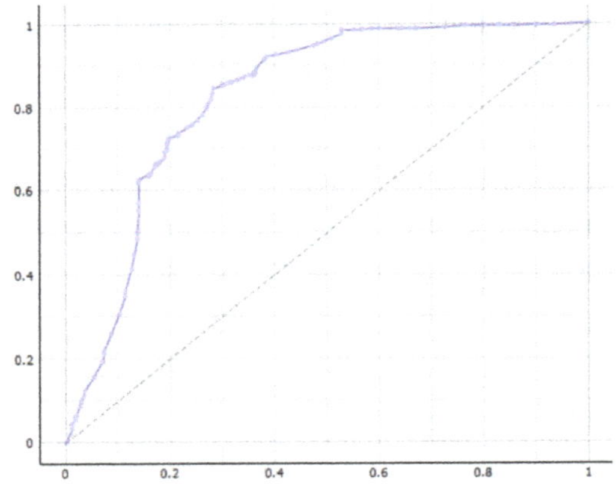

Receiver Operating Characteristic (ROC) curves provide a graphical representation of model performance across different classification thresholds. The curve plots the true positive rate (recall) against the false positive rate at various threshold settings.

The Area Under the Curve (AUC) summarizes the ROC curve with a single number ranging from 0 to 1. An AUC of 0.5 indicates random performance, while an AUC of 1.0 indicates perfect classification. AUC is particularly useful for comparing models because it's threshold-independent.

ROC curves are most informative for balanced datasets. For imbalanced datasets, precision-recall curves may provide more meaningful insights because they focus on the positive class performance.

Modern classification tools often provide interactive ROC curves that allow you to explore different threshold settings and their impact on precision and recall, helping you choose optimal operating points for your specific application.

6.9.5 Cross-Validation

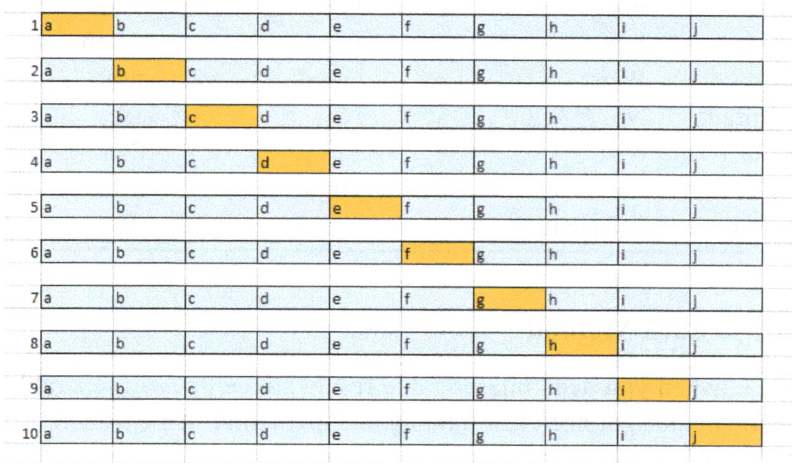

Cross-validation provides a more robust evaluation of model performance by testing the model on multiple subsets of the data. K-fold cross-validation divides the data into K equal parts, trains the model on K-1 parts, and tests on the remaining part. This process repeats K times, with each part serving as the test set once.

The final performance estimate is the average across all K folds, providing a more stable and reliable assessment than a single train-test split. Cross-validation also helps detect overfitting by showing how consistently the model performs across different data subsets.

Stratified cross-validation ensures that each fold maintains the same proportion of classes as the original dataset, which is particularly important for imbalanced datasets.

Leave-one-out cross-validation (LOOCV) is an extreme case where K equals the number of instances, providing the most thorough evaluation but at high computational cost.

6.10 Comparing Classification Methods

Each classification algorithm has strengths and weaknesses that make it more suitable for certain types of problems. Understanding these characteristics helps you choose the most appropriate method for your specific situation.

Table 6.1: Algorithm Comparison Summary

Aspect	Logistic Regression	Decision Trees	KNN
Interpretability	High	Very High	Medium
Training Speed	Fast	Fast	Instant
Prediction Speed	Fast	Fast	Slow
Memory Usage	Low	Low	High
Handling Nonlinearity	Poor	Good	Excellent
Feature Scaling Required	No	No	Yes
Handles Missing Values	No	Yes	No
Overfitting Tendency	Low	High	Medium
Large Dataset Performance	Excellent	Good	Poor

6.10.1 When to Use Each Method

Use logistic regression when you need interpretable results, have linearly separable data, want probabilistic outputs, or need fast training and prediction. It's excellent for baseline models and situations where understanding feature importance is crucial.

Choose decision trees when interpretability is paramount, you have mixed data types, missing values are present, or you need to identify important features automatically. They work well for rule-based decision making and when you need to explain predictions to non-technical stakeholders.

Select KNN when you have small to medium datasets, irregular decision boundaries, local patterns are important, or you want a simple algorithm that requires minimal assumptions about data distribution.

6.10.2 Practical Algorithm Selection Strategy

Start with logistic regression as your baseline model. It's fast, interpretable, and often performs surprisingly well. If the relationship between features and outcomes appears nonlinear, try decision trees next.

Use KNN when the first two methods don't capture the patterns in your data, particularly when you suspect that local similarity is important for classification.

Modern AI platforms like Orange and WEKA can automatically test all three methods and help you compare their performance using appropriate evaluation metrics.

6.11 Key Terms

Supervised Learning – Machine learning using labeled data to predict outcomes.

Target Variable (Dependent Variable/Label) – The outcome we aim to predict in classification tasks.

Binary Classification – Predicting between two classes (e.g., spam/not spam).

Multiclass Classification – Predicting among three or more classes.

Feature Selection – Choosing relevant variables that improve model performance.

Training/Testing Split – Dividing data to build and evaluate models.

Logistic Regression – A probabilistic classification algorithm for binary/multiclass outcomes.

Decision Trees – A rule-based, interpretable classification model with nodes and branches.

K-Nearest Neighbors (KNN) – A similarity-based, "lazy learning" classification algorithm.

Confusion Matrix – A table showing true/false positives and negatives.

Accuracy – Proportion of correctly predicted instances.

Precision – Proportion of predicted positives that are correct.

Recall (Sensitivity) – Proportion of actual positives correctly identified.

F1-Score – Harmonic mean of precision and recall.

ROC Curve & AUC – Graphical and numeric methods for evaluating model performance across thresholds.

Cross-Validation – Technique to assess model stability and prevent overfitting.

6.12 Review Questions

1. What distinguishes classification analysis from clustering and regression?
2. Explain why splitting data into training and testing sets is important.
3. Describe how logistic regression predicts class membership and the role of the sigmoid function.
4. What are the main advantages and limitations of decision trees?
5. How does KNN make predictions, and why is feature scaling important for it?
6. Define precision, recall, and F1-score, and explain when each is most useful.
7. How can ROC curves and AUC help in evaluating classification models?
8. When would you choose logistic regression over decision trees or KNN?

9. What strategies prevent overfitting in decision trees?
10. Give examples of real-world applications for logistic regression, decision trees, and KNN.

6.13 Lab 6: Classification Analysis

Classification analysis represents one of the most powerful and widely used techniques in business intelligence and data mining. Unlike clustering, which is an unsupervised method that identifies patterns without predefined labels, classification is a supervised learning approach that relies on labeled training data to predict categories or classes for new, unseen data.

In this comprehensive lab, you will gain hands-on experience with three fundamental classification algorithms that form the backbone of predictive analytics in business. Logistic Regression provides probability-based predictions and is valued for its clear interpretability, allowing analysts to understand how each feature contributes to the predicted outcome. Decision Trees generate rule-based models that closely mirror human decision-making, making them intuitive and easy to visualize. K-Nearest Neighbors (KNN) predicts outcomes by comparing new observations to historical cases, assigning class labels based on similarity, which makes it flexible and straightforward for a wide range of classification problems. Together, these algorithms offer complementary strengths for solving real-world business classification challenges.

6.13.1 Demonstration

6.13.1.1 Required Libraries and Initial Setup

```
# Essential libraries for classification analysis
import pandas as pd
import numpy as np
import matplotlib.pyplot as plt
import seaborn as sns
from sklearn.model_selection import train_test_split, cross_val_score
from sklearn.linear_model import LogisticRegression
from sklearn.tree import DecisionTreeClassifier, plot_tree
from sklearn.neighbors import KNeighborsClassifier
from sklearn.metrics import classification_report, confusion_matrix,
 ↪ accuracy_score
from sklearn.preprocessing import StandardScaler, LabelEncoder
import warnings
warnings.filterwarnings('ignore')

# Set display options for better output formatting
```

```
pd.set_option('display.max_columns', None)
pd.set_option('display.width', None)
plt.style.use('default')
```

6.13.1.2 Creating Our Business Dataset

We'll work with a comprehensive employee performance dataset that demonstrates real-world classification challenges:

```
# Create a realistic employee performance dataset
np.random.seed(42)  # For reproducible results

# Generate employee data with realistic business relationships
n_employees = 500

# Base employee characteristics
experience = np.random.exponential(5, n_employees)  # Years of
↪ experience
age = 25 + experience + np.random.normal(0, 2, n_employees)
education_level = np.random.choice([1, 2, 3, 4], n_employees, p=[0.1,
↪ 0.3, 0.4, 0.2])
training_hours = np.random.gamma(2, 10, n_employees)
project_count = np.random.poisson(3, n_employees) + 1

# Create performance score based on realistic business logic
performance_base = (
    0.3 * experience +
    0.2 * education_level +
    0.1 * training_hours/10 +
    0.2 * project_count +
    np.random.normal(0, 1, n_employees)
)

# Convert to performance categories (our target variable)
performance_category = pd.cut(performance_base,
                              bins=[-np.inf, -0.5, 0.5, np.inf],
                              labels=['Needs Improvement',
↪ 'Satisfactory', 'Excellent'])

# Create the complete dataset
employee_data = pd.DataFrame({
    'employee_id': range(1, n_employees + 1),
    'age': np.round(age, 1),
    'experience_years': np.round(experience, 1),
```

```
    'education_level': education_level,
    'training_hours': np.round(training_hours, 1),
    'project_count': project_count,
    'performance_score': np.round(performance_base, 2),
    'performance_category': performance_category
})

# Display dataset overview
print("Employee Performance Dataset Overview")
print("=" * 50)
print(f"Dataset shape: {employee_data.shape}")
print(f"Features: {list(employee_data.columns[:-1])}")
print(f"Target variable: performance_category")
print("\nFirst 10 rows:")
print(employee_data.head(10))
```

Output:

```
First 10 rows:
   employee_id   age  experience_years  education_level  training_hours
0            1  28.0               2.3                2            19.3
1            2  43.8              15.1                4            13.0
2            3  33.5               6.6                3            27.6
3            4  28.4               4.6                3            32.3
4            5  24.1               0.8                4             8.4
5            6  26.8               0.8                4             4.7
6            7  22.7               0.3                3             2.4
7            8  38.7              10.1                4            24.1
8            9  32.0               4.6                3            22.2
9           10  30.2               6.2                3            74.0

   project_count  performance_score performance_category
0              2               2.16            Excellent
1              8               4.97            Excellent
2              5               3.76            Excellent
3              4               2.94            Excellent
4              4               1.61            Excellent
5              1               0.26         Satisfactory
6              4               0.34         Satisfactory
7              4               5.32            Excellent
8              2               2.05            Excellent
9              1               3.70            Excellent
```

6.13.1.3 Exploratory Data Analysis

Before building any classification models, it's important to first explore and understand your dataset. Exploratory Data Analysis (EDA) helps you identify patterns, spot anomalies, and assess the distribution of both your features and target variable. In this example, we begin by generating a statistical summary of the employee dataset to understand key metrics like mean, standard deviation, and range for each numerical feature. We then examine the distribution of the target variable, performance_category, to see how balanced the classes are. Here, most employees are categorized as "Excellent" (93.2%), with very few in "Satisfactory" or "Needs Improvement," indicating a highly imbalanced dataset. Recognizing such imbalances is crucial, as it can influence model performance and the choice of appropriate evaluation metrics.

```
# Comprehensive data exploration
print("\nDataset Statistical Summary")
print("=" * 40)
print(employee_data.describe())

print("\nTarget Variable Distribution")
print("=" * 35)
performance_counts =
↪ employee_data['performance_category'].value_counts()
print(performance_counts)
print(f"\nPercentage distribution:")
print(performance_counts / len(employee_data) * 100)
```

Output:

```
Target Variable Distribution
===================================
performance_category
Excellent            466
Satisfactory          29
Needs Improvement      5
Name: count, dtype: int64

Percentage distribution:
performance_category
Excellent            93.2
Satisfactory          5.8
Needs Improvement     1.0
Name: count, dtype: float64
```

To understand class balance, we can visualize employee performance categories using both a clear, accessible bar chart and a pie chart to highlight the number and proportion of each category.

```
# Visualize
# Accessible, high-contrast color palette
accessible_colors = ['#0072B2', '#E69F00', '#009E73'] # blue, orange,
 ↪ green (colorblind-safe)

plt.figure(figsize=(10, 6))

# --- Bar Chart ---
plt.subplot(1, 2, 1)
performance_counts.plot(
kind='bar',
color=accessible_colors,
edgecolor='black' # improves contrast
)
plt.title('Employee Performance Distribution')
plt.xlabel('Performance Category')
plt.ylabel('Number of Employees')
plt.xticks(rotation=45)

# --- Pie Chart ---
plt.subplot(1, 2, 2)
plt.pie(
performance_counts.values,
labels=performance_counts.index,
autopct='%1.1f%%',
colors=accessible_colors,
wedgeprops={'edgecolor': 'black'} # adds separation for visibility
)
plt.title('Performance Category Percentages')

plt.tight_layout()
plt.show()
```

Output:

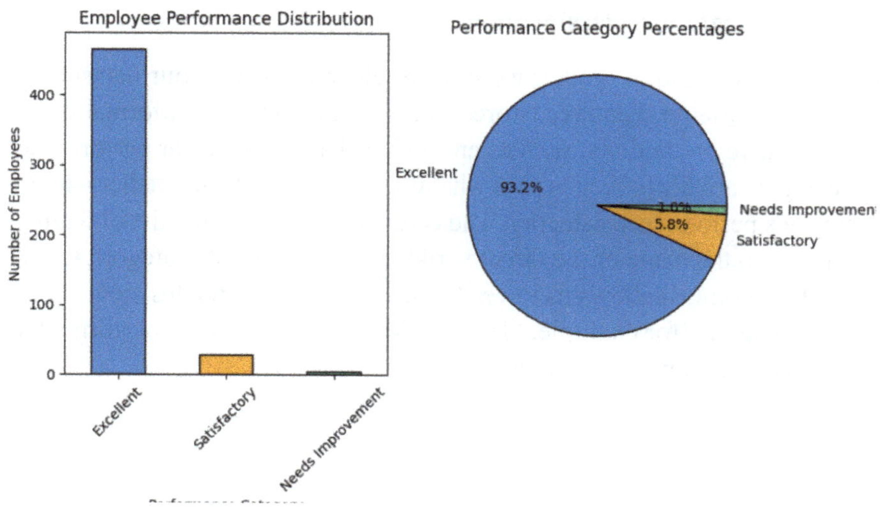

This visualization highlights the extreme imbalance in our dataset, with the vast majority of employees classified as "Excellent" and very few in "Satisfactory" or "Needs Improvement," illustrating the challenges this poses for training and evaluating classification models. However, this is a common and realistic scenario.

6.13.1.4 Understanding Supervised Learning

Supervised learning is a type of machine learning where the model is trained using labeled data, meaning that each example in the dataset already has a known, correct answer. The goal is for the model to learn the relationship between the input variables (features) and the output (label), so it can make accurate predictions on new, unseen data. For example, in email spam detection, the model is trained on emails that are already labeled as "spam" or "not spam," allowing it to learn patterns that distinguish between the two. Other common applications include medical diagnosis, where past patient data includes known outcomes, and credit approval, where historical records indicate whether applicants were approved or denied.

In contrast, unsupervised learning works with unlabeled data, meaning there are no predefined answers provided to guide the model. Instead of predicting a specific outcome, the goal is to explore the data and uncover hidden patterns, structures, or groupings. For instance, clustering techniques can be used to group customers based on similar purchasing behavior, helping businesses identify different market segments. Another example is market basket analysis, which examines purchasing patterns to discover which products are frequently bought together. While supervised learning focuses on prediction, unsupervised learning is primarily concerned with discovery and insight.

6.13.1.5 Preparing Data for Classification

Before building a classification model, we need to clearly separate our dataset into features and a target variable. Features (stored in X) are the pieces of information the model will use to make predictions, such as employee characteristics or performance indicators. The target variable (stored in y) is what we want the model to predict—in this case, the employee's performance category. The code then prints out the list of features being used, along with the name of the target variable and its possible categories. This is an important checkpoint. It allows us to verify that the correct variables are included and that the target classes (for example, "High," "Medium," or "Low" performance) are properly defined before moving forward.

```
# Prepare features (X) and target variable (y)
# Remove non-predictive columns
X = employee_data.drop(['employee_id', 'performance_score',
 ↪  'performance_category'], axis=1)
y = employee_data['performance_category']

print("Features for Classification:")
print("=" * 30)
for i, feature in enumerate(X.columns, 1):
    print(f"{i}. {feature}")

print(f"\nTarget Variable: {y.name}")
print(f"Classes: {list(y.unique())}")
```

Output:

```
Features for Classification:
==============================
1. age
2. experience_years
3. education_level
4. training_hours
5. project_count

Target Variable: performance_category
Classes: ['Excellent', 'Satisfactory', 'Needs Improvement']
```

Next, the dataset is split into training and testing sets using train_test_split. The training set (70% of the data) is used to teach the model, while the testing set (30%) is used to evaluate how well the model performs on new, unseen data. The random_state=42 ensures that the split is reproducible, meaning you will get the same results each time you run the code. The stratify=y argument is especially important because it preserves the proportion of each performance category in both the training and testing sets, preventing imbalances that could bias the evaluation.

After splitting the data, the code prints a summary showing how many employees are in the training and testing sets, as well as the number of features being used. This helps confirm that the split worked as expected and that the dataset is ready for modeling.

```
from sklearn.model_selection import train_test_split
# Split data into training and testing sets
X_train, X_test, y_train, y_test = train_test_split(
    X,
    y,
    test_size=0.3,
    random_state=42,
    stratify=y
)

print(f"\nData Split Summary:")
print(f"Training set: {X_train.shape[0]} employees")
print(f"Testing set: {X_test.shape[0]} employees")
print(f"Features: {X_train.shape[1]}")
```

Output:

```
Data Split Summary:
Training set: 350 employees
Testing set: 150 employees
Features: 5
```

Next, by comparing the percentage distribution of performance categories in both the training and testing sets, we can check whether they are similar. When the distributions closely match, it means the testing set is a good representation of the overall data. This leads to a more reliable evaluation of the model's performance. If the distributions were very different, the model's results could be misleading. This helps us detect overfitting (when a model memorizes training data but fails on new data).

```
# Demonstrate the importance of data splitting
print("Training Set Target Distribution:")
print(y_train.value_counts(normalize=True) * 100)

print("\nTesting Set Target Distribution:")
print(y_test.value_counts(normalize=True) * 100)
print("\n Both sets have similar distributions - good for reliable
↪  evaluation!")
```

Output:

```
Training Set Target Distribution:
performance_category
Excellent            93.142857
Satisfactory          5.714286
Needs Improvement     1.142857
Name: proportion, dtype: float64

Testing Set Target Distribution:
performance_category
Excellent            93.333333
Satisfactory          6.000000
Needs Improvement     0.666667
Name: proportion, dtype: float64

 Both sets have similar distributions - good for reliable evaluation!
```

6.13.1.6 Logistic Regression Analysis

Logistic regression is one of the most important methods for classification problems. The goal is not to predict a number but to predict which category an observation belongs to. What the model actually does is estimate the probability that an observation falls into a particular class, such as whether an employee will be classified as "Excellent" or not. At its core, logistic regression takes the input features (your variables) and combines them into a single score using learned weights. That score can be any real number, so the model then passes it through a sigmoid function, which squeezes the value into a range between 0 and 1. This allows the output to be interpreted as probability. Values close to 1 indicate high likelihood of belonging to a class, while values close to 0 indicate low likelihood.

Another important aspect of logistic regression is that its coefficients are interpretable. Each coefficient represents how much a feature contributes to increasing or decreasing the likelihood of a particular outcome. This makes the model especially useful when understanding the relationship between variables is just as important as making predictions. Logistic regression also works best when the classes can be reasonably separated using a linear boundary, meaning a straight-line (or flat surface in higher dimensions) can divide the groups.

6.13.1.6.1 Implementing Logistic Regression

In this section, the logistic regression model is created and trained using the training dataset. The model learns patterns by adjusting its internal coefficients so that the predicted probabilities match the actual class labels as closely as possible. The fit() function performs this learning process.

After training, the model is used to make predictions on new, unseen data stored in the test set. The predict() function returns the final predicted class for each observation, while predict_proba() provides the probability that each observation belongs to each possible class. This distinction is important because it allows us to see not just what the model predicts, but how confident it is in those predictions.

Finally, the model's performance is evaluated using accuracy scores on both the training and testing datasets. The training accuracy shows how well the model learned from the data it was given, while the testing accuracy indicates how well it generalizes to new data.

```
from sklearn.linear_model import LogisticRegression

log_reg = LogisticRegression(random_state=42, max_iter=1000)

# Create and train logistic regression model
print("LOGISTIC REGRESSION ANALYSIS")
print("=" * 50)

# Initialize the model
log_reg = LogisticRegression(random_state=42, max_iter=1000)

# Train the model
log_reg.fit(X_train, y_train)

# Make predictions
y_pred_log = log_reg.predict(X_test)
y_pred_proba_log = log_reg.predict_proba(X_test)

print("Model Training Complete!")
print(f"Training Accuracy: {log_reg.score(X_train, y_train):.3f}")
print(f"Testing Accuracy: {log_reg.score(X_test, y_test):.3f}")
```

Output:

```
Model Training Complete!
Training Accuracy: 0.931
Testing Accuracy: 0.933
```

6.13.1.6.2 Interpreting Logistic Regression Coefficients

In this section, the model's coefficients are examined to understand how each feature influences the predictions. When the model was trained, it assigned a weight to every feature, and these weights are stored in log_reg.coef_. By organizing these values into a table, we can clearly see how each variable contributes to predicting each class.

```
# Analyze feature importance through coefficients
feature_names = X.columns
classes = log_reg.classes_

print("\nLogistic Regression Coefficients Analysis")
print("=" * 45)

# Create coefficient interpretation table

coef_df = pd.DataFrame(
    log_reg.coef_.T,
    index=feature_names,
    columns=[f'Coef_{c}' for c in classes]
)

print("Coefficient Values (impact on log-odds):")
print(coef_df.round(3))
```

Output:

```
Coefficient Values (impact on log-odds):
                  Coef_Excellent  Coef_Needs    Coef_
                                  Improvement  Satisfactory
age                       -0.166    0.176           -0.010
experience_years           0.676   -0.402           -0.275
education_level            0.161   -0.255            0.094
training_hours             0.058   -0.092            0.034
project_count              0.218   -0.209           -0.009
```

Each coefficient represents the impact of a feature on the model's internal scoring system. A positive coefficient means that as the feature increases, the likelihood of the associated class also increases. A negative coefficient means that higher values of the feature reduce the likelihood of that class. Values close to zero indicate that the feature has little influence on the prediction.

The loop at the end translates these numerical coefficients into simple interpretations. Instead of requiring the reader to interpret raw numbers, it classifies each feature as increasing, decreasing, or having minimal impact on the probability of "Excellent" performance. This step bridges the gap between mathematical output and practical understanding.

```
# Interpret the most important features
print("\nFeature Impact Interpretation:")
print("-" * 35)
```

```
for feature in feature_names:
  excellent_coef = coef_df.loc[feature, 'Coef_Excellent']
  if excellent_coef > 0.1:
      print(f"• {feature}: INCREASES probability of Excellent
       ↪ performance")
  elif excellent_coef < -0.1:
      print(f"• {feature}: DECREASES probability of Excellent
       ↪ performance")
  else:
      print(f"• {feature}: Minimal impact on performance prediction")
```

Output:

```
Feature Impact Interpretation:
• age: DECREASES probability of Excellent performance
• experience_years: INCREASES probability of Excellent performance
• education_level: INCREASES probability of Excellent performance
• training_hours: Minimal impact on performance prediction
• project_count: INCREASES probability of Excellent performance
```

6.13.1.6.3 Probability Analysis

This section focuses on one of the most valuable aspects of logistic regression: probability outputs. Instead of only providing a final prediction, the model shows the probability associated with each possible class. The code creates a table displaying these probabilities for the first ten test cases, along with the predicted class, the actual class, and whether the prediction was correct.

By examining these probabilities, it becomes easier to understand how confident the model is in each decision. For example, a prediction with a probability of 0.95 indicates strong confidence, while a probability closer to 0.55 suggests uncertainty. This information is especially useful in real-world scenarios where decisions may depend on how confident the model is, not just what it predicts.

```
# Analyze prediction probabilities
print("\nProbability Analysis for First 10 Test Cases")
print("=" * 50)

prob_df = pd.DataFrame(
y_pred_proba_log[:10],
columns=[f'P({c})' for c in classes]
)
prob_df['Predicted'] = y_pred_log[:10]
prob_df['Actual'] = y_test.iloc[:10].values
prob_df['Correct'] = prob_df['Predicted'] == prob_df['Actual']
```

```
print(prob_df.round(3))
```

Output:

```
  P(Excellent)  P(Needs Improvement)  P(Satisfactory)  Predicted  \
0        0.933                 0.013            0.055  Excellent
1        1.000                 0.000            0.000  Excellent
2        0.985                 0.006            0.009  Excellent
3        0.982                 0.003            0.015  Excellent
4        0.910                 0.000            0.090  Excellent
5        0.946                 0.002            0.052  Excellent
6        0.998                 0.001            0.001  Excellent
7        1.000                 0.000            0.000  Excellent
8        1.000                 0.000            0.000  Excellent
9        0.813                 0.018            0.168  Excellent

        Actual  Correct
0    Excellent     True
1    Excellent     True
2    Excellent     True
3    Excellent     True
4    Excellent     True
5    Excellent     True
6    Excellent     True
7    Excellent     True
8    Excellent     True
9 Satisfactory    False
```

6.13.1.7 Decision Tree Classification

Decision trees are a classification method that make predictions by breaking data into smaller and smaller groups using a sequence of simple decisions. Instead of relying on a complex equation, the model works by asking a series of yes/no questions about the features. This structure closely resembles how humans make decisions, which is why decision trees are often considered one of the most intuitive machine learning methods.

The model begins with the entire dataset and looks for the best feature and split point to divide the data into more homogeneous groups. Each split is chosen to improve how well the data is separated into classes. This process continues step by step, creating branches until the model reaches final predictions. Because of this structure, decision trees can naturally handle both numerical and categorical data, and they do not require assumptions about how the data is distributed.

As the tree grows, it forms a hierarchy of decisions. The top of the tree, called the root node, represents the entire dataset. Each internal node represents a decision based on a feature, and each branch represents the outcome of that decision. The process ends at leaf nodes, which contain the final predicted class. The quality of each split is determined using measures such as Gini impurity or entropy, which evaluate how well the split separates the data into distinct classes.

6.13.1.7.1 Implementing Decision Trees

In this section, the decision tree model is created and trained using the training dataset. The model works by repeatedly selecting the best feature and split point to divide the data into smaller groups that are more similar in terms of the target outcome. The parameters such as max_depth, min_samples_split, and min_samples_leaf are used to control how large and complex the tree becomes. These settings help prevent overfitting, which occurs when the model becomes too tailored to the training data and performs poorly on new data.

Once the model is trained using the fit() function, it is applied to the test dataset to generate predictions. The predict() function assigns a class label to each observation based on the path it follows through the tree. The accuracy scores are then calculated for both the training and testing datasets to evaluate how well the model has learned patterns and how well it generalizes to new data.

The feature importance values provide insight into which variables were most influential in building the tree. These values are calculated based on how much each feature contributed to improving the quality of the splits. Features with higher importance values played a larger role in determining the final predictions, while features with low importance had little impact on the model's decisions.

```
print("DECISION TREE ANALYSIS")
print("=" * 40)

# Create and train decision tree
tree_model = DecisionTreeClassifier(
    random_state=42,
    max_depth=5,  # Prevent overfitting
    min_samples_split=20,  # Minimum samples to split a node
    min_samples_leaf=10    # Minimum samples in leaf nodes
)

# Train the model
tree_model.fit(X_train, y_train)

# Make predictions
```

```
y_pred_tree = tree_model.predict(X_test)

print("Decision Tree Training Complete!")
print(f"Training Accuracy: {tree_model.score(X_train, y_train):.3f}")
print(f"Testing Accuracy: {tree_model.score(X_test, y_test):.3f}")
```

Output:

```
Decision Tree Training Complete!

Training Accuracy: 0.931

Testing Accuracy: 0.933
```

```
# Analyze feature importance
feature_importance = pd.DataFrame({
    'Feature': X.columns,
    'Importance': tree_model.feature_importances_
}).sort_values('Importance', ascending=False)

print("\nFeature Importance in Decision Tree:")
print("=" * 40)
print(feature_importance.round(3))
```

Output:

```
Feature Importance in Decision Tree:
========================================
            Feature  Importance
1  experience_years       0.439
3    training_hours       0.319
4     project_count       0.128
0               age       0.114
2   education_level       0.000
```

6.13.1.7.2 Visualizing the Decision Tree

This section visualizes the structure of the trained decision tree, allowing us to see how the model makes its decisions. Each node in the diagram represents a question about a feature, and each branch shows the outcome of that question. By limiting the depth of the visualization, the most important top-level decisions can be examined without overwhelming detail. The colors and labels help indicate how the data is being split and which classes dominate each region of the tree.

```
# Create a simplified tree visualization
plt.figure(figsize=(15, 10))
plot_tree(tree_model,
          feature_names=X.columns,
          class_names=tree_model.classes_,
          filled=True,
          rounded=True,
          fontsize=10,
          max_depth=3)  # Show only top 3 levels for clarity
plt.title('Decision Tree Structure (Top 3 Levels)', fontsize=16)
plt.tight_layout()
plt.show()
```

The tree shows how the model classifies employee performance using only the top three levels of splits. It begins by dividing everyone based on years of experience, because that feature explains most of the variation in the data; employees with more than about two and a half years of experience are almost always predicted as Excellent, so that entire side of the tree becomes extremely pure with very little additional branching.

On the low-experience side, the model needs more information, so it looks at training hours, age, and project count to separate the few cases that differ from the dominant class. Even there, the structure shows that most outcomes remain Excellent, but the model is carving out the small pockets where performance varies.

6.13.1.8 K-Nearest Neighbors (KNN)

KNN is a "lazy learning" algorithm that makes predictions based on the similarity of new instances to stored training examples. K-nearest neighbors (KNN) is a classification method that makes predictions based on similarity rather than learning an explicit model. Instead of estimating coefficients or building a tree, KNN stores the training data and compares new observations to it. The idea is simple: observations that are similar to each other are likely to belong to the same class. Because similarity is measured using distance, the scale of the features becomes extremely important. This first step prints the minimum and maximum values of each feature to show that different variables may be on very different scales, which would distort distance calculations if left unadjusted.

6.13.1.8.1 Feature Scaling in KNN

To address the issue of differing feature scales, the data is standardized using a scaling process. This transformation centers each feature around zero and rescales it so that all variables have a similar range. As a result, no single feature dominates the distance calculation simply because of its magnitude. The scaling is applied to the training data and then consistently applied to the test data using the same transformation. The printed output shows the first few rows after scaling, illustrating how the values are now balanced and comparable across features.

```
print("K-NEAREST NEIGHBORS ANALYSIS")
print("=" * 40)

# Demonstrate why scaling is important
print("Feature Scales Before Scaling:")
print(X_train.describe().loc[['min', 'max']])
```

Output:

```
Feature Scales Before Scaling:

     age  experience  education  training  project
          years       level      hours     count
---- ---- ---------- ---------- --------- -------
min  21.0       0.0        1.0       0.5      1.0
max  47.9      23.1        4.0      77.9     10.0
```

```
# Scale the features for KNN
scaler = StandardScaler()
X_train_scaled = scaler.fit_transform(X_train)
X_test_scaled = scaler.transform(X_test)

print("\nFeature Scales After Scaling (first 5 samples):")
scaled_df = pd.DataFrame(X_train_scaled[:5], columns=X.columns)
print(scaled_df.round(3))
```

Output:

```
Feature Scales After Scaling (first 5 samples):

Standardized Features (First 5 Rows):

     age  experience  education  training  project
          years       level      hours     count
--- ------ ---------- ---------- --------- -------
0   -0.287    -0.168      0.332    -0.580   -0.615
1    0.762     0.132      0.332     1.956   -0.615
2   -0.366    -0.919      0.332     0.660   -0.615
3   -1.177    -0.983      0.332    -0.039   -0.019
4    0.327     0.411      0.332    -1.033   -1.211
```

6.13.1.8.2 Finding the Optimal K Value

In this section, the model is evaluated using different values of K, which represents the number of nearest neighbors used to make a prediction. For each value of K, the model looks at the K closest training observations to a test point and assigns the most common class among them. Smaller values of K make the model more sensitive to local patterns and noise, while larger values create smoother, more generalized predictions. By testing a range of values, the code measures how accuracy changes and collects the results for comparison.

```
# Test different K values to find the optimal one
k_values = range(1, 21)
k_scores = []

print("\nTesting Different K Values:")
print("=" * 30)

for k in k_values:
    knn = KNeighborsClassifier(n_neighbors=k)
    knn.fit(X_train_scaled, y_train)
    score = knn.score(X_test_scaled, y_test)
    k_scores.append(score)
    if k <= 10 or k % 5 == 0:  # Print selected values
        print(f"K={k:2d}: Accuracy = {score:.3f}")

# Find optimal K
optimal_k = k_values[np.argmax(k_scores)]
print(f"\nOptimal K value: {optimal_k}")
print(f"Best accuracy: {max(k_scores):.3f}")
```

Output:

```
Optimal K value: 2

Best accuracy: 0.933
```

After evaluating multiple values of K, the code selects the one that produces the highest accuracy on the test data. This value is considered optimal because it provides the best balance between overfitting and underfitting for this particular dataset. The corresponding accuracy is also displayed to show the model's best observed performance.

```
# Visualize K selection
plt.figure(figsize=(10, 6))
plt.plot(k_values, k_scores, 'bo-', linewidth=2, markersize=8)
```

```
plt.axvline(x=optimal_k, color='red', linestyle='--', alpha=0.7)
plt.xlabel('K Value (Number of Neighbors)')
plt.ylabel('Accuracy')
plt.title('KNN Performance vs. K Value')
plt.grid(True, alpha=0.3)
plt.show()
```

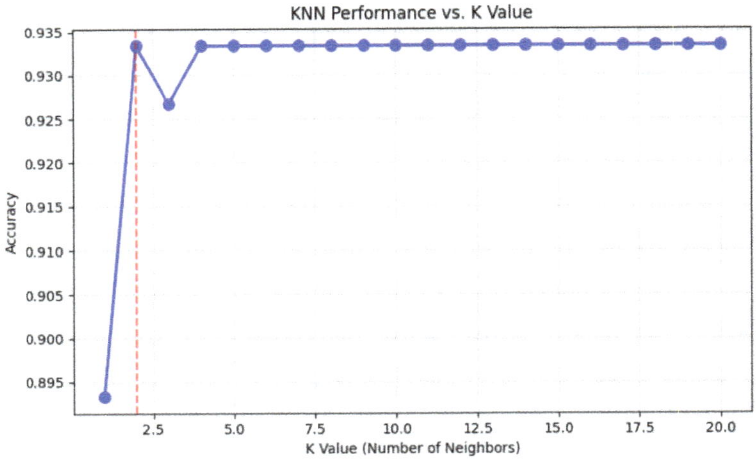

This visualization shows how model accuracy changes as the value of K increases. Each point represents a different model, and the line connects them to reveal the overall trend. The vertical line highlights the optimal K value, making it easy to see where performance peaks. This graph helps illustrate the trade-off involved in choosing K and reinforces why testing multiple values is necessary.

6.13.1.8.3 Implementing KNN with Optimal Parameters

Using the optimal value of K, the final KNN model is trained on the scaled training data. The model does not learn parameters in the traditional sense but instead stores the training observations and uses them for comparison during prediction. When predictions are made, each test point is assigned a class based on the majority class among its nearest neighbors. The training and testing accuracy values provide insight into how well this final model performs and whether it generalizes effectively to new data.

```
# Train KNN with optimal K
knn_model = KNeighborsClassifier(n_neighbors=optimal_k)
knn_model.fit(X_train_scaled, y_train)

# Make predictions
y_pred_knn = knn_model.predict(X_test_scaled)
```

```
print(f"\nKNN Model Performance (K={optimal_k}):")
print("=" * 35)
print(f"Training Accuracy: {knn_model.score(X_train_scaled,
    y_train):.3f}")
print(f"Testing Accuracy: {knn_model.score(X_test_scaled,
    y_test):.3f}")
```

Output:

```
KNN Model Performance (K=2):

===================================

Training Accuracy: 0.937

Testing Accuracy: 0.933
```

This final section demonstrates how KNN makes an individual prediction. For a single test observation, the model identifies the nearest neighbors from the training data and calculates their distances. These distances represent how similar the observations are based on the feature values. The indices are then used to retrieve the corresponding class labels of those neighbors. The model assigns the final prediction based on the most common class among these neighbors, effectively using a majority vote. This example makes the prediction process transparent by showing exactly which data points influenced the decision and how similarity drives the outcome.

```
# Demonstrate how KNN makes predictions
print(f"\nHow KNN Makes Predictions (Example):")
print("=" * 40)
test_example = X_test_scaled[0:1]
distances, indices = knn_model.kneighbors(test_example)

print(f"For test employee #1:")
print(f"Nearest {optimal_k} neighbors have distances:
    {distances[0][:5].round(3)}")
print(f"Their performance categories:
    {y_train.iloc[indices[0][:5]].values}")
print(f"Prediction: {y_pred_knn[0]}")
```

Output:

```
How KNN Makes Predictions (Example):
========================================
For test employee #1:
```

```
Nearest 2 neighbors have distances: [0.326 0.593]
Their performance categories: ['Excellent', 'Satisfactory']
Categories (3, str):
  ['Needs Improvement' < 'Satisfactory' < 'Excellent']
Prediction: Excellent
```

6.13.1.9 Model Evaluation and Comparison

This code performs a systematic evaluation and comparison of three different classification models: Logistic Regression, Decision Tree, and K-Nearest Neighbors (KNN). Its goal is to summarize their predictive performance using multiple metrics and visualizations so you can determine which model performs best on the test data. The process is broken into several steps, each with a clear purpose.

The first section calculates the accuracy of each model on the test set. Accuracy measures the proportion of correct predictions out of all predictions, providing a simple overall metric of performance. These values are stored alongside the predicted labels for each model in a dictionary. Then, the code creates a comparison table using a pandas DataFrame, which neatly lists each model and its corresponding accuracy. Printing this table allows for a quick, side-by-side comparison of the models' overall performance.

Next, the code generates detailed classification reports for each model using classification_report. This report goes beyond accuracy and includes metrics like precision, recall, and F1-score for each class. Precision measures how many of the predicted positives are actually correct, recall measures how many of the actual positives were correctly identified, and F1-score balances the two. This provides a more nuanced understanding of how each model performs, especially if the dataset is imbalanced.

```
print("COMPREHENSIVE MODEL COMPARISON")
print("=" * 50)

# Calculate accuracy for all models
models = {
    'Logistic Regression': (y_pred_log, log_reg.score(X_test, y_test)),
    'Decision Tree': (y_pred_tree, tree_model.score(X_test, y_test)),
    'K-Nearest Neighbors': (y_pred_knn, knn_model.score(X_test_scaled,
     ↪ y_test))
}

# Create comparison table
comparison_df = pd.DataFrame({
    'Model': list(models.keys()),
    'Accuracy': [score for _, score in models.values()]
})
```

```
print("Model Accuracy Comparison:")
print("=" * 30)
print(comparison_df.round(3))
```

Output:

```
Model Accuracy Comparison:

Model Accuracy

0 Logistic Regression 0.933

1 Decision Tree 0.933

2 K-Nearest Neighbors 0.933
```

```
# Detailed classification reports
for model_name, (predictions, _) in models.items():
    print(f"\n{model_name} - Detailed Performance:")
    print("-" * 45)
    print(classification_report(y_test, predictions))
```

Output:

```
Logistic Regression - Detailed Performance:
---------------------------------------------
                   precision    recall  f1-score   support

        Excellent       0.93      1.00      0.97       140
Needs Improvement       0.00      0.00      0.00         1
     Satisfactory       0.00      0.00      0.00         9

         accuracy                           0.93       150
        macro avg       0.31      0.33      0.32       150
     weighted avg       0.87      0.93      0.90       150


Decision Tree - Detailed Performance:
---------------------------------------------
                   precision    recall  f1-score   support

        Excellent       0.93      1.00      0.97       140
Needs Improvement       0.00      0.00      0.00         1
```

```
     Satisfactory       0.00      0.00      0.00         9

         accuracy                           0.93       150
        macro avg       0.31      0.33      0.32       150
     weighted avg       0.87      0.93      0.90       150


K-Nearest Neighbors - Detailed Performance:
--------------------------------------------
                   precision    recall  f1-score   support

        Excellent       0.93      1.00      0.97       140
Needs Improvement       0.00      0.00      0.00         1
     Satisfactory       0.00      0.00      0.00         9

         accuracy                           0.93       150
        macro avg       0.31      0.33      0.32       150
     weighted avg       0.87      0.93      0.90       150
```

6.13.1.9.1 Confusion Matrix Analysis

The final part focuses on confusion matrix analysis, which visualizes where each model is making correct versus incorrect predictions. A confusion matrix shows actual classes along one axis and predicted classes along the other. The diagonal values represent correct predictions, while off-diagonal values indicate misclassifications. The code plots all three confusion matrices side by side using heatmaps, making it easier to compare model performance visually.

Overall, this workflow helps not only to quantify how well each model performs but also to interpret the types of errors each model makes. By combining accuracy scores, classification reports, and confusion matrices, you get a comprehensive picture of model strengths and weaknesses, enabling informed decisions about which model to choose for deployment or further tuning.

```
# Create confusion matrices for all models
print("\nCONFUSION MATRICES (TABLE FORMAT)")
print("=" * 40)

for model_name, (predictions, _) in models.items():
    cm = confusion_matrix(y_test, predictions)

    print(f"\n{model_name}")
    print("-" * len(model_name))
    print(pd.DataFrame(
        cm,
```

```
        index=[f"Actual {cls}" for cls in log_reg.classes_],
        columns=[f"Pred {cls}" for cls in log_reg.classes_]
    ))
```

Output:

```
Logistic Regression
-------------------
                          Pred Excellent  Pred Needs Improvement  \
Actual Excellent                     140                       0
Actual Needs Improvement               1                       0
Actual Satisfactory                    9                       0

                          Pred Satisfactory
Actual Excellent                          0
Actual Needs Improvement                  0
Actual Satisfactory                       0

Decision Tree
-------------
                          Pred Excellent  Pred Needs Improvement  \
Actual Excellent                     140                       0
Actual Needs Improvement               1                       0
Actual Satisfactory                    9                       0

                          Pred Satisfactory
Actual Excellent                          0
Actual Needs Improvement                  0
Actual Satisfactory                       0

K-Nearest Neighbors
-------------------
                          Pred Excellent  Pred Needs Improvement  \
Actual Excellent                     140                       0
Actual Needs Improvement               1                       0
Actual Satisfactory                    9                       0

                          Pred Satisfactory
Actual Excellent                          0
Actual Needs Improvement                  0
Actual Satisfactory                       0
```

6.13.2 Practice

In this practice, you will work with a simulated employee dataset to practice key data analytics and machine learning skills. You will explore the dataset, prepare features and target variables, and build predictive models—including Logistic Regression, Decision Tree, and K-Nearest Neighbors (KNN)—to classify employee performance into categories (Needs Improvement, Satisfactory, Excellent).

Here is the code to create the dataset.

```
# Import libraries
import pandas as pd
import numpy as np

# Set seed for reproducibility
np.random.seed(42)

# Number of observations
n = 400

# Generate features
experience = np.random.exponential(5, n)
age = 25 + experience + np.random.normal(0, 2, n)
education_level = np.random.choice([1, 2, 3, 4], n, p=[0.1, 0.3, 0.4,
 ↪  0.2])
training_hours = np.random.gamma(2, 10, n)
project_count = np.random.poisson(3, n) + 1

# Create performance score
performance_score = (
    0.3 * experience +
    0.2 * education_level +
    0.1 * training_hours/10 +
    0.2 * project_count +
    np.random.normal(0, 1, n)
)

# Convert to categories
performance_category = pd.cut(
    performance_score,
    bins=[-np.inf, -0.5, 0.5, np.inf],
    labels=['Needs Improvement', 'Satisfactory', 'Excellent']
)
```

```
# Create DataFrame
df = pd.DataFrame({
    'age': np.round(age, 1),
    'experience_years': np.round(experience, 1),
    'education_level': education_level,
    'training_hours': np.round(training_hours, 1),
    'project_count': project_count,
    'performance_category': performance_category
})

# View data
print(df.head())
print(df.info())
```

6.13.2.1 Lab 6 Questions

1. What is the shape of the dataset (rows and columns)?

2. List all feature variables and identify the target variable.

3. What type of variable is performance_category (categorical or numerical)?

4. Display the distribution of the target variable. Is the dataset balanced or imbalanced? Explain.

5. Create feature matrix X and target vector y. Which columns did you include in each?

6. Split the dataset into training and testing sets (70/30 split). How many observations are in each set?

7. Train a Logistic Regression model. What is the training accuracy and testing accuracy?

8. Examine the model coefficients. Which feature appears to have the strongest positive impact on predicting "Excellent"?

9. Train a Decision Tree model. What is the testing accuracy?

10. Which feature has the highest importance in the Decision Tree model?

11. Why is feature scaling necessary before applying KNN?

12. Test multiple values of K (e.g., 1–10). Which K gives the best accuracy?

13. Compare the accuracy of all three models. Which model performs best?

14. Based on your results, which model would you recommend and why?

6.14 Conclusion

Classification analysis represents one of the most practical and immediately applicable techniques in data mining. The three core algorithms covered in this chapter - logistic regression, decision trees, and K-nearest neighbors - form the foundation that every data analyst should master before exploring more advanced methods.

The beauty of these fundamental algorithms lies in their interpretability and accessibility. Logistic regression provides clear probabilistic predictions with understandable coefficients. Decision trees offer transparent, rule-based classifications that anyone can follow. KNN captures local patterns through intuitive similarity concepts that mirror human reasoning.

Modern AI-enhanced tools like Orange and WEKA have transformed how we implement these algorithms, making sophisticated analysis accessible through visual interfaces and automated evaluation. However, the tools amplify rather than replace understanding. By grasping how these algorithms work conceptually, you can interpret results meaningfully and make informed decisions about which approach fits your specific problem.

The evaluation techniques we've explored - confusion matrices, precision, recall, F1-scores, and cross-validation - provide the foundation for assessing any classification model. These metrics help you move beyond simple accuracy to understand how well your model performs for each class and in different scenarios.

As you continue your data mining journey, you'll encounter more sophisticated techniques like neural networks and ensemble methods. However, the three core algorithms often perform surprisingly well and should always be your starting point. They provide baselines for comparison and insights into your data that inform decisions about whether more complex methods are necessary.

The hands-on experience with modern tools prepares you for real-world classification projects. Whether you're predicting customer churn, classifying products, or solving other business problems, you now have both the conceptual understanding and practical skills to tackle these challenges effectively.

Remember that successful classification starts with understanding your data and problem domain. The most sophisticated algorithm won't compensate for poor data quality or inappropriate problem formulation. By combining the solid foundation provided by these three core methods with modern AI-enhanced tools, you're well-equipped to extract valuable insights and make accurate predictions that drive business decisions.

The future of classification lies in the intelligent combination of human understanding and AI capabilities. You now have the foundation to participate in this future, whether as a business analyst leveraging automated tools or as a data scientist building custom solutions.

Chapter 7

Association Analysis

7.1 Learning Outcomes

7-1. Explain the purpose of association analysis and how it differs from clustering and classification.

7-2. Understand transactional data and how itemsets and frequent patterns form the basis of association rules.

7-3. Apply metrics such as support, confidence, and lift to evaluate the strength and significance of association rules.

7-4. Describe the Apriori algorithm and its steps for generating frequent itemsets and association rules.

7-5. Interpret association rules to make actionable business decisions and identify opportunities for cross-selling or promotions.

7.2 Introduction

Association analysis represents the second major category of unsupervised data mining techniques, complementing the clustering methods we explored in Chapter 5. While clustering groups similar data points together, association analysis discovers relationships between different items or events that frequently occur together. This technique has become increasingly powerful with modern AI-enhanced tools that can automatically identify meaningful patterns and provide business-friendly interpretations of complex relationships.

7.3 Introduction to Association Analysis

Association analysis, also known as market basket analysis or affinity analysis, seeks to identify relationships between items based on their co-occurrence patterns. The fundamental question it answers is: "What items tend to appear together?" This seemingly simple question has profound implications for business strategy, customer understanding, and decision-making across numerous industries.

7.3.1 Understanding Transactional Data

Association analysis works with transactional data, which differs significantly from the traditional row-and-column datasets we've used in previous chapters. In transactional data, each transaction represents a collection of items purchased, viewed, or otherwise associated together at a specific point in time.

Consider our grocery store example dataset shown in Table 7.1. Rather than having rows representing customers and columns representing different products, transactional data represents each shopping trip as a separate transaction containing the list of items purchased together.

Table 7.1: Transactional Dataset

TransactionID	Items
1	bread, milk, eggs
2	bread, butter, jam
3	milk, eggs, cheese
4	bread, milk, butter
5	bread, butter, jam, milk
6	diapers, beer
7	diapers, beer, chips
8	bread, milk, eggs, butter
9	milk, eggs
10	bread, butter

This format captures the essential information needed for association analysis: which items appear together in the same transaction. Transaction 1 contains {bread, milk, eggs}, Transaction 2 contains {bread, butter, jam}, and so forth.

Modern AI-enhanced tools can automatically convert various data formats into transactional format and suggest appropriate preprocessing steps. Platforms like Orange, WEKA, or specialized retail analytics tools can handle the data transformation seamlessly, allowing analysts to focus on interpreting results rather than data preparation.

7.3.2 Association Rules

Association rules express relationships between items in the form "If X, then Y" or more formally, X → Y. These rules suggest that when items in set X appear in a transaction, items in set Y are likely to appear as well. For instance, the rule {bread, butter} → {jam} suggests that customers who buy bread and butter are likely to also purchase jam.

It's crucial to understand that association rules identify correlation, not causation. The rule doesn't imply that buying bread and butter causes someone to buy jam, but rather that these items frequently appear together in transactions. This distinction is important for proper interpretation and business application of association analysis results.

Association rules consist of two parts: the antecedent (left-hand side or LHS) and the consequent (right-hand side or RHS). The antecedent represents the condition or items that are already present, while the consequent represents the items that are likely to occur given the antecedent.

7.3.3 Applications Beyond Retail

While market basket analysis in retail settings provides the most intuitive examples, association analysis has applications across many domains. In web analytics, it can identify pages that are frequently visited together, helping optimize website navigation and content placement. In healthcare, it can discover symptoms or treatments that commonly occur together, supporting diagnostic and treatment decisions.

Streaming services use association analysis to understand viewing patterns, identifying shows or movies that audiences tend to watch together. This information drives recommendation algorithms and content acquisition strategies. Social media platforms apply these techniques to understand user behavior patterns and optimize content delivery.

Modern AI platforms have expanded these applications by automatically identifying relevant transaction structures in various data types and suggesting appropriate association analysis approaches for different business contexts.

7.4 Itemsets and Frequent Patterns

Before diving into association rules, we must understand itemsets and how to identify frequent patterns within transactional data. This foundation is essential for generating meaningful association rules.

7.4.1 Understanding Itemsets

An itemset is simply a collection of items that appear together in transactions. Itemsets can contain one item (1-itemset), two items (2-itemset), three items (3-itemset), and so on. Looking at our dataset, examples include:

- 1-itemsets: {bread}, {milk}, {eggs}, {butter}, {jam}, {cheese}, {diapers}, {beer}, {chips}
- 2-itemsets: {bread, milk}, {bread, butter}, {milk, eggs}, {diapers, beer}
- 3-itemsets: {bread, milk, eggs}, {bread, butter, jam}, {diapers, beer, chips}

The size of an itemset, also called its length, determines its complexity and the strength of the relationship it represents. Larger itemsets represent more specific patterns but occur less frequently in the data. This creates a natural trade-off between pattern specificity and frequency.

7.4.2 Frequent Itemsets

A frequent itemset is one that appears in a sufficient number of transactions to be considered significant. The definition of "sufficient" depends on a threshold called minimum support. In our example, we use a minimum support of 0.2 (20%), meaning an itemset must appear in at least 2 out of 10 transactions to be considered frequent.

From this dataset, several frequent itemsets emerge. Single items such as **bread** and **milk** each appear in six of the ten transactions, giving them a frequency (support) of 60 percent, while **butter** appears in five transactions, or 50 percent frequency (support). Common item combinations are also evident. The pair of **bread and milk** occur together in four transactions, corresponding to 40 percent frequency (support), and **bread and butter** also appear in four transactions. These frequent itemsets highlight both popular individual products and commonly purchased item pairs, forming the foundation for subsequent association rule generation.

The process of finding frequent itemsets involves examining all possible combinations of items and counting how often each combination appears in the transaction database.

7.4.3 The Apriori Property

The Apriori property is a fundamental principle that makes association analysis computationally feasible. It states that if an itemset is frequent, then all of its subsets must also be frequent. Conversely, if an itemset is not frequent, then none of its supersets can be frequent.

This property allows algorithms to prune the search space efficiently. If {bread, milk} is not a frequent 2-itemset, then {bread, milk, eggs} cannot be a frequent 3-itemset. This pruning dramatically reduces the number of itemsets that need to be examined, making the analysis practical for large datasets.

7.5 Support, Confidence, and Lift

Three key metrics form the foundation of association analysis: support, confidence, and lift. These measures help evaluate the strength and significance of association rules, enabling analysts to identify the most meaningful patterns in their data.

7.5.1 Support: Measuring Frequency

Support measures how frequently an itemset appears in the transaction database. It's calculated as the number of transactions containing the itemset divided by the total number of transactions. Support is typically expressed as a decimal between 0 and 1.

For example, the itemset **{bread, milk}** appears in 4 of the 10 transactions. Support is calculated as the proportion of transactions containing the itemset:
support({bread, milk}) = 4 / 10 = 0.40 (40%).

Support serves two important purposes in association analysis. First, it helps identify frequent itemsets by filtering out combinations that occur too rarely to be meaningful. Second, it provides a measure of the general popularity or prevalence of item combinations.

7.5.2 Confidence: Measuring Reliability

Confidence measures the reliability of an association rule by calculating the conditional probability that the consequent occurs given the antecedent. For a rule $X \rightarrow Y$, confidence is calculated as the support of {X, Y} divided by the support of {X}.

Using our dataset, we evaluate the rule **{bread}** → **{milk}** as follows. The itemset {bread, milk} appears in 40 percent of transactions, giving a support value of 0.4. Bread alone appears in 60 percent of transactions, giving a support value of 0.6. Confidence measures how often milk appears given that bread appears and is calculated as 0.4 divided by 0.6. This results in a confidence of 0.667, or 66.7 percent.

This means that 66.7% of customers who buy bread also buy milk. Confidence provides insight into the strength of the relationship between items. Higher confidence values indicate stronger associations, suggesting that the rule is more reliable for prediction or recommendation purposes.

7.5.3 Lift: Measuring Interest

Lift measures how much more likely the consequent is to occur when the antecedent is present, compared to its overall frequency. Lift is calculated as confidence divided by the support of the consequent.

Consider the rule **{bread}** → **{milk}**. Lift measures how much more likely milk is purchased when bread is purchased compared to the overall likelihood of buying milk. In our dataset, the lift for this rule is 1.111. This means that when a customer buys bread, they are about 11% more likely to also buy milk than the average customer in the dataset.

Lift values indicate the strength and direction of the relationship between items:

- A lift greater than 1 shows a positive association, meaning the items are purchased together more often than expected by chance.
- A lift equal to 1 indicates independence, so buying one item does not affect the likelihood of buying the other.
- A lift less than 1 indicates a negative association, meaning the items are purchased together less often than expected.

In this case, the lift of 1.111 tells us that bread and milk are slightly positively associated. This insight can guide decisions such as product placement, promotions, or cross-selling, highlighting items that customers are more likely to purchase together.

7.6 The Apriori Algorithm

The Apriori algorithm is the most widely used method for association rule mining. It efficiently discovers frequent itemsets and generates association rules by leveraging the Apriori property to prune the search space.

7.6.1 Algorithm Steps

The Apriori algorithm is a systematic method for discovering meaningful associations within transactional data, and it operates in two main phases. The first phase focuses on **finding frequent itemsets**. It begins by examining all individual items (1-itemsets) and counting how often each appears across transactions. Only those itemsets that meet a minimum support threshold are retained as frequent. The algorithm then combines these frequent itemsets to form candidate sets of the next size (k+1)-itemsets and counts their frequency in the dataset. This iterative process continues, generating larger candidate itemsets and filtering them by support, until no additional frequent itemsets can be found. By building up from smaller to larger itemsets, the algorithm efficiently identifies combinations of items that occur together frequently.

The second phase involves **generating association rules** from the frequent itemsets identified in the first phase. For each frequent itemset, the algorithm considers all possible ways to split it into an antecedent (the "if" part) and a consequent (the "then" part). It then evaluates each potential rule against a minimum confidence threshold, keeping only those that are reliable. Additional measures, such as lift, can be calculated to understand the strength and significance of relationships. Together, these phases allow the Apriori algorithm to systematically uncover patterns in transactional data, helping businesses identify which items are commonly purchased together and make data-driven decisions.

7.6.2 Applying Apriori to Our Dataset

Using our grocery store dataset with minimum support = 0.2 and minimum confidence = 0.6, the Apriori algorithm generates the following association rules (sorted by lift):

Table 7.2: Association Rules Generated by Apriori Algorithm

LHS	RHS	Support	Confidence	Lift	Count
{butter}	{bread}	0.40	0.80	1.33	4
{jam}	{bread}	0.20	1.00	1.67	2
{jam}	{butter}	0.20	1.00	2.00	2
{bread,butter}	{jam}	0.20	0.50	2.50	2
{bread}	{milk}	0.40	0.67	1.11	4
{milk}	{bread}	0.40	0.67	1.11	4

These association rules reveal several interesting patterns in the dataset. The strongest relationship is observed in the rule where customers who buy both bread and butter also purchase jam, with a lift value of 2.5, indicating a strong positive association. Notably, every customer who buys jam also purchases bread, resulting in a confidence of 1.0. Similarly, every customer who buys jam also buys butter, with the same confidence of 1.0. In contrast, bread and milk show a more moderate positive association, with a lift of 1.111, suggesting that customers who buy bread are slightly more likely to purchase milk compared to the general probability of buying milk.

7.6.3 Interpreting the Results

The results show clear purchasing patterns in our dataset. The high lift values for jam-related rules suggest that jam is typically purchased as part of a breakfast combination with bread and butter. The moderate association between bread and milk indicates these are commonly purchased together, though not as strongly as the jam combinations.

These insights can guide several important business decisions. For product placement, stores might position jam near bread and butter to encourage combined purchases. Promotional strategies could include breakfast combo deals featuring bread, butter, and jam. In terms of inventory management, ensuring adequate stock of these complementary items can prevent stockouts and lost sales. Additionally, cross-selling opportunities arise by recommending jam to customers who are purchasing bread and butter.

7.7 Key Terms

Association Analysis – Identifying relationships between items that frequently occur together.

Market Basket Analysis / Affinity Analysis – Common names for association analysis in retail.

Transactional Data – Data organized by individual transactions containing sets of items.

Itemset – A set of items appearing together in a transaction.

Frequent Itemset – An itemset that appears in transactions above a minimum support threshold.

Support – Proportion of transactions containing a specific itemset.

Confidence – Probability that the consequent occurs given the antecedent in a rule.

Lift – Measures how much more likely the consequent is to occur with the antecedent compared to its baseline probability.

Apriori Property – If an itemset is frequent, all its subsets are also frequent; used to prune the search space.

Apriori Algorithm – Method for finding frequent itemsets and generating association rules.

Antecedent (LHS) – The "if" part of an association rule.

Consequent (RHS) – The "then" part of an association rule.

7.8 Review Questions

1. What is the main difference between association analysis and clustering?
2. Explain what transactional data is and how it differs from typical row-and-column datasets.
3. Define itemset, frequent itemset, and explain why minimum support is important.
4. How do support, confidence, and lift help evaluate the strength of an association rule?
5. What is the Apriori property and how does it make association analysis computationally feasible?
6. Describe the main steps of the Apriori algorithm for generating association rules.
7. Give an example of a practical business application of association analysis.

8. How can lift values guide decisions for product placement or promotions?
9. Why does association analysis identify correlation rather than causation?
10. Explain why larger itemsets are less frequent and what trade-offs this creates in analysis.

7.9 Lab 7: Association Analysis

Have you ever noticed how peanut butter and jelly, or chips and salsa, often appear together in shopping carts? That's exactly what association analysis uncovers — patterns of items that frequently occur together in transactional data. This technique helps answer the question: "If a customer buys X, what else are they likely to buy?"

Association analysis is important in many business contexts. Retailers and e-commerce sites can use it to place complementary products near each other and increase sales. Recommendation systems use it to suggest products customers are likely to want next. Marketing teams can create bundles or targeted promotions based on buying patterns. Inventory managers can stock related items together to avoid missing sales opportunities.

The core idea is simple: association rules are "If-Then" statements, such as "If a customer buys bread, then they are likely to buy butter." In this lab, you will explore a dataset of transactions, generate association rules, and discover which item combinations are the most profitable or surprising. By the end, you'll know how to spot patterns that can directly inform business decisions.

7.9.1 Demonstration

We'll start by importing the essential Python libraries for our analysis:

```
# Essential libraries for association analysis
import pandas as pd
import numpy as np
import matplotlib.pyplot as plt
import seaborn as sns
from itertools import combinations
from collections import defaultdict, Counter
import warnings
warnings.filterwarnings('ignore')

# For advanced association rule mining
try:
    from mlxtend.frequent_patterns import apriori, association_rules
    from mlxtend.preprocessing import TransactionEncoder
    print("✓ MLxtend library available for advanced analysis")
except ImportError:
```

```
    print("⚠ MLxtend not available - we'll implement algorithms from
     ↪ scratch")

# Set display options
pd.set_option('display.max_columns', None)
plt.style.use('default')

print("Association Analysis Lab - Setup Complete!")
```

7.9.1.1 Creating Our Transactional Dataset

Before beginning any formal analysis, it is important to understand the type of data we are working with. In this case, we are using a transactional dataset, which is commonly used in association analysis. A transactional dataset records individual events—in this context, customer purchases—where each transaction contains a group of items that were bought together. Unlike traditional datasets that organize information into fixed columns, transactional data is flexible and focuses on sets of items within each observation.

```
# Create realistic grocery store transaction data
transactions = [
    ['bread', 'milk', 'eggs'],                          # Transaction 1
    ['bread', 'butter', 'jam'],                         # Transaction 2
    ['milk', 'eggs', 'cheese'],                         # Transaction 3
    ['bread', 'milk', 'butter'],                        # Transaction 4
    ['bread', 'butter', 'jam', 'milk'],                 # Transaction 5
    ['diapers', 'beer'],                                # Transaction 6
    ['diapers', 'beer', 'chips'],                       # Transaction 7
    ['bread', 'milk', 'eggs', 'butter'],                # Transaction 8
    ['milk', 'eggs'],                                   # Transaction 9
    ['bread', 'butter']                                 # Transaction 10
]

print(f"Dataset Summary:")
print(f"Total transactions: {len(transactions)}")

# Display transactions
for i, transaction in enumerate(transactions, 1):
    print(f"Transaction {i:2d}: {transaction}")
```

Output:

```
Dataset Summary:
Total transactions: 10
```

```
Transaction  1: ['bread', 'milk', 'eggs']
Transaction  2: ['bread', 'butter', 'jam']
Transaction  3: ['milk', 'eggs', 'cheese']
Transaction  4: ['bread', 'milk', 'butter']
Transaction  5: ['bread', 'butter', 'jam', 'milk']
Transaction  6: ['diapers', 'beer']
Transaction  7: ['diapers', 'beer', 'chips']
Transaction  8: ['bread', 'milk', 'eggs', 'butter']
Transaction  9: ['milk', 'eggs']
Transaction 10: ['bread', 'butter']
```

In the dataset above, each transaction represents a single shopping trip made by a customer at a grocery store. The items listed within each transaction correspond to the products purchased during that visit. For example, one customer may buy bread, milk, and eggs, while another may purchase bread, butter, and jam. Some transactions are small and contain only two items, while others include several products. This variation reflects realistic shopping behavior, where different customers have different needs and purchasing habits.

The structure of this dataset is intentionally simple: it is a list of transactions, where each transaction is itself a list of items. This format allows us to easily examine which items appear together within the same transaction. At this stage, we are not applying any algorithms or calculations. Instead, the goal is to become familiar with the data and begin thinking about relationships between items. By observing the transactions, we can start to ask questions such as whether certain items tend to appear together more frequently than others.

Even without formal analysis, some patterns may begin to stand out. For instance, items like bread and milk appear together in multiple transactions, and milk and eggs also occur together several times. There are also repeated pairings such as diapers and beer, which appear in more than one transaction. These observations suggest that certain items may be related in terms of customer purchasing behavior. However, at this point, these are only informal observations and have not yet been measured or confirmed.

This dataset serves as the foundation for association analysis by providing the raw information needed to explore relationships between items. The key idea is that value lies not just in individual items, but in combinations of items that occur within the same transaction. By organizing the data in this way, we prepare it for deeper analysis, where we can systematically identify and evaluate patterns of co-occurrence.

7.9.1.2 Data Structure Analysis

This step looks at the structure of the transactional data in a way that directly supports association analysis. First, we identify all unique items across transactions. This defines the full set of products that could potentially form item combinations. Association analysis works by examining combinations of these items, so knowing the total item set tells us the scope of possible relationships.

Next, we look at transaction length, which is the number of items in each transaction. The average of about 2.9 items per transaction tells us that most baskets are small. This matters because it limits the size of meaningful item combinations. In this dataset, most associations will involve pairs or possibly triples of items, rather than large groups.

```
# Get all unique items
all_items = set()

for transaction in transactions:
    all_items.update(transaction)

print(f"Total unique items: {len(all_items)}")
print(f"Items: {sorted(list(all_items))}")

# Transaction length distribution
transaction_lengths = [len(t) for t in transactions]

print(f"Average items per transaction:
↪  {np.mean(transaction_lengths):.2f}")
```

Output:

```
Average items per transaction: 2.90
```

Finally, we count how often each item appears across transactions. This is directly related to support, which is a key concept in association analysis. Items like bread and milk appear in 60% of transactions, making them strong candidates for forming associations with other items. In contrast, items with low frequency, like jam, will have fewer opportunities to form strong relationships because they appear in fewer transactions.

```
# Item frequency analysis
item_counts = Counter()

for transaction in transactions:
    item_counts.update(transaction)

print("Top 5 Most Frequent Items:")

for item, count in item_counts.most_common(5):
    percentage = (count / len(transactions)) * 100
    print(f"{item:12s}: {count:3d} transactions ({percentage:5.1f}%)")
```

Output:

```
Top 5 Most Frequent Items:

bread : 6 transactions ( 60.0%)

milk : 6 transactions ( 60.0%)

butter : 5 transactions ( 50.0%)

eggs : 4 transactions ( 40.0%)

jam : 2 transactions ( 20.0%)
```

Overall, this step establishes which items exist, how transactions are structured, and which items occur often enough to matter. These factors directly influence which item combinations are likely to produce meaningful associations in later analysis.

7.9.1.3 Support, Confidence, and Lift

Association analysis relies on three core metrics—support, confidence, and lift—to measure relationships between items. These metrics move us from simple observation to quantifiable evidence. Support tells us how often a combination of items appears in the dataset. Confidence tells us how reliable a rule is, meaning how often the consequent appears when the antecedent is present. Lift goes one step further by comparing the observed relationship to what we would expect if the items were independent. Together, these metrics allow us to evaluate whether a pattern is frequent, reliable, and meaningful.

7.9.1.3.1 Essential Metrics Computed

```
def calculate_support(itemset, transactions):
    """Calculate support for a given itemset"""

    count = 0

    for transaction in transactions:
        if set(itemset).issubset(set(transaction)):
            count += 1

    return count / len(transactions)
```

The support function checks how many transactions contain a given itemset and divides that count by the total number of transactions. This gives a proportion between 0 and 1. In association analysis, support is important because it filters out rare combinations that are not useful for decision-making. If an itemset appears only once, it is usually not considered meaningful.

```
def calculate_rule_metrics(antecedent, consequent, transactions):
    """Calculate support, confidence, and lift for an association
    ↪  rule"""

    # Support calculations
    antecedent_support = calculate_support(antecedent, transactions)
    consequent_support = calculate_support(consequent, transactions)
    rule_support = calculate_support(list(antecedent) +
↪   list(consequent), transactions)

    # Confidence calculation
    confidence = rule_support / antecedent_support if
↪   antecedent_support > 0 else 0

    # Lift calculation
    lift = confidence / consequent_support if consequent_support > 0
↪   else 0

    return {
        'antecedent_support': antecedent_support,
        'consequent_support': consequent_support,
        'rule_support': rule_support,
        'confidence': confidence,
        'lift': lift
    }
```

This function brings the three metrics together for a rule of the form X → Y. It first calculates how often the antecedent and consequent appear individually, and then how often they appear together. Confidence is computed by dividing the joint support by the support of the antecedent, which tells us how often Y occurs when X occurs. Lift adjusts this value by comparing it to how often Y appears overall, helping us determine whether the relationship is stronger than random chance.

```
# Example: bread → milk

metrics = calculate_rule_metrics(['bread'], ['milk'], transactions)
print("Rule: bread → milk")
print(f"Support: {metrics['rule_support']:.3f}")
print(f"Confidence: {metrics['confidence']:.3f}")
print(f"Lift: {metrics['lift']:.3f}")
print(f"Interpretation: {metrics['confidence']:.1%} of bread buyers
 ↪  also buy milk")
```

In this example, we evaluate the rule "bread → milk," which asks whether customers who buy bread also tend to buy milk. The code calculates all three metrics for this specific relationship.

Output:

```
Rule: bread → milk

Support: 0.400

Confidence: 0.667

Lift: 1.111

Interpretation: 66.7% of bread buyers also buy milk
```

The support of 0.400 means that 40% of all transactions contain both bread and milk. This tells us the combination is relatively common in the dataset. The confidence of 0.667 means that among customers who bought bread, about two-thirds also bought milk, indicating a fairly strong rule. The lift of 1.111 shows that this relationship is slightly stronger than what we would expect if bread and milk were purchased independently. A lift greater than 1 suggests a positive association, meaning the presence of bread increases the likelihood of milk being purchased.

This example shows how support, confidence, and lift work together. Support ensures the pattern is frequent enough to matter, confidence measures the reliability of the rule, and lift helps determine whether the relationship is genuinely meaningful or just a result of overall item popularity.

7.9.1.4 Apriori Algorithm Implementation

The Apriori class is a complete implementation of the Apriori algorithm, which is a widely used method for discovering associations between items in a transactional dataset. At a high level, the algorithm has two main goals: first, to find combinations of items that appear frequently together across transactions, and second, to generate association rules that describe relationships between these items. For beginners, the key idea is that it turns raw transaction data into actionable insights, like identifying which products tend to be purchased together.

The algorithm works in two phases. In the first phase, it identifies frequent itemsets, which are groups of items that occur together in the dataset often enough to meet a minimum support threshold. It starts by examining individual items, then progressively considers larger combinations, pruning candidate sets that contain infrequent subsets. This pruning step is critical because it dramatically reduces the number of item combinations to evaluate, making the algorithm efficient even as the dataset grows. By the end of this phase, the algorithm has a collection of all itemsets that are frequent enough to be meaningful.

In the second phase, the algorithm generates association rules from these frequent itemsets. Each rule describes a potential relationship, such as “customers who buy bread and butter also buy milk.” For every possible split of a frequent itemset into an antecedent (if part) and a consequent (then part), the algorithm calculates support, confidence, and lift. Confidence measures the reliability of the rule, while lift indicates whether the relationship is stronger than what would be expected by chance. Finally, rules that meet the minimum confidence threshold are retained and sorted by lift, producing a ranked list of actionable associations. This process allows businesses or analysts to understand not just which items are popular, but which items are meaningfully linked in customer purchasing behavior.

```
class AprioriAlgorithm:
    def __init__(self, min_support=0.2, min_confidence=0.6):
        self.min_support = min_support
        self.min_confidence = min_confidence
        self.transactions = []
        self.frequent_itemsets = {}
        self.association_rules = []

    def fit(self, transactions):
        """Run the complete Apriori algorithm"""
        self.transactions = transactions
        print(f"Running Apriori Algorithm:")
        print(f"  Minimum Support: {self.min_support}")
        print(f"  Minimum Confidence: {self.min_confidence}")
        print(f"  Total Transactions: {len(transactions)}")

        # Phase 1: Find frequent itemsets
        self._find_frequent_itemsets()

        # Phase 2: Generate association rules
        self._generate_association_rules()

        return self

    def _find_frequent_itemsets(self):
        """Phase 1: Find all frequent itemsets using Apriori
         ↪ property"""
        print("\nPHASE 1: Finding Frequent Itemsets")
        print("=" * 35)

        # Get all unique items
        all_items = sorted(set(item for transaction
```

```
            in self.transactions
            for item in transaction))

        # Start with 1-itemsets
        current_itemsets = [(item,) for item in all_items]
        k = 1

        while current_itemsets:
            print(f"\nProcessing {k}-itemsets:")
            print(f"  Candidates to evaluate: {len(current_itemsets)}")

            # Calculate support for current candidates
            frequent_k = []
            for itemset in current_itemsets:
                support = self._calculate_support(itemset)
                if support >= self.min_support:
                    frequent_k.append(itemset)
                    print(f"    {str(itemset):25s}: support =
                     ↪  {support:.3f} ✓")

            if frequent_k:
                self.frequent_itemsets[k] = frequent_k
                print(f"  Found {len(frequent_k)} frequent
                 ↪  {k}-itemsets")

                # Generate candidates for next iteration
                current_itemsets =
                  self._generate_candidates(frequent_k)
                k += 1
            else:
                print(f"  No frequent {k}-itemsets found - stopping")
                break

        # Summary
        total_frequent = sum(len(itemsets) for itemsets in
↪   self.frequent_itemsets.values())
        print(f"\nFrequent Itemsets Summary:")
        for k, itemsets in self.frequent_itemsets.items():
            print(f"  {k}-itemsets: {len(itemsets)}")
        print(f"  Total: {total_frequent}")

    def _generate_candidates(self, frequent_k):
        """Generate candidate (k+1)-itemsets from frequent
         ↪  k-itemsets"""
```

```
        candidates = []
        n = len(frequent_k)

        for i in range(n):
            for j in range(i + 1, n):
                # Join two k-itemsets if they differ by only one item
                itemset1 = frequent_k[i]
                itemset2 = frequent_k[j]

                # For k-itemsets, check if first k-1 items are the same
                if itemset1[:-1] == itemset2[:-1]:
                    candidate =
                        tuple(sorted(set(itemset1) | set(itemset2)))

                    # Prune: check if all k-subsets are frequent
                    if not self._has_infrequent_subset(candidate):
                        candidates.append(candidate)

        return candidates

    def _has_infrequent_subset(self, candidate):
        """Check if candidate has any infrequent subset (Apriori
         ↪ pruning)"""
        k = len(candidate) - 1
        if k not in self.frequent_itemsets:
            return True

        # Check all k-subsets
        for i in range(len(candidate)):
            subset
              = tuple(item for j, item in enumerate(candidate) if j !=
               ↪ i)
            if subset not in self.frequent_itemsets[k]:
                return True

        return False

    def _calculate_support(self, itemset):
        """Calculate support for an itemset"""
        count = 0
        for transaction in self.transactions:
            if set(itemset).issubset(set(transaction)):
                count += 1
```

```
        return count / len(self.transactions)

    def _generate_association_rules(self):
        """Phase 2: Generate association rules from frequent
         ↪  itemsets"""
        print(f"\nPHASE 2: Generating Association Rules")
        print("=" * 40)

        rules = []

        # Generate rules from itemsets of size 2 and above
        for k in range(2, max(self.frequent_itemsets.keys()) + 1):
            for itemset in self.frequent_itemsets[k]:
                # Generate all possible rules from this itemset

↪   rules.extend(self._generate_rules_from_itemset(itemset))

        # Filter by confidence and sort by lift
        self.association_rules = [rule for rule in rules
                                  if rule['confidence'] >=
                                   ↪  self.min_confidence]
        self.association_rules.sort(key=lambda x: x['lift'],
         ↪  reverse=True)

        print(f"Generated {len(self.association_rules)} rules with
         ↪  confidence >= {self.min_confidence}")

        return self.association_rules

    def _generate_rules_from_itemset(self, itemset):
        """Generate all possible association rules from a frequent
         ↪  itemset"""
        rules = []

        # Generate all possible antecedent-consequent splits
        for i in range(1, len(itemset)):
            for antecedent in combinations(itemset, i):
                consequent
                = tuple(item for item in itemset if item not in
                 ↪  antecedent)

                # Calculate metrics
                antecedent_support =
```

```
            self._calculate_support(antecedent)
          consequent_support =
          `self._calculate_support(consequent)
          rule_support = self._calculate_support(itemset)

          confidence
          `= rule_support / antecedent_support if
↪ antecedent_support > 0 else 0
          lift = confidence / consequent_support if
↪ consequent_support > 0 else 0

          rules.append({
              'antecedent': list(antecedent),
              'consequent': list(consequent),
              'support': rule_support,
              'confidence': confidence,
              'lift': lift,
              'count': int(rule_support * len(self.transactions))
          })

        return rules

    def get_rules_summary(self):
        """Get a formatted summary of association rules"""
        if not self.association_rules:
            return "No association rules generated"

        summary_data = []
        for rule in self.association_rules:
            summary_data.append({
                'LHS': ' & '.join(rule['antecedent']),
                'RHS': ' & '.join(rule['consequent']),
                'Support': f"{rule['support']:.3f}",
                'Confidence': f"{rule['confidence']:.3f}",
                'Lift': f"{rule['lift']:.3f}",
                'Count': rule['count']
            })

        return pd.DataFrame(summary_data)

# Run the Apriori implementation
apriori = AprioriAlgorithm(min_support=0.2, min_confidence=0.6)
apriori.fit(transactions)
```

```
# Display results
print(f"\nFINAL ASSOCIATION RULES")
print("=" * 30)
rules_summary = apriori.get_rules_summary()
print(rules_summary.to_string(index=False))
```

When the Apriori algorithm starts, it first prints out the settings and size of your dataset. Here, the minimum support is set at 0.2, meaning only itemsets that appear in at least 20% of transactions will be considered "frequent." The minimum confidence is 0.6, so only rules that are correct at least 60% of the time will be kept. The algorithm sees that there are 10 transactions in total.

7.9.1.4.1 Phase 1: Finding Frequent Itemsets

The algorithm begins by examining individual items (1-itemsets) to see which ones appear frequently enough. It finds 7 frequent 1-itemsets, such as bread, milk, and butter. Then it combines these frequent items to form 2-itemsets (pairs) and checks which of these pairs meet the minimum support. For example, bread & milk occurs in 40% of transactions, so it is included. This process continues to 3-itemsets (triples), such as bread, butter, milk, which occurs in 30% of transactions. The algorithm stops when no larger frequent combinations can be found.

By the end of Phase 1, the algorithm has 18 frequent itemsets: 7 single items, 8 pairs, and 3 triples. This is important because only frequent itemsets can generate meaningful association rules.

Output:

```
Running Apriori Algorithm:

Minimum Support: 0.2

Minimum Confidence: 0.6

Total Transactions: 10

PHASE 1: Finding Frequent Itemsets

===================================

Processing 1-itemsets:

Candidates to evaluate: 9
```

```
('beer',) : support = 0.200 ✓

('bread',) : support = 0.600 ✓

('butter',) : support = 0.500 ✓

('diapers',) : support = 0.200 ✓

('eggs',) : support = 0.400 ✓

('jam',) : support = 0.200 ✓

('milk',) : support = 0.600 ✓

Found 7 frequent 1-itemsets

Processing 2-itemsets:

Candidates to evaluate: 21

('beer', 'diapers') : support = 0.200 ✓

('bread', 'butter') : support = 0.500 ✓

('bread', 'eggs') : support = 0.200 ✓

('bread', 'jam') : support = 0.200 ✓

('bread', 'milk') : support = 0.400 ✓

('butter', 'jam') : support = 0.200 ✓

('butter', 'milk') : support = 0.300 ✓

('eggs', 'milk') : support = 0.400 ✓

Found 8 frequent 2-itemsets

Processing 3-itemsets:

Candidates to evaluate: 3

('bread', 'butter', 'jam'): support = 0.200 ✓
```

```
('bread', 'butter', 'milk'): support = 0.300 ✓

('bread', 'eggs', 'milk'): support = 0.200 ✓

Found 3 frequent 3-itemsets

Frequent Itemsets Summary:

1-itemsets: 7

2-itemsets: 8

3-itemsets: 3

Total: 18
```

7.9.1.4.2 Phase 2: Generating Association Rules

Next, the algorithm takes the frequent itemsets and generates rules by splitting each itemset into two parts, forming statements such as "if X, then Y." For each possible rule, it evaluates three measures: support, confidence, and lift. Support indicates how often the combination of items appears in the dataset overall. Confidence measures how often Y appears in transactions that already contain X, reflecting how reliable the rule is. Lift compares this relationship to what would be expected by chance, helping determine whether the association is meaningful.

For example, the rule "beer leads to diapers" appears in 20 percent of all transactions, so its support is 0.2. Every transaction that includes beer also includes diapers, so the confidence is 1.0, meaning the rule is perfectly reliable in this dataset. The lift is 5.0, which means this combination occurs five times more often than would be expected if the two items were unrelated. Another rule, "bread leads to milk," appears in 40 percent of transactions, has a confidence of about 0.667, and a lift of about 1.111, suggesting a moderate positive relationship between the two items.

After all possible rules are generated, the algorithm filters out weaker ones by keeping only those that meet a minimum confidence threshold, such as 0.6. The remaining rules are then sorted by lift so that the strongest and most meaningful associations appear first.

Output:

```
PHASE 2: Generating Association Rules

========================================
```

```
Generated 19 rules with confidence \>= 0.6

FINAL ASSOCIATION RULES

==============================

LHS RHS Support Confidence Lift Count

beer diapers 0.200 1.000 5.000 2

diapers beer 0.200 1.000 5.000 2

jam butter 0.200 1.000 2.000 2

jam bread & butter 0.200 1.000 2.000 2

bread & jam butter 0.200 1.000 2.000 2

bread butter 0.500 0.833 1.667 5

butter bread 0.500 1.000 1.667 5

jam bread 0.200 1.000 1.667 2

eggs milk 0.400 1.000 1.667 4

milk eggs 0.400 0.667 1.667 4

butter & jam bread 0.200 1.000 1.667 2

butter & milk bread 0.300 1.000 1.667 3

bread & eggs milk 0.200 1.000 1.667 2

butter bread & milk 0.300 0.600 1.500 3

bread & milk butter 0.300 0.750 1.500 3

bread milk 0.400 0.667 1.111 4

milk bread 0.400 0.667 1.111 4

butter milk 0.300 0.600 1.000 3
```

```
bread & butter milk 0.300 0.600 1.000 3
```

The final output of the process is a set of actionable insights derived from transaction data. These insights reveal how items are commonly purchased together and can be used to guide decisions such as product placement, promotions, or recommendations. For example, beer and diapers may be found to be purchased together very frequently, suggesting a strong relationship that a store might use for marketing or shelf organization. Similarly, bread and butter often appear together, and in one direction the relationship may show that about 83 percent of customers who buy bread also purchase butter, indicating a high level of reliability in that pattern. Lift values help interpret the strength of these relationships by showing whether the association is stronger than what would occur by random chance. Values greater than one indicate a meaningful connection between items, while values close to one suggest little or no real relationship. Overall, the Apriori algorithm identifies frequent combinations of items and translates them into clear rules that describe how products are related, which is the main goal of association analysis.

7.9.2 Practice

```
# Python imports for association analysis
import pandas as pd           # For data manipulation and tables
import numpy as np            # For numeric calculations
from itertools import combinations  # For generating itemsets
from collections import Counter      # For counting items

# Coffee Shop Transactions Dataset
student_transactions = [
    ['coffee', 'sugar', 'cream'],
    ['coffee', 'sugar'],
    ['tea', 'honey', 'lemon'],
    ['coffee', 'cream'],
    ['tea', 'sugar'],
    ['coffee', 'sugar', 'cream', 'pastry'],
    ['tea', 'honey'],
    ['coffee', 'pastry'],
    ['tea', 'lemon', 'honey'],
    ['coffee', 'sugar', 'pastry']
]

print("Total transactions:", len(student_transactions))
for i, t in enumerate(student_transactions, 1):
    print(f"Transaction {i}: {t}")
```

7.9.2.1 Lab 7 Questions

1. List all unique items in the dataset.
2. Which item appears most frequently across all transactions?
3. Calculate the support for coffee.
4. Calculate the support for tea.
5. Calculate the support for the itemset coffee and sugar.
6. Calculate the support for the itemset tea and honey.
7. Calculate the support for the itemset coffee and pastry.
8. Compute the confidence for the rule coffee leads to sugar.
9. Compute the confidence for the rule tea leads to honey.
10. Compute the lift for the rule coffee leads to sugar.
11. Compute the lift for the rule tea leads to lemon.
12. Identify one rule with confidence greater than or equal to 0.6 and explain why it is considered strong.
13. Identify one rule with lift close to 1 and explain why it is weak or not meaningful.
14. If the minimum support threshold is 0.3, which individual items qualify as frequent?
15. Based on the patterns in the dataset, suggest one product placement strategy for the coffee shop and explain your reasoning.

7.10 Conclusion

Association analysis provides powerful insights into the relationships between items, events, and behaviors in transactional data. From our simple grocery store example with 10 transactions, we discovered meaningful patterns like the strong association between bread, butter, and jam purchases, demonstrating how even small datasets can yield actionable insights.

The technique's strength lies in its ability to uncover hidden patterns that might not be obvious through casual observation. The systematic approach of the Apriori algorithm, combined with metrics like support, confidence, and lift, provides a rigorous framework for identifying and evaluating relationships in data.

Modern AI-enhanced tools have made association analysis more accessible and powerful, enabling automatic pattern discovery, natural language interpretation of results, and integration with business processes. However, successful implementation requires understanding both the technical aspects of the algorithms and the business context in which they're applied.

As you apply association analysis in your own projects, remember that the goal is not just to find statistically significant patterns, but to discover actionable insights that can improve business outcomes. The most valuable association rules are those that lead to better customer experiences, more effective marketing strategies, and improved operational efficiency.

The future of association analysis lies in its integration with other data mining techniques and AI capabilities. By combining association analysis with clustering, classification, and predictive modeling, organizations can develop more comprehensive understanding of customer behavior and market dynamics. This integrated approach, supported by modern AI tools, will continue to unlock new opportunities for data-driven decision making across industries.

Chapter 8

AI-Enhanced Data Mining

8.1 Learning Outcomes

8-1. Explain how AI enhances traditional data mining techniques such as clustering, classification, and association analysis.

8-2. Describe automated feature engineering and feature selection, and their impact on model performance and interpretability.

8-3. Understand AI applications in mining unstructured data types, including text (NLP) and images/videos (computer vision).

8-4. Identify ethical considerations in AI-enhanced data mining, including bias mitigation, privacy protection, and explainable AI.

8-5. Recognize emerging AI technologies and trends, such as generative AI, federated learning, quantum computing, and human-AI collaboration

8.2 Introduction

This final chapter explores how AI is revolutionizing data mining techniques and what the future holds for this rapidly evolving field. As we've journeyed through clustering, classification, and association analysis, you've built a solid foundation in data mining fundamentals. Now, let's discover how AI amplifies these techniques and opens entirely new possibilities for extracting insights from data.

The integration of AI with data mining isn't just about making existing methods faster or more accurate—it's about fundamentally transforming how we approach data analysis. From automated feature engineering that discovers patterns humans might miss, to natural language processing that unlocks insights from text, to computer vision that analyzes images and videos, AI is expanding the boundaries of what's possible in data mining.

8.3 The AI Revolution in Data Mining

8.3.1 From Traditional to AI-Enhanced Approaches

Traditional data mining required significant human expertise at every step. Data scientists spent countless hours cleaning data, engineering features, selecting algorithms, and tuning parameters. While these skills remain valuable, AI is automating many of these tasks, allowing analysts to focus on higher-level strategy and interpretation.

Consider how clustering has evolved. Traditional k-means clustering required you to specify the number of clusters in advance and manually tune parameters. AI-enhanced clustering can automatically determine optimal cluster numbers, suggest appropriate distance metrics, and even provide natural language descriptions of what each cluster represents. Instead of seeing "Cluster 1" and "Cluster 2," you might see "Budget-conscious families" and "Tech-savvy professionals."

This transformation extends across all data mining techniques. Classification algorithms can now automatically select features, tune hyperparameters, and even explain their decisions in plain English. Association analysis can identify not just what items are purchased together, but why these associations exist and how they might change over time.

8.3.2 Democratized Data Mining

Perhaps the most exciting aspect of AI-enhanced data mining is its democratizing effect. Previously, effective data mining required deep technical expertise in statistics, programming, and domain knowledge. AI tools are making sophisticated analysis accessible to business users, domain experts, and students who may not have extensive technical backgrounds.

Modern platforms like Orange, WEKA, and cloud-based AutoML services allow users to perform complex analyses through intuitive interfaces. You can upload data, specify your goals, and let AI handle the technical complexities while you focus on interpreting results and making decisions.

This democratization doesn't diminish the importance of understanding fundamental concepts—quite the opposite. As AI handles more technical details, human insight becomes even more crucial for asking the right questions, interpreting results correctly, and ensuring ethical use of these powerful tools.

8.3.3 The Expanding Universe of Data Types

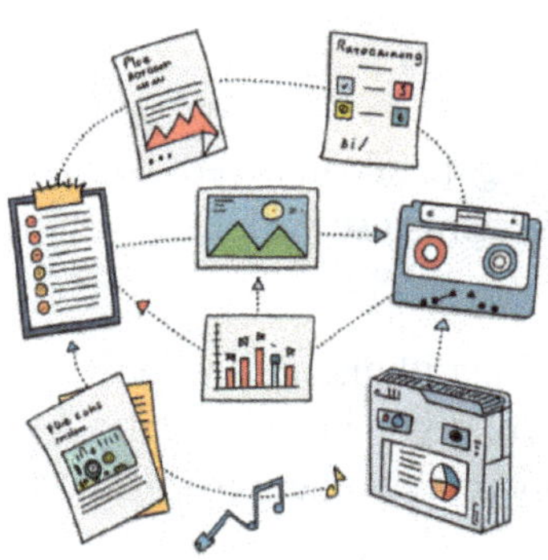

AI has dramatically expanded the types of data we can mine effectively. Traditional data mining focused primarily on structured, numerical data stored in databases. Today's AI-enhanced tools can analyze text documents, images, videos, audio recordings, sensor data, and even complex network structures.

This expansion means data mining applications now span virtually every industry and domain. Healthcare organizations analyze medical images and patient records simultaneously. Retailers combine transaction data with customer reviews and social media sentiment. Manufacturers integrate sensor data from equipment with maintenance logs and environmental conditions.

The convergence of different data types creates opportunities for richer, more comprehensive analyses that provide deeper insights than any single data source could offer alone.

8.4 Automated Feature Engineering

8.4.1 Understanding Feature Engineering's Importance

Feature engineering—the process of creating, transforming, and selecting the most relevant variables for analysis—has traditionally been considered more art than science. Experienced data scientists develop intuition about which features might be predictive, how to combine variables, and what transformations might reveal hidden patterns.

This process is crucial because the quality of features often determines the success of data mining projects more than the choice of algorithm. Great features can make simple algorithms perform exceptionally well, while poor features can cause even sophisticated algorithms to fail.

Consider a simple example: predicting house prices. Raw data might include square footage, number of bedrooms, and lot size. A skilled data scientist might create new features like "price per square foot," "bedroom density" (bedrooms per square foot), or "lot utilization" (house footprint divided by lot size). These engineered features often prove more predictive than the original variables.

8.4.2 How AI Automates Feature Creation

AI-powered feature engineering tools can automatically generate hundreds or thousands of potential features from your original data. These systems use various techniques to create new variables:

Mathematical transformations apply functions like logarithms, square roots, or polynomial combinations to existing variables. For instance, if you have variables A and B, the system might create A^2, $\sqrt{B}$, log(A), A×B, A/B, and many other combinations.

Temporal features extract patterns from time-based data. If you have transaction timestamps, AI might automatically create features like "day of week," "hour of day," "time since last transaction," or "seasonal patterns."

Aggregation features summarize data across different groupings. For customer data, AI might automatically calculate "average purchase amount per month," "number of unique products purchased," or "time between first and last purchase."

Interaction features capture relationships between variables that might not be obvious. The system might discover that the combination of customer age and product category is highly predictive, even if neither variable alone shows strong patterns.

8.4.3 Intelligent Feature Selection

Creating thousands of features is only half the battle—selecting the most useful ones is equally important. Too many features can lead to overfitting, where models perform well on training data but poorly on new data. AI-enhanced feature selection uses sophisticated algorithms to identify the most predictive features while avoiding redundancy.

Modern AutoML platforms combine multiple feature selection techniques. They might use statistical tests to identify features with strong relationships to the target variable, employ machine learning algorithms to assess predictive power, and use domain knowledge to ensure selected features make business sense.

The result is a curated set of features that maximizes predictive performance while remaining interpretable and actionable for business users.

8.4.4 Real-World Impact and Examples

The impact of automated feature engineering extends across industries. In healthcare, AI systems automatically extract features from medical images, patient histories, and lab results to support diagnosis and treatment planning. These systems can identify subtle patterns that human experts might miss while processing information much faster than manual analysis.

Financial services use automated feature engineering for fraud detection, creating features that capture spending patterns, geographic anomalies, and temporal irregularities. These systems continuously adapt as fraudsters develop new techniques, automatically generating new features to detect emerging threats.

E-commerce platforms employ automated feature engineering to power recommendation systems, creating features that capture user preferences, product similarities, and contextual factors like seasonality or trending topics.

8.5 Natural Language Processing: Unlocking Text Data

8.5.1 The Text Data Explosion

We live in an age of unprecedented text generation. Every day, billions of emails are sent, social media posts are published, customer reviews are written, and documents are created. This vast repository of textual information contains invaluable insights about customer sentiment, market trends, operational issues, and emerging opportunities.

Traditional data mining struggled with text data because it's unstructured and highly variable. The same concept can be expressed in countless ways, making it difficult to identify patterns using conventional techniques. AI-powered natural language processing (NLP) has transformed text from a challenging data type into one of the richest sources of business intelligence.

Consider customer feedback analysis. Traditional approaches might count positive and negative words or look for specific keywords. Modern NLP can understand context, detect sarcasm, identify specific aspects of products or services being discussed, and even predict customer behavior based on the language they use.

8.5.2 Core NLP Techniques in Data Mining

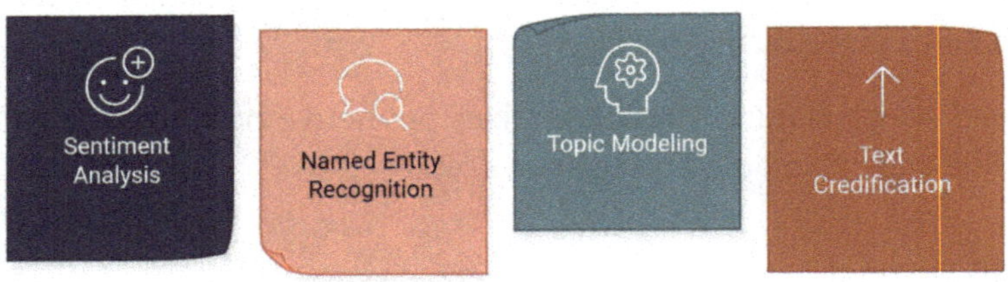

Sentiment analysis determines the emotional tone of text, going beyond simple positive/negative classifications to identify specific emotions like frustration, excitement, or confusion. Modern systems can analyze sentiment at different levels—overall document sentiment, sentence-level sentiment, or aspect-based sentiment that identifies feelings about specific features or topics.

Named entity recognition automatically identifies and categorizes important elements in text, such as people, organizations, locations, dates, and product names. This capability enables automatic extraction of structured information from unstructured text, making it possible to analyze patterns across large document collections.

Topic modeling discovers hidden themes in large text collections without requiring predefined categories. These algorithms can automatically identify that a collection of customer reviews discusses themes like "product quality," "shipping experience," and "customer service," even if these exact phrases don't appear in the text.

Text classification automatically categorizes documents into predefined groups. This might involve sorting customer emails by department, classifying news articles by topic, or identifying spam messages. Modern systems can handle complex, multi-label classifications where documents might belong to multiple categories simultaneously.

8.5.3 Advanced NLP Applications

Modern NLP extends far beyond basic text analysis, enabling systems to understand meaning, context, and intent. Semantic search, for example, interprets the intent behind queries rather than relying solely on keyword matches. A search for "affordable family cars" will return vehicles that are budget-friendly and suitable for families, even if those exact words do not appear in product descriptions. Text summarization automatically condenses lengthy documents, allowing analysts to quickly grasp key points from large collections of research papers, legal documents, or customer feedback. Question answering systems can respond directly to user queries by retrieving relevant information from vast text databases, transforming customer service, technical support, and organizational knowledge management. Additionally, language translation and multilingual analysis empower organizations to process and understand text across different languages, breaking down barriers to global insights.

8.5.4 Practical Implementation and Tools

Implementing NLP in data mining has become increasingly accessible. Cloud platforms like Google Cloud Natural Language, Amazon Comprehend, and Microsoft Text Analytics provide powerful NLP capabilities through simple APIs. These services handle the complexity of language processing while providing business-friendly results.

Open-source libraries like spaCy, NLTK, and Hugging Face Transformers offer more customization for organizations with specific needs. These tools provide pre-trained models that can be fine-tuned for specific domains or use cases.

The key to successful NLP implementation is starting with clear business objectives. Whether you're analyzing customer feedback, monitoring social media sentiment, or extracting insights from internal documents, defining specific goals helps guide tool selection and implementation strategies.

8.6 Computer Vision: Mining Visual Data

8.6.1 The Visual Data Revolution

Images and videos represent one of the fastest-growing data types in our digital world.

From social media photos and security camera footage to medical images and satellite imagery, visual data contains rich information that was previously difficult to analyze systematically.

Computer vision—the AI field focused on enabling machines to interpret and understand visual information—has transformed how we approach visual data mining. What once required human experts to manually analyze images can now be automated, scaled, and integrated with other data sources to provide comprehensive insights.

Consider retail applications. Traditional inventory management relied on manual counts and visual inspections. Computer vision systems can now automatically monitor shelf stock levels, identify product placement issues, and even analyze customer behavior patterns from security camera footage. This visual data mining provides insights that complement traditional sales data analysis.

8.6.2 Core Computer Vision Techniques

Image classification automatically categorizes images into predefined groups. This might involve identifying product types in e-commerce, classifying medical images by condition, or sorting photos by content. Modern systems achieve human-level accuracy on many classification tasks while processing thousands of images per minute.

Object detection goes beyond classification to identify and locate specific objects within images. Security systems use this capability to detect unauthorized personnel or suspicious activities. Manufacturing applications identify defects or quality issues in products. Retail systems track inventory levels and product placement.

Image segmentation divides images into meaningful regions, enabling detailed analysis of different components. Medical applications use segmentation to identify specific anatomical structures or abnormalities. Agricultural systems analyze crop health by segmenting plant areas from soil and background elements.

Optical Character Recognition (OCR) extracts text from images, enabling analysis of documents, signs, labels, and handwritten notes. Modern OCR systems handle multiple languages, various fonts, and even challenging conditions like poor lighting or skewed text.

8.6.3 Advanced Visual Analytics

Facial recognition and analysis can identify individuals and assess demographic characteristics, emotional expressions, and attention patterns. In retail, these systems help analyze customer demographics and engagement, while security applications provide access control and threat detection. Marketing research uses facial analysis to study emotional responses to advertisements or products. Motion analysis in video data uncovers patterns of movement and behavior, supporting traffic management through vehicle flow analysis, sports analytics by tracking player movements and performance, and manufacturing by monitoring worker safety and efficiency. Quality inspection systems automatically detect defects, inconsistencies, or anomalies in products and processes, often surpassing human accuracy and operating continuously without fatigue. Scene understanding integrates multiple computer vision techniques to analyze complex visual environments, enabling smart city applications to monitor traffic patterns, pedestrian flow, and urban planning needs, as well as environmental monitoring systems to track wildlife populations and habitat changes.

8.6.4 Integration with Traditional Data Mining

The real power of computer vision emerges when visual analysis integrates with traditional data mining techniques. Retailers combine visual analysis of customer behavior with transaction data to understand shopping patterns. Healthcare organizations integrate medical image analysis with patient records and lab results for comprehensive diagnosis support.

Manufacturing companies combine visual quality inspection with sensor data and production metrics to optimize processes and predict maintenance needs. Social media platforms integrate image analysis with user behavior data to improve content recommendations and advertising targeting.

This integration creates opportunities for richer, more comprehensive analyses that provide insights impossible to achieve with any single data source.

8.7 Ethical AI and Responsible Data Mining

8.7.1 The Imperative for Ethical AI

As AI-enhanced data mining becomes more powerful and pervasive, ethical considerations become increasingly critical. The ability to automatically analyze vast amounts of data and make decisions that affect people's lives carries significant responsibilities.

Ethical AI isn't just about avoiding obvious harms—it's about ensuring that AI systems are fair, transparent, accountable, and aligned with human values. This responsibility extends to everyone involved in data mining, from data scientists and business analysts to executives and policymakers.

Consider hiring algorithms that analyze resumes and predict job performance. If these systems inadvertently discriminate against certain groups, they can perpetuate or amplify existing inequalities. The automated nature of these systems can make bias less visible while affecting thousands of decisions, making ethical considerations paramount.

Understanding Bias in AI Systems Bias in AI can arise from several sources. Data bias occurs when training data is unrepresentative or reflects historical inequalities, such as a hiring dataset that favors one gender. Algorithmic bias can emerge from design choices, feature selection, or model structure that inadvertently favor certain groups. Confirmation bias happens when AI reinforces existing assumptions, overlooking important patterns. Deployment bias appears when AI is applied in contexts different from its training environment or when outputs are misinterpreted.

Strategies for Bias Mitigation Mitigating bias starts with diverse and representative data to ensure all relevant groups are included. Algorithmic fairness techniques help maintain equitable treatment across groups, while regular bias audits detect unfair outcomes over time. Diverse development teams bring multiple perspectives that can uncover potential biases that homogeneous teams might miss. Together, these strategies create a more robust and fair AI system.

Transparency and Explainability Explainable AI (XAI) provides understandable reasons for AI decisions, building trust and enabling oversight. Proper documentation and auditability maintain records of system development, training, and deployment, supporting accountability. Involving stakeholders, including affected users, in the development process ensures AI systems reflect real-world concerns and ethical standards.

Privacy and Data Protection Protecting privacy starts with data minimization, collecting only what is necessary for the task. Anonymization and pseudonymization safeguard identities, though care is needed to prevent re-identification. Consent and user control give individuals clarity and authority over how their data is used. Strong security measures, including access controls and incident response protocols, further protect sensitive information from misuse or breaches.

8.8 Emerging Trends and Future Possibilities

8.8.1 Generative AI in Data Mining

Generative AI—systems that can create new content rather than just analyzing existing data—is opening exciting new possibilities for data mining. These systems can generate synthetic data for training when real data is scarce or sensitive, create realistic scenarios for testing algorithms, and even generate insights and explanations in natural language.

Synthetic data generation addresses one of data mining's biggest challenges: obtaining sufficient, high-quality data for analysis. Generative AI can create realistic synthetic datasets that preserve statistical properties of original data while protecting privacy. This enables analysis in sensitive domains like healthcare or finance where real data sharing is restricted.

Automated insight generation goes beyond traditional analysis to automatically generate human-readable reports, explanations, and recommendations. Instead of presenting charts and statistics, future systems might generate executive summaries that explain what the data means and what actions should be taken.

Interactive data exploration enables natural language conversations with data. Users might ask questions like "Why did sales drop last quarter?" and receive comprehensive analyses that combine multiple data sources and analytical techniques.

8.8.2 Federated Learning and Distributed Analytics

Federated learning enables collaborative data mining without centralizing data. Multiple organizations can jointly train models while keeping their data private and secure. This approach is particularly valuable in healthcare, where hospitals can collaborate on research without sharing patient data, or in finance, where banks can jointly detect fraud patterns without exposing customer information.

This technology addresses growing privacy concerns while enabling more comprehensive analyses than any single organization could achieve alone. The result is better models and insights while maintaining data sovereignty and privacy.

Edge computing brings data mining capabilities closer to data sources, enabling real-time analysis with reduced latency and bandwidth requirements. Smart cities can analyze traffic patterns locally, manufacturing systems can detect quality issues immediately, and mobile applications can provide personalized experiences without sending data to central servers.

8.8.3 Quantum Computing and Advanced Analytics

Quantum computing promises to revolutionize certain types of data mining problems, particularly those involving optimization, pattern recognition, and complex simulations. While practical quantum computers for general data mining are still years away, early applications are emerging in specific domains.

Quantum algorithms might enable analysis of datasets too large or complex for classical computers, solve optimization problems that are currently intractable, and discover patterns that classical algorithms cannot detect.

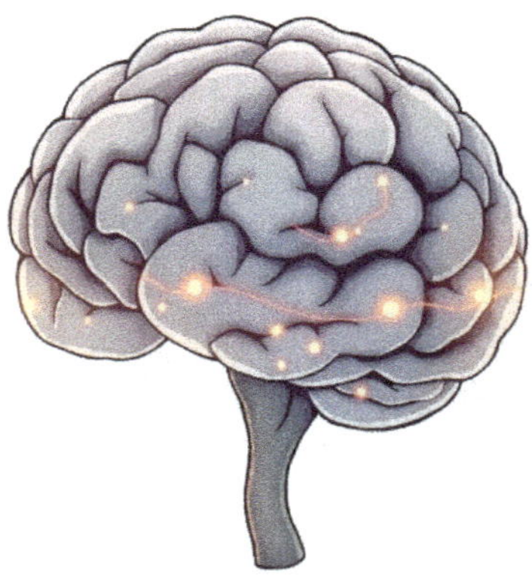

Neuromorphic computing mimics brain structures to create more efficient AI systems. These approaches might enable continuous learning, better handling of uncertainty, and more energy-efficient processing of large datasets.

8.8.4 Human-AI Collaboration

The future of data mining isn't about AI replacing human analysts—it's about creating powerful partnerships between human insight and AI capabilities. **Augmented analytics** combines AI automation with human expertise, enabling analysts to focus on strategy, interpretation, and decision-making while AI handles routine tasks.

Interactive machine learning enables continuous collaboration between humans and AI systems. Analysts can provide feedback, correct mistakes, and guide learning processes, creating systems that improve through use.

Citizen data science empowers domain experts who aren't technical specialists to perform sophisticated analyses. Teachers might analyze student performance data, doctors might explore treatment effectiveness, and marketers might investigate customer behavior patterns—all using AI-enhanced tools that don't require programming expertise.

8.9 Key Terms

AI-Enhanced Data Mining – Using artificial intelligence to improve or automate data mining tasks.

Automated Feature Engineering – AI-driven creation of new variables to improve predictive performance.

Feature Selection – Identifying the most relevant variables for analysis to avoid overfitting and improve interpretability.

Natural Language Processing (NLP) – AI techniques for analyzing and extracting insights from text data.

Sentiment Analysis – Determining emotional tone or opinion from text.

Named Entity Recognition (NER) – Identifying and classifying key elements in text, such as names, dates, or products.

Topic Modeling – Discovering hidden themes in large text datasets.

Computer Vision – AI methods to interpret and analyze images and videos.

Image Classification / Object Detection / Image Segmentation / OCR – Core computer vision techniques for analyzing visual data.

Ethical AI – AI designed to be fair, transparent, accountable, and aligned with human values.

Explainable AI (XAI) – Methods that make AI decision-making understandable to humans.

Federated Learning – Collaborative machine learning without centralizing data.

Generative AI – AI that can create new content or synthetic data for training and analysis.

Human-AI Collaboration / Augmented Analytics – Combining AI capabilities with human expertise for better insights and decisions.

8.10 Review Questions

1. How does AI enhance traditional data mining techniques like clustering and classification?

2. What is automated feature engineering, and why is it important for predictive modeling?
3. Explain the difference between NLP and computer vision in AI-enhanced data mining.
4. What are some key techniques used in NLP for data mining applications?
5. How does computer vision transform analysis of image and video data?
6. Why is ethical AI important, and what types of bias can occur in AI systems?
7. Describe strategies for mitigating bias and ensuring transparency in AI-enhanced data mining.
8. How can generative AI be used to create synthetic data or generate insights?
9. What is federated learning, and why is it useful for privacy-sensitive domains?
10. Explain the concept of human-AI collaboration and how it supports augmented analytics.

8.11 Lab 8: AI Enhanced Data Mining

This lab demonstrates three core areas:

Automated Feature Engineering – Learn how AI-inspired methods can generate new variables from raw data, capture complex relationships, and improve the predictive potential of datasets. Students will practice creating mathematical transformations, interaction features, aggregation metrics, and categorical bins, followed by intelligent feature selection using statistical methods.

Natural Language Processing (NLP) for Text Mining – Examine how unstructured text data, such as customer reviews, can be transformed into structured insights. Students will use automated sentiment analysis, compute polarity and subjectivity, and generate word frequency summaries and word clouds to quantify and visualize textual data.

Ethical AI and Bias Detection – Investigate how AI systems can unintentionally reflect bias in decision-making. Using synthetic selection data, students will calculate group-level outcomes, compute disparate impact ratios, perform chi-square tests, and visualize differences to detect potential inequities.

Throughout the lab, students will work with synthetic datasets specifically designed to illustrate the core techniques. The focus is on replicating AI-enhanced processes exactly as demonstrated, including data preparation, automated feature creation, feature selection, sentiment scoring, and bias detection. All exercises emphasize reproducible outputs and practical Python implementation, with no extra interpretation required beyond the printed results.

By the end of this lab, students will gain hands-on experience in using AI methods to make data mining more efficient, accurate, and responsible. The lab prepares learners to apply these techniques systematically while ensuring the ethical evaluation of AI-driven analyses.

8.11.1 Demonstration

Before starting the labs, ensure you have the following installed:

```
# Required Python packages
pip install pandas numpy scikit-learn matplotlib seaborn
pip install textblob nltk wordcloud
pip install opencv-python pillow
pip install plotly dash

# Data manipulation and analysis
import pandas as pd
import numpy as np
import matplotlib.pyplot as plt
import seaborn as sns

# Machine learning and feature engineering
from sklearn.preprocessing import StandardScaler, LabelEncoder
from sklearn.feature_selection import SelectKBest, f_classif
from sklearn.model_selection import train_test_split
from sklearn.ensemble import RandomForestClassifier

# Text processing
from textblob import TextBlob
import nltk
from wordcloud import WordCloud

# Warnings control
import warnings
warnings.filterwarnings('ignore')
```

8.11.2 Part 1: Feature Engineering

The first step in this demonstration is to simulate a real-world data mining scenario by creating a synthetic customer dataset. Using random number generation, 1,000 customer records are generated, each containing key attributes such as age, income, spending score, years as a customer, number of purchases, and average purchase amount. These features represent the types of data businesses typically collect to understand customer behavior and spending patterns. To ensure reproducibility, a random seed is set, so that the same dataset can be generated consistently for analysis or demonstration purposes.

A target variable called `high_value` is then introduced to classify customers. Customers are labeled as high-value if they have both a spending score above 70 and an average purchase amount greater than 150. This step transforms the dataset into a supervised learning context, making it suitable for classification tasks. By defining a clear outcome, we can later identify which features are most predictive of high-value customer status.

```
np.random.seed(42)
n_customers = 1000

customer_data = pd.DataFrame({
    'age': np.random.randint(18, 80, n_customers),
    'income': np.random.normal(50000, 20000, n_customers),
    'spending_score': np.random.randint(1, 100, n_customers),
    'years_customer': np.random.randint(1, 20, n_customers),
    'num_purchases': np.random.poisson(12, n_customers),
    'avg_purchase_amount': np.random.normal(150, 50, n_customers)
})

# Create target variable: high-value customer
customer_data['high_value'] = (
    (customer_data['spending_score'] > 70) &
    (customer_data['avg_purchase_amount'] > 150)
).astype(int)

print("Original Dataset Shape:", customer_data.shape)
print("\nFirst 5 rows:")
print(customer_data.head())
```

Output:

```
Original Dataset Shape: (1000, 7)

First 5 rows:
   age        income  spending_score  years_customer  num_purchases  \
0   56  77447.555931              58               6             17
1   69  36444.278140              60               4             14
2   46  73070.637440              21              18             15
3   32  42499.787433              28               9             17
4   60  36117.080930              75              17              7

   avg_purchase_amount  high_value
0            88.696470           0
1           214.324103           0
```

```
2           157.696510          0
3           175.951804          0
4           200.910479          1
```

8.11.2.1 Automated Feature Creation

Next, the dataset is enriched using automated feature creation, a process inspired by AI-driven feature engineering. Traditionally, feature engineering requires deep domain knowledge and careful manual effort to derive meaningful variables. Automated approaches, however, can systematically generate new features from existing data, uncovering relationships that may not be obvious at first glance.

Several types of features are created in this process:

Mathematical transformations: Variables such as income are converted to a logarithmic scale to reduce skewness, and age is squared to capture non-linear effects. A new variable, `spending_income_ratio`, measures customer spending relative to income, providing a normalized view of purchasing behavior.

Interaction features: Combining existing variables can reveal important relationships. For example, multiplying age by income creates an `age_income_interaction` feature, and multiplying years as a customer by spending score creates a `loyalty_spending` metric, capturing the interplay between loyalty and spending habits.

Aggregation features: Summary measures, such as `purchase_frequency` (number of purchases per year as a customer) and `total_spent_estimate` (total estimated spending), summarize behavior over time.

Categorical binning: Continuous variables like age and income are grouped into categories (`age_group` and `income_tier`) to capture broader trends, enabling models to detect patterns across defined ranges.

```python
def create_automated_features(df):
    df_enhanced = df.copy()

    # Mathematical transformations
    df_enhanced['income_log'] = np.log1p(df['income'])
    df_enhanced['age_squared'] = df['age'] ** 2
    df_enhanced['spending_income_ratio']
      = df['spending_score'] / (df['income'] / 1000)

    # Interaction features
    df_enhanced['age_income_interaction']
      = df['age'] * df['income'] / 10000
    df_enhanced['loyalty_spending']
      = df['years_customer'] * df['spending_score']
```

```
    # Aggregation features
    df_enhanced['purchase_frequency']
      = df['num_purchases'] / df['years_customer']
    df_enhanced['total_spent_estimate']
      = df['num_purchases'] * df['avg_purchase_amount']

    # Categorical binning
    df_enhanced['age_group'] = pd.cut(df['age'], bins=[0, 30, 50, 100],
 ↪
                                      labels=['Young', 'Middle', 'Senior'])
    df_enhanced['income_tier'] = pd.cut(df['income'], bins=3,
                                      labels=['Low', 'Medium', 'High'])

    return df_enhanced

enhanced_data = create_automated_features(customer_data)

# Optionally, print just the new features to highlight them
new_features = [col for col in enhanced_data.columns if col not in
 ↪  customer_data.columns]
print("\nNewly created features:")
print(enhanced_data[new_features].head())
```

Output:

```
Newly Created Features (Part 1)

row  inc_log  age_sq  spend/inc  age×inc
--- ------- ------- ---------- --------
0    11.257    3136      0.749  433.706
1    10.504    4761      1.646  251.466
2    11.199    2116      0.287  336.125
3    10.657    1024      0.659  135.999
4    10.495    3600      2.077  216.702

Newly Created Features (Part 2)

row  loyalty  freq/mo  total_spent  age_grp  inc_tier
--- -------- -------- ------------ -------- --------
0        348    2.833     1507.840  Senior   High
1        240    3.500     3000.537  Senior   Medium
2        378    0.833     2365.448  Middle   High
3        252    1.889     2991.181  Middle   Medium
4       1275    0.412     1406.373  Senior   Medium
```

After applying these transformations, the dataset expands from 7 original features to 16 features, adding 9 new variables automatically. These new features enrich the data and provide additional signals that can improve model performance when predicting high-value customers.

8.11.2.2 Intelligent Feature Selection

While automated feature creation provides a richer dataset, not all features are equally predictive. To focus on the most informative variables, intelligent feature selection is applied using the SelectKBest method with the ANOVA F-test (`f_classif`).

Before applying feature selection, only numeric variables are considered, as categorical columns cannot be processed directly with this method. Any infinite values are replaced, and missing values are filled with the mean of each column to ensure compatibility with the algorithm.

SelectKBest evaluates each numeric feature individually against the target variable, ranking them based on their ability to distinguish high-value customers. By selecting the top 8 features, the process retains the most predictive variables while discarding less informative ones.

```
# Select only numeric features for SelectKBest (exclude categorical)
numeric_cols =
↪ enhanced_data.select_dtypes(include=[np.number]).columns.tolist()
numeric_cols.remove('high_value')  # remove target
X = enhanced_data[numeric_cols]
y = enhanced_data['high_value']

# Clean numeric data
X = X.replace([np.inf, -np.inf], np.nan)
X = X.fillna(X.mean())

# Apply SelectKBest
selector = SelectKBest(score_func=f_classif, k=8)
X_selected = selector.fit_transform(X, y)

# Get top selected feature names
selected_features = X.columns[selector.get_support()].tolist()
print("\nTop 8 Selected Features:")
for i, feature in enumerate(selected_features, 1):
    print(f"{i}. {feature}")

# Feature importance scores
feature_scores = pd.DataFrame({
    'Feature': X.columns,
```

```
    'Score': selector.scores_
}).sort_values('Score', ascending=False)

print("\nTop 5 Feature Importance Scores:")
print(feature_scores.head())
```

Output:

```
Top 8 Selected Features:
1. spending_score
2. years_customer
3. num_purchases
4. avg_purchase_amount
5. spending_income_ratio
6. loyalty_spending
7. purchase_frequency
8. total_spent_estimate

Top 5 Feature Importance Scores:
                 Feature       Score
2         spending_score  380.622907
10      loyalty_spending  214.991663
5    avg_purchase_amount  135.158727
12  total_spent_estimate   71.790804
3         years_customer    6.889390
```

The results highlight both traditional and newly generated features as important predictors. Features like `spending_score`, `years_customer`, and `num_purchases` remain highly influential, while automated features such as `loyalty_spending`, `spending_income_ratio`, `purchase_frequency`, and `total_spent_estimate` also rank among the top predictors. This demonstrates that AI-driven feature engineering can generate meaningful insights that complement traditional business metrics.

Starting from a synthetic customer dataset, we first create new features automatically, then select the most predictive numeric variables for modeling. This process showcases how modern data mining tools can efficiently identify patterns and relationships in data, ensuring models focus on variables that truly matter for predicting high-value customers. By combining automated feature creation with intelligent selection, analysts can build more robust and effective predictive models while minimizing noise and redundancy in the data.

8.11.3 Part 2: Natural Language Processing for Text Mining

Traditional data mining struggled with text because it's unstructured. AI-powered NLP transforms text into structured insights about sentiment, topics, and patterns.

Text data presents a unique challenge for traditional data mining approaches because it is inherently unstructured. Unlike numeric or categorical data, text is composed of words, sentences, and context that machines cannot easily quantify. This is where AI-powered natural language processing (NLP) comes into play. NLP techniques can transform raw textual content into structured insights, enabling analysis of sentiment, identification of common themes, and discovery of patterns that would be difficult to detect manually.

In this demonstration, we examine a small sample of customer reviews to illustrate the process. The dataset contains ten customer reviews, each labeled with a unique review ID. These reviews reflect a variety of opinions—some highly positive, others negative, and a few neutral or mixed. By structuring the text into a DataFrame, we can systematically analyze it using NLP tools, preparing it for tasks like sentiment scoring or keyword extraction.

```
# Sample customer reviews dataset
reviews_data = [
    "This product is amazing! Great quality and fast shipping.",
    "Terrible experience. Product broke after one day.",
    "Good value for money. Would recommend to others.",
    "Customer service was unhelpful. Very disappointed.",
    "Excellent product! Exceeded my expectations completely.",
    "Average quality. Nothing special but does the job.",
    "Love this! Will definitely buy again soon.",
    "Poor packaging. Product arrived damaged unfortunately.",
    "Outstanding quality and great customer support team.",
    "Not worth the price. Found better alternatives elsewhere."
]

reviews_df = pd.DataFrame({
    'review_text': reviews_data,
    'review_id': range(1, len(reviews_data) + 1)
})

print("Sample Reviews Dataset:")
print(reviews_df.head())
```

Output:

```
Sample Reviews Dataset:
                                         review_text  review_id
0  This product is amazing! Great quality and fas...          1
1  Terrible experience. Product broke after one day.          2
2   Good value for money. Would recommend to others.          3
3  Customer service was unhelpful. Very disappoin...          4
4  Excellent product! Exceeded my expectations co...          5
```

The printed sample shows the first five reviews, giving a sense of the diversity in customer feedback. For example, review 1 praises product quality and shipping speed, while review 2 reports a broken product and a negative experience. This variation demonstrates why automated analysis is so valuable: manually reading and summarizing even a small dataset is feasible, but scaling this process to thousands or millions of reviews would be impossible without AI.

8.11.3.1 Automated Sentiment Analysis

Automated sentiment analysis is a key application of AI in text data mining, allowing machines to assess the emotional tone of textual content without manual intervention. In this demonstration, we use TextBlob, a Python library that applies natural language processing techniques to quantify sentiment. Each review is analyzed to compute two primary measures: polarity, which ranges from -1 (very negative) to +1 (very positive), and subjectivity, which ranges from 0 (completely objective) to 1 (highly subjective). These measures provide a structured way to understand customer opinions.

Once the polarity and subjectivity are calculated, the text is classified into one of three sentiment categories: Positive, Negative, or Neutral. For example, strongly positive reviews such as “This product is amazing! Great quality and fast shipping” receive a high positive polarity and are labeled Positive. Conversely, reviews expressing frustration or disappointment, like “Terrible experience. Product broke after one day,” have strongly negative polarity and are labeled Negative. Reviews that are balanced or moderate would fall under the Neutral category.

By appending these results to the original dataset, we can directly see how each review is interpreted by the AI. The printed output shows the first five reviews, along with their assigned sentiment and polarity scores. This structured representation allows businesses to quickly summarize customer satisfaction trends, identify areas needing improvement, and make data-driven decisions without manually reading each review.

Ultimately, automated sentiment analysis transforms subjective text into actionable insights, enabling organizations to scale their understanding of customer feedback efficiently and consistently.

```
def analyze_sentiment(text):
    """
    Perform automated sentiment analysis using TextBlob
    This demonstrates how AI can understand emotional tone
    """
    blob = TextBlob(text)

    # Get polarity (-1 to 1: negative to positive)
    polarity = blob.sentiment.polarity

    # Get subjectivity (0 to 1: objective to subjective)
```

```
    subjectivity = blob.sentiment.subjectivity

    # Classify sentiment
    if polarity > 0.1:
        sentiment = 'Positive'
    elif polarity < -0.1:
        sentiment = 'Negative'
    else:
        sentiment = 'Neutral'

    return sentiment, polarity, subjectivity

# Apply sentiment analysis to all reviews
sentiment_results = []
for review in reviews_df['review_text']:
    sentiment, polarity, subjectivity = analyze_sentiment(review)
    sentiment_results.append({
        'sentiment': sentiment,
        'polarity': polarity,
        'subjectivity': subjectivity
    })

# Add results to dataframe
sentiment_df = pd.DataFrame(sentiment_results)
reviews_analysis = pd.concat([reviews_df, sentiment_df], axis=1)

print("Sentiment Analysis Results:")
print(reviews_analysis[['review_text', 'sentiment',
↪  'polarity']].head())
```

Output:

```
Sentiment Analysis Results

row  review                    sent  pol
---  ------------------------  ---- ------
0    This product is amazing!  Pos   0.583
     Great quality and
     fast shipping.

1    Terrible experience.      Neg  -1.000
     Product broke after
     one day.
```

```
2     Good value for money.      Pos    0.700
      Would recommend
      to others.

3     Customer service was       Neg   -0.975
      unhelpful. Very
      disappointing.

4     Excellent product!         Pos    0.550
      Exceeded my
      expectations.
```

```
# Sentiment summary
print("Sentiment Analysis Summary:\n")

# Count of each sentiment
sentiment_counts = reviews_analysis['sentiment'].value_counts()
print("Sentiment Counts:")
print(sentiment_counts)

# Average polarity and subjectivity
print("\nAverage Polarity:", reviews_analysis['polarity'].mean())
print("Average Subjectivity:", reviews_analysis['subjectivity'].mean())
```

Output:

```
Sentiment Analysis Summary:

Sentiment Counts:
sentiment
Positive    7
Negative    3
Name: count, dtype: int64

Average Polarity: 0.06494047619047619
Average Subjectivity: 0.6973214285714285
```

This sentiment summary provides a quick overview of the emotional tone across all customer reviews. The Sentiment Counts show that most reviews (7 out of 10) are classified as Positive, while 3 are Negative, and none are Neutral, indicating that overall customer feedback is largely favorable.

The Average Polarity of approximately 0.065 suggests that, on average, the sentiment is slightly positive, but close to neutral, reflecting some mixed opinions. The Average Subjectivity of around 0.70 indicates that most reviews are subjective in nature, meaning they express personal opinions and feelings rather than purely objective statements. Together, these metrics give a concise, quantifiable snapshot of customer sentiment, allowing businesses to understand overall satisfaction and identify areas for improvement at a glance.

8.11.4 Part 3: Ethical AI and Bias Detection

As AI becomes more powerful, we must ensure it's used responsibly. This lab demonstrates how to detect and address bias in AI systems. This demonstration illustrates the importance of AI ethics, particularly in detecting and mitigating bias in decision-making systems. Here, we simulate a hiring dataset to show how AI models can inadvertently reflect human or systemic biases. The dataset includes standard features used in hiring decisions—experience, education, interview performance, along with demographic attributes like gender and age.

To model bias, we deliberately favor male applicants by adding a small "bias factor" to their hiring probability. The resulting `hired` column therefore reflects both legitimate qualifications and an artificial gender bias. By examining this dataset, students can see how even subtle biases in the data can skew AI predictions and lead to unfair outcomes.

This example sets the stage for discussions about responsible AI: before deploying models, it's essential to check for potential biases, ensure fairness across groups, and take corrective actions such as reweighting features or using bias-mitigation techniques. It emphasizes that AI ethics is not just theoretical—it has tangible consequences in real-world applications like hiring.

```
# Create synthetic hiring dataset with potential bias
np.random.seed(42)
n_applicants = 1000

# Generate biased hiring data
hiring_data = pd.DataFrame({
    'experience_years': np.random.randint(0, 20, n_applicants),
    'education_score': np.random.randint(1, 10, n_applicants),
    'interview_score': np.random.randint(1, 10, n_applicants),
    'gender': np.random.choice(['Male', 'Female'], n_applicants),
    'age': np.random.randint(22, 65, n_applicants)
})

# Introduce bias: slightly favor males in hiring decisions
bias_factor = np.where(hiring_data['gender'] == 'Male', 0.2, 0)
hiring_probability = (
    0.3 * hiring_data['experience_years'] / 20 +
    0.3 * hiring_data['education_score'] / 10 +
    0.4 * hiring_data['interview_score'] / 10 +
```

```
    bias_factor
)

hiring_data['hired'] = (hiring_probability > 0.6).astype(int)

print("Hiring Dataset Sample:")
print(hiring_data.head())
```

Output:

```
Hiring Dataset Sample

     exp  edu  int
     yrs  scr  scr   gender   age  hired
---  ---  ---  ---  -------  ---  -----
0      6    7    4   Male     27     1
1     19    2    2   Female   62     0
2     14    2    6   Male     57     1
3     10    1    2   Male     23     0
4      7    3    7   Male     50     1
```

8.11.4.1 Automated Bias Detection

This section demonstrates automated bias detection in AI systems, highlighting how algorithms can identify inequities in decision-making. Using the synthetic hiring dataset, the `detect_bias` function evaluates whether a protected attribute—here, gender—influences the outcome (hired).

The analysis first calculates the hiring rates for each gender group. From the output, we see a stark difference: male applicants are hired at a rate of 69%, while female applicants are hired only 22% of the time. To quantify fairness, the function computes the disparate impact ratio, which is the ratio of the lower hiring rate to the higher one. In this case, the ratio is 0.318, well below the commonly used 0.8 threshold, indicating significant bias against female applicants.

Additionally, the function performs a chi-square test to assess statistical significance. The result confirms that the observed difference is unlikely due to chance, reinforcing that the bias is real and measurable. This demonstration underscores the importance of systematically checking AI models for bias before deployment, as automated detection tools can quickly flag disparities that might otherwise go unnoticed. It also illustrates how AI ethics practices can be operationalized through quantitative metrics.

```
def detect_bias(data, protected_attribute, outcome):
    """
    Automatically detect potential bias in dataset
```

```
    """
    bias_analysis = {}

    # Calculate hiring rates by protected attribute
    group_stats =
↪   data.groupby(protected_attribute)[outcome].agg(['count', 'sum',
↪   'mean'])
    group_stats['hiring_rate'] = group_stats['mean']

    print(f"Hiring Rates by {protected_attribute}:")
    print(group_stats[['count', 'sum', 'hiring_rate']])

    # Calculate disparate impact ratio
    rates = group_stats['hiring_rate']
    max_rate = rates.max()
    min_rate = rates.min()
    disparate_impact = min_rate / max_rate

    bias_analysis['disparate_impact_ratio'] = disparate_impact
    bias_analysis['bias_detected'] = disparate_impact < 0.8  # 80% rule

    # Statistical significance test
    from scipy.stats import chi2_contingency
    contingency_table = pd.crosstab(data[protected_attribute],
↪   data[outcome])
    chi2, p_value, _, _ = chi2_contingency(contingency_table)

    bias_analysis['statistical_significance'] = p_value < 0.05
    bias_analysis['p_value'] = p_value

    return bias_analysis, group_stats

# Detect gender bias
gender_bias, gender_stats = detect_bias(hiring_data, 'gender', 'hired')

print(f"\nBias Analysis Results:")
print(f"Disparate Impact Ratio:
↪   {gender_bias['disparate_impact_ratio']:.3f}")
print(f"Bias Detected (< 0.8): {gender_bias['bias_detected']}")
print(f"Statistically Significant:
↪   {gender_bias['statistical_significance']}")
```

Output:

```
Hiring Rates by gender:
        count  sum  hiring_rate
gender
Female    487  107     0.219713
Male      513  354     0.690058

Bias Analysis Results:
Disparate Impact Ratio: 0.318
Bias Detected (< 0.8): True
Statistically Significant: True
```

8.11.5 Practice

In this lab, you will work with three datasets to practice key data mining techniques covered in class. Start by running the provided Python code to load and create the datasets. Then, complete the numbered exercises, performing operations such as feature engineering, text analysis, and bias detection.

```python
# ------------------------
# Part 1: Feature Engineering - Customer Dataset
# ------------------------
import numpy as np
import pandas as pd

np.random.seed(42)
n_customers = 1000

customer_data = pd.DataFrame({
    'age': np.random.randint(18, 80, n_customers),
    'income': np.random.normal(50000, 20000, n_customers),
    'spending_score': np.random.randint(1, 100, n_customers),
    'years_customer': np.random.randint(1, 20, n_customers),
    'num_purchases': np.random.poisson(12, n_customers),
    'avg_purchase_amount': np.random.normal(150, 50, n_customers)
})

# Target variable: high-value customer
customer_data['high_value'] = ((customer_data['spending_score'] > 70) &
                               (customer_data['avg_purchase_amount'] >
↪ 150)).astype(int)

# ------------------------
# Part 2: NLP - Customer Reviews Dataset
# ------------------------
```

```
from textblob import TextBlob

reviews_data = [
    "This product is amazing! Great quality and fast shipping.",
    "Terrible experience. Product broke after one day.",
    "Good value for money. Would recommend to others.",
    "Customer service was unhelpful. Very disappointed.",
    "Excellent product! Exceeded my expectations completely.",
    "Average quality. Nothing special but does the job.",
    "Love this! Will definitely buy again soon.",
    "Poor packaging. Product arrived damaged unfortunately.",
    "Outstanding quality and great customer support team.",
    "Not worth the price. Found better alternatives elsewhere."
]

reviews_df = pd.DataFrame({
    'review_text': reviews_data,
    'review_id': range(1, len(reviews_data)+1)
})

# ------------------------
# Part 3: Ethical AI - Hiring Dataset
# ------------------------
np.random.seed(42)
n_applicants = 1000

hiring_data = pd.DataFrame({
    'experience_years': np.random.randint(0, 20, n_applicants),
    'education_score': np.random.randint(1, 10, n_applicants),
    'interview_score': np.random.randint(1, 10, n_applicants),
    'gender': np.random.choice(['Male', 'Female'], n_applicants),
    'age': np.random.randint(22, 65, n_applicants)
})

# Introduce gender bias
bias_factor = np.where(hiring_data['gender'] == 'Male', 0.2, 0)
hiring_prob = (0.3*hiring_data['experience_years']/20 +
               0.3*hiring_data['education_score']/10 +
               0.4*hiring_data['interview_score']/10 +
               bias_factor)
hiring_data['hired'] = (hiring_prob > 0.6).astype(int)
```

8.11.5.1 Lab 8 Questions

1. Print the shape and first 5 rows of `customer_data`.
2. Write a function to create new features in `customer_data`: `income_log`, `age_squared`, `spending_income_ratio`, `age_income_interaction`, `loyalty_spending`, `purchase_frequency`, `total_spent_estimate`, `age_group`, and `income_tier`.

Apply the function and print the first 5 rows of the new features.

3. Convert any categorical features in `customer_data` to numeric codes.
4. Use SelectKBest with ANOVA F-test to select the top 8 numeric features for predicting `high_value`. Print the names of the selected features.
5. Print all numeric features and their F-scores. Display the top 5 features.
6. Write a function to compute polarity, subjectivity, and a sentiment label (Positive, Negative, Neutral) for each review in `reviews_df`.
7. Apply the sentiment function to all reviews and add the results as new columns.
8. Print the `review_text`, `sentiment`, and `polarity` columns from `reviews_df`.
9. Compute and print the count of each sentiment category, average polarity, and average subjectivity.
10. Group `hiring_data` by gender and compute the count, sum, and mean of the `hired` column.
11. Compute the disparate impact ratio for `hiring_data` and indicate whether the 80% rule is violated.
12. Create a contingency table for gender and hired and perform a chi-square test. Print the p-value.
13. Summarize the results: disparate impact ratio, bias detected (True/False), and statistical significance (True/False).
14. Identify which gender is favored based on hiring rates.
15. Plot a bar chart showing hiring rate by gender.

8.12 Conclusion

AI is transforming data mining from a manual, expert-driven process into an automated, scalable, and democratized practice. By integrating AI with traditional techniques, analysts can handle larger and more complex datasets, uncover hidden patterns, and generate actionable insights more efficiently. Automated feature engineering, NLP, and computer vision expand the types of data that can be mined, while ethical considerations, bias mitigation, and explainability ensure responsible use. Emerging technologies like generative AI, federated learning, and quantum computing promise even greater capabilities. The future of data mining emphasizes human-AI collaboration, enabling analysts to leverage AI's computational power while applying critical human insight for strategy, interpretation, and decision-making.

www.ingramcontent.com/pod-product-compliance
Lightning Source LLC
Chambersburg PA
CBHW061354240926
51846CB00007B/1407
9781969233388